How Children Read Biblical Narrative

How Children Read Biblical Narrative

An Investigation of Children's Readings of the Gospel of Luke

Melody R. Briggs

☙PICKWICK *Publications* · Eugene, Oregon

HOW CHILDREN READ BIBLICAL NARRATIVE
An Investigation of Children's Readings of the Gospel of Luke

Copyright © 2017 Melody R. Briggs. All rights reserved. Except for brief quotations in critical publications or reviews, no part of this book may be reproduced in any manner without prior written permission from the publisher. Write: Permissions, Wipf and Stock Publishers, 199 W. 8th Ave., Suite 3, Eugene, OR 97401.

Pickwick Publications
An Imprint of Wipf and Stock Publishers
199 W. 8th Ave., Suite 3
Eugene, OR 97401

www.wipfandstock.com

PAPERBACK ISBN: 978-1-4982-9385-3
HARDCOVER ISBN: 978-1-4982-9387-7
EBOOK ISBN: 978-1-4982-9386-0

Cataloguing-in-Publication data:

Names: Briggs, Melody R.

Title: How children read biblical narrative : an investigation of children's readings of the Gospel of Luke / Melody R. Briggs.

Description: Eugene, OR: Pickwick Publications, 2017 | Includes bibliographical references and index.

Identifiers: ISBN 978-1-4982-9385-3 (paperback) | ISBN 978-1-4982-9387-7 (hardcover) | ISBN 978-1-4982-9386-0 (ebook)

Subjects: LCSH: Bible. Luke—Reading—Children. | Bible. Luke—Criticism, Narrative. | Bible. Luke—Hermeneutics.

Classification: LCC BS2595.52 B7 2017 (print) | LCC BS2595.52 (ebook)

Scriptures [marked GNB] are taken from the Good News Bible published by The Bible Societies/Collins © American Bible Society

Manufactured in the U.S.A.   05/30/17

To my own children, Joshua, Kristin, and Matthew,
with love and in tribute to many happy hours of reading together.

Contents

List of Figures and Tables | viii
List of Readers | ix
Preface | xi
Acknowledgments | xiii
Abbreviations | xv

Part One: The Theoretical Background

1. Introduction | 3
2. Reading Luke | 10
3. The Child Reader | 33
4. Perspectives on Children Reading the Bible | 53

Part Two: The Investigation

5. Research Methodology: The Set-Up | 79
6. Research Methodology: The Empirical Work | 100

Part Three: An Analysis

7. A Framework for Analysis: Participatory Reading | 129
8. Reading by Imagining | 149
9. Reading through Empathy | 171
10. Sense-Orientated Reading | 191
11. Plot-Driven Reading | 212
12. Conclusion | 233

Appendices | 247
Bibliography | 253
Author Index | 265
Scripture Index | 271

List of Figures and Tables

Figure 1 | 20

Table 1 | 104

Table 2 | 108

Table 3 | 110

Table 4 | 117

Table 5 | 119

Table 6 | 120

List of Readers

Listed below are the names of the child readers who participated in this study, along with their age at the time of interview. These readers appear frequently in the following pages. The full demographic information for each reader may be found in Table 2.

Name	Age	Name	Age
Abby	13 years	John	13 years
Allie	12 years	Kit	12 years
B.C.	11 years	Lisa	14 years
Boris	11 years	Lucy	12 years
Ebby	14 years	Michael	12 years
Elaine	12 years	Percy	13 years
Fishy	11 years	Rachel	13 years
Grace	12 years	Robyn	11 years
Hannah C.	11 years	Sophie A.	14 years
Hannah M.	12 years	Sophie M.	14 years
Jack	11 years	Stephanie	12 years
Jake	14 years	Tarquin	12 years
James A.	13 years	Trevor	14 years
James S.	14 years	Vanessa	12 years
Jenny	14 years	Zak	12 years
Jeremy	14 years		

Preface

This book grows out of a question that has puzzled me for years: "How do children read the Bible?" Or, to be more precise, how do children *interpret* what they encounter in the Bible? My particular area of interest here is in Bible stories, which are, after all, the key staple that we provide for our children's biblical diet. We serve out an array of vibrant characters—Daniel, Ruth, David, and of course Jesus—and heap on plenty of wildlife, from the birds in Eden to the donkey who carries Jesus into Jerusalem. All of these are usually served in a smorgasbord of enticing tales. But what do children make of all this? What tools do they use to take in and digest what they hear and read?

A quick perusal of books on this subject reveals only a few answers to my question, and most of these are anecdotal. In fact, much of the material, whether paper or electronic, that deals with the interaction of the child and the Bible seems to be guided by the Mary Poppins' principle. Find a story or interesting character to sugarcoat the medicinal lesson and the child may well swallow it and benefit. But do we really want children to learn to view Bible stories as a form of theological or moral medicine? Reading the Bible with my own children when they were younger was always rewarding and clearly suggested that children had a few things of their own to say about what they found in its pages.

The study in this book, then, is my attempt to provide a few, tentative answers to the question of how children read Bible stories. I hope that these answers will begin to help those who work with children and the Bible to be aware of how children might approach their engagement with Bible stories, and thus to make that engagement spiritually nourishing for all who are involved.

Melody Briggs

September 2016

Acknowledgments

I would like to thank Professors Hugh Pyper and Jan Horwath for guiding me through this research. Hugh responded enthusiastically to my initial research proposal and served as a source of inspiration throughout, stretching my thinking and introducing me to a range of others working in this area. Jan came on board to supervise the empirical work, but her steady hand and clear thinking guided all aspects of this study. It was a privilege to discuss my work with both of them. I am also grateful to Alison Bygrave for her untiring help and for keeping me supplied with an array of relevant documents.

A number of friends and co-researchers provided invaluable assistance. Kate Wright, working in the field of children's literature theory, listened patiently to my ideas and gave me feedback during the early part of the research. Emma England drew me further into the circle of those working with the Bible and children. Discussions with Kris Miller about the epistemology of participation helped to clarify the theological framework for my research. Patricia Briggs loaned me books on literary theory and helped to develop my knowledge of that field. Caz Weir proved an invaluable conversation partner when I was preparing for the school-based focus groups.

I am indebted to the staff of the comprehensive school in which I conducted the focus groups. For the sake of preserving participant anonymity, they must remain unnamed. Thank you to all of the pupils who participated in those groups. Special thanks goes to the Religious Education Department for making time in their schedule for the focus groups, to the head teacher for welcoming me into the school, and to the English teacher who advised me on the literary approaches used with Key Stage 3 pupils. Thank you as well to Nicola Rogers and Nicola Cadet de Fontaney for serving as assistants for these focus groups.

I also wish to acknowledge the support, encouragement, and assistance in many and various ways of: Hugh and Barbara Mason, Robert and Maureen Briggs, Edith and Steve Light, Susanne and Kristian Bendoraitis, Jon and Amelia Parker, Ruth Perrin, Christina and John Castling, Joss Bryan, Alasdair and Rachel Hicks, and Ruth and Mark Bonnington. I would like to thank Chris Spinks, Dave Belcher, Calvin Jaffarian, and everyone at Pickwick Publications for their help in bringing this book to publication.

My husband Richard has been unwavering in his support throughout, making cups of tea and repeatedly assuring me that I would one day finish this project. Our children, Joshua, Kristin, and Matthew have reminded me that life is much more than research, even research that concerns their reading habits. Our youngest, Matthew, has grown up believing that conducting research is a key part of motherhood.

Finally, I want specially to thank the children who gave of their time and energy to participate in this study: Elaine, Kit, Rachel, James S., Vanessa, Sophie A., Fishy, Sophie M., Jeremy, Jenny, Jake, Zak, Ebby, Allie, Abby, Trevor, Percy, James A., Hannah M., Jack, Stephanie, John, Lucy, Tarquin, Boris, Robyn, B.C., Hannah C., Grace, Lisa, and Michael. You know who you are. This study would not have been possible without you, and you are the true stars of all that follows.

Abbreviations

GNB	Good News Bible
IFG	Interviewee Focus Group
JSNTS Supplement	Journal for the Study of the New Testament: Supplement Series
NCV	New Century Version
SBL	Society of Biblical Literature
RVG	Respondent Validation Group
WBC	Word Biblical Commentary
{ }	The notations in { } brackets indicate the reader's body language and other forms of non-verbal response.

Part One

The Theoretical Background to the Children's Readings of Luke

Chapter 1

Introduction

Trevor: "What I've read in Luke, it's really different."

The Question

How do children read the Bible? This is a question that does not often seem to come up in the circles where children and the Bible generally mix. The two key formal institutions in Britain that include these circles are the church and school, and their concern often appears to be determining what child readers *ought* to take from the biblical text, rather than asking the more basic question of what happens when the Bible and child meet, free of any imposed *oughts*. Even if these oughts, or boundaries, are necessary (and I am not certain that they are), how can we accurately draw the boundary lines if we have not first worked out the location of the field?

This study seeks to locate that field. It does not ask *if* children should be reading the Bible, but, rather, what happens when they *do*? This question should undergird the encounters between the Bible and the child that are initiated by the adults of any institution. It allows these adults to be more effective in their work with children and the Bible since it enables them to know their starting point. Importantly, this question also respects the child. As this study will show, children may well bring their own orientations and reading strategies to the biblical text. If we respect the position of children as people with a particular set of developmental interests and contextual concerns, and if we respect the Bible with its challenging and often subversive approach to the interests and concerns of any group, then we need to give child readers a voice to articulate their readings of the Bible. How else will we get a glimpse of the field?

This question matters because children, and especially churched children, are repeatedly exposed to the Bible not only in church-based groups and school, but also at home and through various forms of media. If these various parties are to handle the biblical text wisely with their young charges, they need to understand what young readers make of the Bible. It may be salutary at this point to provide a few examples of the clash between adult provision of the Bible and children's expectations. One of the child participants in this study, Robyn, found herself reading through the Gospel of Luke at the same time as, but independently of, her church: "My church is reading Luke's Gospel [for Lent] and I just assumed that when the church would read a whole Gospel, that they'd read the entire thing. When I finished Luke . . . I realized that they were missing verses out and how much that I hadn't known." Robyn responded with indignation to her discovery that her church was not exposing her to the entirety of the Gospel. She particularly bemoaned her church's omission of what she deemed to be some of the most interesting parables: "They missed the Widow and the Judge out." This discovery led her to an unsettling conclusion: "So now I realize how much the church doesn't teach you."

Note that Robyn's discovery took place in the midst of an adult congregation. It was not in a children's group where the Bible tends to be even more truncated and tamed. Another participant in this study, Trevor, lamented the discrepancy between the portrait of Jesus provided by Luke and the view of Jesus that he had developed through attendance at his church's children's work: "I found there was a lot of contradiction between what's been drummed into me for ages at church, like, 'Jesus was amazing. Jesus was perfect.' Then what I've read in Luke, it's really different." This discrepancy left Trevor questioning his church tradition. The views expressed by Robyn and Trevor may perhaps not be views that the average churched adult would like children to have of their church's handling of the Bible, but they may be unavoidable if children's perspectives on the biblical text are not taken seriously.

Developing the Question

It would be misleading to present my study as the product of a self-evident research question that generated a particular way of investigating children's readings of the Bible. I will now give a brief account of how my central question, "how do children read the Bible?" led to the development and shape of this study. Robyn and Trevor's views resonate with me. Professionally, I straddle two academic disciplines: youth and children's work as an area of practical theology, and biblical studies. I have found that the material and methods used in the former discipline in its approach to the Bible often diverge from the hermeneutical theories and interpretive methods advocated by the discipline of biblical studies. This divergence raised an array of related questions for me. Is it appropriate? Do the disciplines of practical theology, particularly the area of youth and children's work, and biblical studies not have more to say to each other? What are the implications of this divergence for the children and youth with whom I have worked, as well as for the students whom I have trained to work with them?

It seemed to me that asking how children read the Bible might draw these two disciplines together, since analyzing the encounter of a real reader with the biblical text would overlap the interests of both. An area within biblical studies that particularly interests me is how ordinary readers handle the Bible, and children are one sub-group of these non-theologically trained readers. My central question has been largely neglected by the academy: biblical scholars have shown only minimal interest in the reading strategies of ordinary readers in general, let alone in those of children. A key exception here is the burgeoning interest in Contextual Bible Study with particular people groups.[1]

My research in the discipline of children's literature theory further stimulated my pursuit of the central question. Children's literature theorists regularly ask questions about how children interpret texts.[2] It occurred to me as I explored their research that asking similar questions about children's interpretation of the Bible could be a fruitful enterprise, both for the practices of youth and children's work, and for the discipline of biblical studies. I duly went in search of any existing fruit, but found only a few, rather under-developed specimens. I discovered that either the relevant interpretive questions had not been asked, or on the few occasions when they were, they were often formed in such a way that their answers came with an array of in-built biases. The fruit was not necessarily rotten, but it certainly did not make for a satisfying repast.

I concluded that I needed to cultivate some fruit of my own. This study, accordingly, seeks to explore how children read the Bible. Such exploration means working out how one group of readers approach the biblical text. That approach may have implications for how the Bible is used with children, but it may also have implications for how other groups of people encounter the Bible. That is, child readers may have a thing or two to reveal about how to read the Bible in a way that goes beyond the bounds of their particular field.

---

1. See, for example, Riches, *What Is Contextual Bible Study?*; Lawrence, *The Word in Place*; Rowland and Roberts, *The Bible for Sinners*.

2. See, for example, Tatar, *Enchanted Hunters*; Mikkelsen, *Powerful Magic*; Appleyard, *Becoming a Reader*; Applebee, *The Child's Concept of Story*.

Narrowing the Field

The question, "How do children read the Bible?" opens up a field that is far too large for one study. The Bible is a big book, a library of books to be precise, which vary greatly in length, literary genre, and theological concern. Likewise children cannot be classified as a homogenous unit. They too vary greatly due to differences in age, context, gender, developmental phase, level of education, socio-economic background, as well as their religious background, an area that is particularly pertinent to a study concerned with the Bible. In order to make the study manageable, I had to narrow its range considerably.

First, I narrowed the study down to one book in the biblical canon. My area of familiarity in biblical studies is with the New Testament. Sticking to this part of the canon significantly reduced the range of books I could use for the study. The common use of Bible stories with children led me to seek a narrative, which again narrowed my options. Out of the remaining options, I decided to work with the Gospel of Luke, for a variety of reasons. Luke provides an account of the life of Jesus from beginning to end, allowing child readers to encounter a full-length story within the canon. While all four Gospels broadly fit this description, only Luke and Matthew include both a birth narrative and a resurrection account, and of these two, only Luke includes an extended resurrection account. Its account of Jesus' life makes Luke an accessible introduction to the world of biblical narrative, providing inexperienced readers of the Bible with a coherent starting point.[3]

Using Luke as the focus text had a number of benefits. It contains a variety of genres and is multi-layered, mixing its account of Jesus' life with fictional, parabolic sections and metaphoric teaching. Navigating Luke, then, demands complex reading strategies whose differences served as a litmus test for working out the make-up of the children's readings. Luke also contains some of the most culturally familiar passages in the whole canon, such as the parables of the Good Samaritan and of the Lost Son, the story of Zacchaeus, and Jesus' birth narrative, alongside numerous unfamiliar passages. This mix of the familiar with the unfamiliar seemed an appropriate blend for child readers, with the familiar passages potentially providing

---

3. Jonathan Pennington even suggests that the Gospels serve as the keystone holding the biblical canon together. He writes: "The Gospel accounts complete and make ultimate sense of the story of God's work in the world as found in the Jewish Scriptures, while at the same time they serve as the fountainhead for the rest of the apostolic witness and teaching." On this basis, a Gospel may even be an *optimal* starting point for an inexperienced reader of the Bible. See Pennington, *Reading the Gospels Wisely*, 231.

them with a toehold in the book while the unfamiliar ensured that they would encounter fresh material.

Secondly, I narrowed the range of potential child participants. The focus of this study is not upon the acquisition of the skill of reading but upon how children interpret the Bible. I wanted to avoid issues related to reading fluency and so decided to investigate the readings of older children. Due to my professional interest in youth and children's ministry, I further narrowed the sample parameters by limiting my participants to those with some type of church background or affiliation. But this still left a wide range of potential participants.

In order to work with a clearly defined sample, I decided to target one school in one city, a decision which had direct implications for the age range of the participants. Since I was interested in the readings of older children, I had to sample either from the oldest age cohort in a primary school or the youngest age cohort in a secondary school. I had ease of access to a particular comprehensive school in the north-east of England and decided to use it as my target school. In England, the youngest age cohort in a comprehensive school is eleven- to fourteen-year-olds. This age group became the study's target readers.

Having determined the biblical book and the target readership, I then had to work out a means of bringing them together. That is, I needed a method of study. Working with real readers meant empirical research and I rapidly concluded that I would need to interview the child participants if I wanted to understand their readings of Luke. But I also wanted the child readers to engage with the Bible on their own terms, as free of as many constraints as possible. I therefore decided to set up a study which allowed me to give a Gospel of Luke to each child participant to read in her or his own time, and to interview each participant afterwards. To validate the findings from these interviews, I decided to conduct two types of focus groups: the first type of focus group was with the interview participants and the second was with a broader sample of child readers from the target school.

As a result of these decisions, this study is based on over two years of qualitative empirical research with a group of eleven- to fourteen-year-old churched children in one north-eastern comprehensive school and this group of children's readings of the Gospel of Luke. While the empirical research had two principal subjects, the child reader and Luke, its focus was the readings of Luke generated by their interaction. All of the theoretical conclusions in this study derive from the results of this empirical work.

Narrowing the field of research necessarily limited the scope of my study. The study findings are only relevant in the first instance to the demographic of the child participants. Most of the interview participants could be described as "churched," although most of the focus group participants were not "churched." Most of the participants live in the same area of the UK and attend the same school. Within the target school, about one-third of the pupils are from a working class background and two-thirds from a middle-class background, and both the interview cohort and focus groups mirror this demographic.[4]

My narrowed field of research led to a narrowed central question and the working question driving this study is: *what are the key features and strategies that characterize children's readings of the Gospel of Luke?* The central thesis of this study is that the children's interpretive strategies may be described as participatory. In the following pages I seek to describe the nature of this participation and to probe its implications. These implications spill over into three disciplines: biblical studies, children's literature theory, and practical theology. In other words, the answer to my question may well have implications for reading the Gospel of Luke, for views of how children read, and for children as readers of the Bible.

Outline of the Study

The following discussion of how children read the Gospel of Luke is divided into three parts. In the first part, I explore the relevant literature. In the second part, I delineate the methodology I used for seeking an answer to the working question. In the third part, I analyze the findings of this empirical work.

In the first part, the literature reviewed falls into three categories which I discuss in three chapters: literature pertinent to reading Luke, literature pertaining to children as readers, and literature which draws together the two principal subjects, the Bible and the child reader. In the first of these, chapter 2, I examine Luke as a text which invites participation, and then consider theoretical discussions of the relationship between texts and readers. This chapter draws heavily upon the fields of biblical studies and literary theory.

In chapter 3, I look at studies of children as readers. This chapter draws on the fields of childhood development, children's literature theory, and cognitive science. I examine the contributions of developmental stage theories and cognitive science to our understanding of children's reading, and I discuss the nuances of the literary theories concerned with childhood

---

4. The sample demographic is outlined in more detail in chapter 5 under "Profile Parameters." Other limitations of the study are discussed in chapter 12.

reading. This chapter aims to delineate some of the key characteristics of children as readers that may be relevant to this study.

I conclude the literature review by turning in chapter 4 to the field of practical theology. Here I examine empirical studies and theoretical discussions concerned with the Bible and real readers. First I consider empirical studies of ordinary readers engaging with the Bible, and then I examine the literature concerned specifically with children reading the Bible. These foci allow me to highlight some of the key gaps between the features of Luke as narrative and the characteristics of children as readers, as established in chapters 2 and 3, and how the Bible is often presented to children.

The second part of this study explicates the empirical research. This part has two chapters. In chapter 5, I explain the reasons behind my choice of research methodology and explore the implications of working with child participants. I also describe how I set up the empirical research. Chapter 6 then provides an account of how I implemented the research methodology, including details of the interviews, the method of analysis, and the validation of the findings through the focus groups.

The third part of the study is an analysis of the research findings with reference to the discussion established in the literature review. There are five key reading strategies that come out of the research and one over-arching theoretical framework uniting these reading strategies. My discussion in this part is organized around these findings. In chapter 7, I discuss the over-arching framework, which I call participatory reading. The children's interpretations of the Gospel of Luke appeared to derive from an active dialogue with the Gospel, which produced for them an experience of Luke's narrative world. After introducing this framework, I discuss over five chapters the five reading strategies of which the reading dialogue was comprised. These include: reading Luke as a story, the child readers' use of the imagination, their empathetic approach to Luke, their pursuit of the sense of the text, and their orientation to the plot.

One of my aims throughout is to allow the voice of the child participants to be heard whenever possible. As a consequence the third part of the study, in particular, includes numerous quotes from the children as evidence of their readings. These quotes are drawn directly from the interview and focus group transcripts, unless otherwise noted. The previous quotes from Robyn and Trevor provide examples.

I conclude in chapter 12 with a brief summary of the overall study. I suggest some of the implications of this study, including ways forward for using the Bible with child readers. I also note the limitations of my study and propose potential trajectories for building on or testing the findings through future studies.

Chapter 2

Reading Luke

Hannah M.: "I was confused before I read [the Gospel]. Now I realize that Luke's more like a story."

Introduction

This chapter has two sections. Initially, I discuss Luke's narrative features, particularly focusing on those features that may contribute to an analysis of the children's readings. Then I examine some of the literary theories concerned with the transaction between readers and texts, in order to select a theoretical framework which may help to elucidate the children's readings of Luke.

Luke as Narrative

The appropriate literary classification for the Gospel of Luke is a matter of some debate, with some scholars describing Luke as historiography,[1] others labelling it as a form of ancient biography,[2] and one prominent proposal claiming that it belongs to the genre of ancient scientific writing since it seeks to communicate a body of teaching.[3] These classifications have at least one thing in common: they all agree that Luke is a "prose narrative."[4] Indeed, the text presents itself as a narrative, first by reporting that it is a narrative account, and then by assuming standard narrative form. In the prologue,

---

1. Classically: Cadbury, *The Style and Literary Method of Luke.*

2. Burridge, *What Are the Gospels?*, 185–212; Pennington, *Reading the Gospels Wisely*, 23; Talbert, *Literary Patterns.*

3. Alexander, *The Preface to Luke's Gospel.* For a summary of the debate, see Burridge, *What Are the Gospels?*, 3–101.

4. Alexander, "What Is a Gospel," 14. See also Frei, *Eclipse*, 13, 16; Pennington, *Reading the Gospels Wisely*, 21; Green, *Luke*, 1.

Luke 1:1, the writer/redactor refers to the text as an orderly *diēgēsis*, or narrative. After the prologue the Gospel assumes narrative form by beginning with time and location markers, and then establishing a focal character using a standard introductory device: "During the time when Herod was king of Judea, there was a priest named Zechariah" (Luke 1:5).[5] As Joel Green notes, this self-classification "immediately invites a mode of reading appropriate to 'narrative.'"[6] Narrative is fundamental to the nature of this Gospel. The contents of Luke are presented to readers as *storied*.[7]

Reading the Gospel of Luke, then, means reading it in a way that respects its narrative form. "Narrative" may be broadly defined as an account of inter-connected events through time. The literary critic Peter Brooks refers to narrative as "a form of understanding and explanation."[8] Narrative is a means of *knowing* through that which it depicts and therefore may have an epistemological function. Hans Frei argues, in his seminal work *The Eclipse of Biblical Narrative*, that how a biblical narrative makes sense is a function "of the depiction and narrative rendering of the events constituting" it.[9] Luke arranges and expresses its contents in a particular way. Frei refers to the synoptic Gospels as a form of realistic narrative: unlike many ancient narratives, they are stylistically simple and life-like, or mimetic.[10] The narrative of Luke is not given, for instance, to romantic depictions of its characters and events.

A narrative communicates through a variety of modes. Seymour Chatman famously described narrative as consisting of two inter-linked forms: the story or contents, and the discourse or means of expression that is used to communicate those contents. In Chatman's words, "the story is the *what* in a narrative that is depicted, discourse the *how*."[11] Using Chatman's categories, Luke's story is concerned with the birth, life, death, and resurrection of the protagonist, while Luke's discourse is multifaceted and includes literary forms such as micro-narratives, parables, metaphors, and imagery.

---

5. All Bible quotes are from the Good News Bible, unless otherwise specified, for reasons to be discussed in chapter 5.

6. Green, *Luke*, 1.

7. See Powell, *Narrative Criticism*, 4. Powell's discussion is with reference to Auerbach, *Mimesis*.

8. Brooks, *Reading for the Plot*, 10.

9. Frei, *Eclipse*, 13.

10. Ibid., 16.

11. Chatman, *Story and Discourse*, 19; italics in the original. It is worth noting that Genette posits a similar division but applies the terms differently. He labels content as "story," similar to Chatman, but refers to discourse as "narrative." My discussion follows Chatman's use of the terms. See Genette, *Narrative Discourse*.

Discourse devices such as sequence, voice, and perspective contribute to the import of the text. Reading Luke means navigating these different communicative forms.

Luke's structure is episodic: it consists of a macro-narrative constructed out of a series of inter-related micro-narratives, with the infancy and passion stories serving as bookends that initiate and conclude the narrative flow. Loveday Alexander helpfully compares the episodic structure of the Gospels to that of folk tales and ancient teaching stories, both of which "tend to be structured as encounters" between the central figure and other individuals or groups. In folk tales, the action ensues through a series of these encounters while in teaching stories, "the teacher meets and responds to a disciple, or an enquirer, or a patron, or a hostile official."[12] The development of Luke's plot may be compared to the former while the presentation of Luke's teaching sections may be compared to the latter, although in Luke these two are intertwined so that the teaching sections also sometimes function as encounters which propel the plot forward. Luke also differs significantly from these two forms of writing in that it consists of a "connected, theologically coherent narrative," a form that Alexander believes takes the narrative mode of the Hebrew Bible as its model.[13]

Luke's teaching sections are part of its narrative. Mark Allan Powell makes the useful point that conceptions of a Gospel text which divide it between "narrative material" and "sayings material" depend upon too narrow a definition of narrative. Powell points out, for instance, that the speech of a character may function as a narrative event.[14] Accordingly, the teaching sections of Luke may be classified as narrative events in which Jesus functions as the narrator. These sections play an important role in the narrative, for they both show the protagonist in his role as a teacher and reveal his theological, ethical, and pastoral concerns.

The ordering of Luke's episodes may not be chronological, but the overall effect is of a temporal sequence structured around the earthly life of the protagonist. The narrative gives weight to the beginning and end points of Jesus' life by slowing its pace and filling in the details of the infancy stories and the concluding days of Jesus' earthly life. The emphasis on these two points signals the passing of time in the Gospel account. Paul Ricoeur stresses the importance of temporality to narrative: not only do the recounted events represent the passing of time, but the recounting of those

---

12. Alexander, "What Is a Gospel," 18, 24.
13. Ibid., 27–28.
14. Powell, *Narrative Criticism*, 35.

events is a process that takes time.[15] Reading through the Gospel gives the reader the experience of passing through time with the characters and thus of experiencing the narrative events alongside of them.

Plot is a fundamental component of narrative: the story events are connected by some form of causality that gives the narrative unity.[16] The plot of Luke connects its beginning and end points, and encompasses the events that comprise the body of the narrative. Plot consists of actions enacted by characters, who are the actors of the story. Marguerat and Bourquin state that narrative includes the "presence of an agent-hero inspired by an intention which draws the story towards its close."[17] Luke's "agent-hero" is Jesus, who, as Alexander points out in reference to all four Gospels, "is the center not only of the story as a whole but of virtually every individual episode."[18] Jesus is the actor whose agency drives the plot forward. The other characters that are present throughout the narrative usually function as group characters. These include the disciples and the crowds, who represent those who follow Jesus and those who may potentially join him, respectively, and the religious leaders who function as Jesus' opponents.

Luke's Narrative World

A narrative is not merely a series of interconnected events; it also conveys a state of affairs. According to Umberto Eco, to recount a narrative is to "construct a world, furnished as much as possible, down to the smallest detail."[19] Although Eco's statement refers to the construction of fictive worlds, his point has some relevance to narratives in general. A narrative conveys a place or world that is not only the site of the plot, but also the locus of a logic which governs the events of the plot. This logic makes sense of the causality that links the narrative events. Together, the plot and this unifying logic, or worldview, constitute the narrative world.

Like any good narrative, Luke's plot and worldview are inseparable. The worldview of Luke is theological. The machinations of Luke's plot not only reflect but also contribute to the text's theology, while the theology guides interpretation of the plot. I look at each of these in turn.

---

15. As discussed in Marguerat and Bourquin, *How to Read*, 16. See also Ricoeur, *From Text to Action*, 2.

16. Marguerat and Bourquin, *How to Read*, 16.

17. Ibid., 16, summarizing the argument of Adam, "Décrire des Actions," 3–22.

18. Alexander, "What Is a Gospel," 14–15.

19. Eco, *Reflections*, 23.

Luke's Plot

Luke's plot revolves around Jesus yet consists not of a general account of his life, but rather of a selective representation of it. The selected contents are concerned with Jesus' identity and the enactment of his mission. This selectivity is an expression of narrative purpose: the narrative provides an account of who Jesus was and what he did.

The narrator initially discloses Jesus' identity to the reader in the infancy account. Jesus is to be viewed as the Son of God and fulfilment of Messianic promise (e.g., Luke 1:32–33). The remainder of the narrative is built on this collusion between the narrator and the reader, both of whom know the protagonist's true identity while many of the characters do not. The subsequent events tend to demonstrate rather than state Jesus' identity, so that a key function of the narrative is revelation. As C. Kavin Rowe remarks: "The narration of the life of Jesus is . . . for Luke the revelation of God."[20] This discourse technique mirrors Jesus' response to John the Baptist's disciples (Luke 7:18–23): Jesus' words and actions demonstrate the essence of Messiah.

What does the narrative demonstrate about the Messiah? The Messiah displays authority over the demonic realm (e.g., Luke 8:26–39; 9:37–43), the natural elements (Luke 8:22–25), and even over death (Luke 7:11–16; 8:40–56). Reflecting God's role as provider in Hebrew Scripture, Jesus provides food in the wilderness (Luke 9:10–17), and heals his people (e.g., Luke 5:12–15, 17–26; 18:35–43). He is not restricted by human interpretations of the covenant, but rather is the Lord and implementer of that covenant (e.g., Luke 6:1–5; 6:6–11; 13:10–17), as well as the interpreter of Scripture (e.g., Luke 6:27–49; 10:25–37; 18:9–14). He uses parables to explain his identity and mission (Luke 8:4–15; 15:1–32; 19:11–27; 20:9–18).

While the events reveal Jesus' identity, the story they *tell* is of the enactment of his mission. The protagonist overtly states his mission in his first public speech in Luke 4:16–21: the fulfilment of Hebrew Scripture's Messianic hope. Shortly thereafter, Jesus summarizes his mission as preaching the "Good News about the Kingdom of God" (Luke 4:43). The work of the Messiah is to establish the Kingdom, that is, the reign of God in the world, and his central actions testify to and enable that Kingdom. Jesus' identity and mission are intertwined. Only as the Messiah can he establish God's

---

20. Rowe, *Early Narrative Christology*, 218. Rowe provides an extensive discussion of the centrality of Jesus' identity to the purpose of Luke. His key argument is that Luke's author/redactor makes sophisticated narrative use of the title *kyrios* both to establish and to develop Jesus' Christological identity as an embodiment of the visitation and presence of God with his people. See *Early Narrative Christology*, 9, 17, 20, 28, 77, 157.

Kingdom; and the Kingdom he inaugurates is of God and not of earth because he is the Messiah.

Although Jesus is the protagonist, his mission is directed by God. As Douglas McComiskey indicates, Luke portrays God as the divine authority behind Jesus' mission "and thereby legitimates" that mission.[21] God is a character in the Gospel only in that his voice is heard on occasion (Luke 3:22; 9:35). This voice, speaking into the story from outside the boundaries of the narrative's setting, presents God as the off-stage director of the plot. Indeed, Jesus' life demonstrates God's sovereignty in action.[22] The events of Luke are initiated by God: he sends angelic messengers, promises, and then provides the births of John and Jesus (e.g., Luke 1:11–17, 26–37, 57–66; 2:1–15). He guides events through the Holy Spirit, who enables Jesus' conception, initiates his public ministry, and serves as the source of its power (e.g., Luke 1:35; 3:22; 4:14; 6:19). Jesus' miracles are proclaimed as God's handiwork (e.g., Luke 5:21–26; 17:11–19; 18:35–43). Jesus and his disciples defeat the forces of darkness through the power of God (e.g., Luke 8:26–39; 9:1–6; 10:17–24; 11:14–22).

The plot follows Jesus' march towards the fulfilment of God's plan[23] to redeem humanity. Even before his birth, Jesus is hailed as a King, while the trajectory of his unusual royal life is towards the salvation of his people from the oppression of death (Luke 1:32–33, 69–79). This path is characterized by conflict, as Jesus faces opposition at some point from most of the other characters, including the blunderings of his friends (e.g., Luke 9:46–50; 22:47–62). The fulfilment of his mission takes place not merely despite but *through* those who oppose him, and Jesus' clash with the religious leaders, the political authorities, and Satan is a driving force in the plot.

Jesus' first confrontation is with Satan (Luke 4:1–13) and the expulsion of evil spirits is a fundamental part of his ministry (e.g., Luke 4:41, 8:26–39; 9:37–43; 11:14–26), so that Jesus' conflict with the demonic realm pervades the narrative. The religious leaders respond acrimoniously to Jesus' refusal to submit to their interpretation of the Jewish law and practices, and, unable to restrain him, they eventually collude with Satan through the medium of a disciple (Luke 22:1–6). This collusion enables them to arrest and thus gain power over Jesus. The threat of political interference also runs like a thread through the narrative, initially in the form of Herod (Luke 1:5; 3:19–20; 9:7–9; 13:31–35), but expanding to include Roman power under Pilate (Luke 23:1–26). All of these groups combine force to put Jesus to death.

---

21. McComiskey, *Lukan Theology*, 307.
22. Squires, "The Gospel according to Luke," 168.
23. Cf. Kingsbury, *Conflict*, 12.

According to Luke's account of the divine plan, Jesus' death does not equate to defeat. Despite the Lukan penchant for showing rather than telling, beginning in chapter 9, Jesus and the narrator repeatedly articulate that his death and resurrection are part of his mission (e.g., Luke 9:21–22, 30–31; 18:31–33; 24:25–27). The reader therefore knows that when Jesus is rendered powerless in the final stages of the plot, the divine plan is being enacted. The plot concludes with an ironic twist. The Satanic and human powers' seeming victory contributes directly to the fulfilment of Jesus' mission: victory over the forces that suppress humanity and the establishment of his eternal Kingship.

Luke's Theological Worldview

Luke's worldview reflects the divine plan. This worldview is evident in Luke's embedded values, many of which have ethical and social ramifications. Jesus' redemption is of the highest value and is praised openly at the outset (e.g., Luke 1:46–56, 67–79; 2:13–14, 28–32). Also of particular value is the recovery of the lost, those who are deemed sinners (Luke 7:36–50; 15:1–32; 19:1–10). Repentance and the forgiveness of sins receive constant approbation in the narrative as the appropriate responses to this recovery (e.g., Luke 3:7–18; 5:27–32; 18:9–14).

According to the Lukan worldview, the presence of the Kingdom has clear implications for the lives of Jesus' followers. Allegiance to the Kingdom is expressed through faith (e.g., Luke 7:1–10; 8:22–25; 12:41–47; 17:5–6). This faith is lived out in discipleship, which involves following Jesus wholeheartedly whatever the cost (e.g., Luke 5:1–11; 9:57–62; 12:8–12; 14:25–35). Discipleship has ethical implications and much of Jesus' teaching focuses on what it means to live according to the Kingdom (e.g., Luke 6:20–49; 12:22–34; 13:18–21; 14:7–35; 18:15–17). Life in the Kingdom means dependence upon God and prayer is endorsed as a fundamental part of discipleship (e.g., Luke 6:12; 11:1–13; 18:1–14).

The narrative elucidates the values of the Kingdom by contrasting them with, and emphasizing their superiority to, the values of the earthly world. Those on the margins of society are drawn in while those wielding power are challenged (e.g., Luke 5:27–32; 6:6–11; 11:37–54; 19:1–10).

Status is side-lined in favor of servanthood (e.g., Luke 9:46–48; 12:41–48; 17:7–10). The poor[24] are valued but love of wealth is deemed an impediment (e.g., Luke 6:20–25; 12:13–34; 16:19–31; 18:18–30; 21:1–4). Humility is upheld and the emptiness of pride is made explicit (e.g., Luke 7:36–50; 14:7–14; 18:9–17).

Jesus' ministry evokes confrontation between the values of the Kingdom and the values of the earthly world, a confrontation which eventually leads to his death. Fokkelman points out that a narrative world may also conflict with the values of the reader's world.[25] Luke's narrative world does not encourage the reader merely to observe its events. As Pennington indicates, the biblical Gospels "purport to define our reality."[26] The Lukan world is presented not as a place of escape from normal life, but as an alternative vision of the primary world. Its values may challenge the reader just as they challenge the characters in the text.

Luke as Participatory

Like any narrative, Luke invites its readers to see from its point of view. The Gospel does not just present a God-directed world, but seeks, as Green indicates, to "involve its readers" in "an interactive discourse" with that world.[27] This reader participation is a type of immersion experience. As Louise Rosenblatt states, narrative literature in general "provides a *living through*, not simply *knowledge about*."[28] Luke aligns its reader with its embedded worldview, so that the reader interacts with its world from within the framework of that worldview.

The discourse of Luke encourages reader participation in various ways. One of these is Luke's style of narration. Luke frequently conveys its stories through the narration technique of showing the significance of events. This indirect form of narration enhances a reader's experience of the story in a way that its counterpart, telling or the provision of direct information by the narrator, does not. As Timothy Wiarda explains, showing "puts greater demand on the reader, but at the same time tends to exert a more powerful

---

24. Although note that "poor" in Luke is a broader category than economic poverty. It refers to any form of low status that leads to exclusion or social disadvantage. See the discussion in Green, *Theology*, 79–82.
25. Fokkelman, *Reading Biblical Narrative*, 23.
26. Pennington, *Reading the Gospels Wisely*, 146; original italics removed.
27. Green, *Theology*, 23–24.
28. Rosenblatt, *Literature as Exploration*, 38; italics in the original.

impact."[29] To work out the significance of an event, readers may become immersed in the plight of the characters and draw conclusions based on their own evaluation of the situation. Due to this narration method, Luke may be described as an open text for it "encourages—indeed, expects—an interactive dynamic between text and audience, because the author has left the arrangement of some elements of the work to the reader. Therefore it is open to a range of meanings."[30]

A number of other Lukan discourse techniques likewise encourage reader participation. Kathy Maxwell specifies, in her discussion of the role of the ancient audience in hearing/reading Luke-Acts, that Luke's provision of "privileged information, omissions, comparisons, hidden meanings, question and answer situations, and allusions"[31] all augment participation. For instance, omissions may invite readers to fill gaps in the narrative in order to make sense of the story. To interact with such a text on its own terms, the reader cannot simply peruse it for information or moral lessons, but must actively engage with its contents via its internal directives.

This openness to reader participation allows for multiple interpretations. Yet, as Robert C. Tannehill states, such multivalency "need not lead to the extreme view that we can make whatever we want of a text, which would imply that we are communicating only with ourselves."[32] If reading is an act of participation with the text, then the text has a role in how it is read. John A. Darr clarifies that "the text remains a constant in the interpretive equation," and therefore "serves as the prime criterion for narrowing the range of acceptable readings."[33] The interpretation of a text should fall within limits which are determined by the text itself. Otherwise, as Eco so elegantly puts it, "if Jack the Ripper told us that he did what he did on the grounds of his interpretation of the Gospel according to Saint Luke" even the most reader-orientated critics "would be inclined to think that he read Saint Luke in a pretty preposterous way."[34] Following the directives of the text is crucial to reader participation and textual interpretation.

Participation in a narrative world is not a neutral activity. It may affect the reader on multiple levels. Wiarda suggests that the Gospels may

---

29. Wiarda, *Interpreting Gospel Narratives*, 37.

30. Green, "Narrative Criticism," 91–92. Green's discussion is an application of Eco's concept of an open text to the Gospel of Luke. See Eco, *The Role of the Reader*, 33–34, 144–72.

31. Maxwell, *Hearing Between the Lines*, 174–75.

32. Tannehill, "Freedom and Responsibility," 265.

33. Darr, *Character Building*, 171.

34. Eco, *Interpretation and Overinterpretation*, 24.

impact their readers' minds as well as their "senses, feelings, and will,"[35] so that reading is a holistic experience. Participation opens the door to the text persuading the reader and numerous scholars label Luke as "persuasive" literature.[36] What is the reader to be persuaded of? In answer to this question, both Maxwell and Shillington point to Luke's own statement in Luke 1:4: that the reader may know the truth about the things in which she or he has been instructed.[37] Luke seeks to assure the reader of the viability of its narrative world, particularly the viability of viewing Jesus as the bringer of God's Kingdom and the redeemer of the world. This persuasion is not just about cognitive assent. Since the Gospel may impact its readers holistically, it may be life-shaping.

In summary, Luke is a narrative and reading with the grain of Luke means reading it as narrative. Such reading does not approach Luke as a historical fact book or a religious "how to" guide, but rather interacts with the text in its story form. How is this text-reader interaction to be analyzed? The next section of this chapter seeks an answer to this question.

In Search of a Theory

The way that a person reads a narrative may be theorized from a variety of angles, an activity that is usually classified as literary criticism. M. H. Abrams notably divides literary criticism, along with all forms of aesthetic criticism, into four categories, including: the work, mimesis of the "universe," the artist, and the audience.[38] He presents these categories in the form of a diagram, with the work at the center and the other categories radiating out from it. Literary theories tend to address the central work, or text, in relation to at least one of the other categories.

John Barton adapts Abrams's schema for the field of biblical studies and uses it to assess the critical theories in this field. Barton's categories are, respective to Abrams': the text, historical events and theological ideas, the author, and the reader.[39] Although other critics formulate this theoretical discussion differently,[40] the Abrams/Barton schema, shown in Figure 1,

---

35. Wiarda, *Interpreting Gospel Narratives*, 48.

36. See, for example, Maxwell, *Hearing Between the Lines*, 125; Parsons, *Luke*, 45; Shillington, *Luke-Acts*, 10; Green, *Luke*, 115; Powell, *What Are They Saying about Luke?*, 6–7; Karris, *Luke*, 8–9.

37. Maxwell, *Hearing between the Lines*, 1; Shillington, *Luke-Acts*, 10.

38. Abrams, *The Mirror and the Lamp*, 6–7.

39. Barton, "Classifying Biblical Criticism," 23.

40. Marguerat and Bourquin indicate that Ricoeur, for instance, formulates the

provides a useful starting point for framing the literary issues pertinent to my study.

FIGURE 1

Abrams's (Barton's) Schema

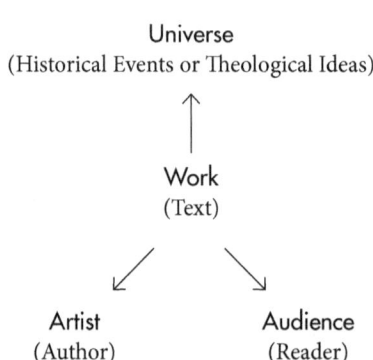

My study has two foci relevant to Abrams's schema, as articulated by Barton: the reader and the text. An important criterion for my theoretical framework is that it does not limit the discussion to one or the other of these two interlocutors, but allows for their interplay. No reader, whether child or adult, views a text free of her or his ideological, contextual, and experiential lenses. Yet the text is the image that the reading seeks to reflect, even if the glass appears a bit distorted at times. As Richard Bauckham helpfully states, "meaning does not reside in the text . . . nor is it simply created by readers . . . It happens in interaction between the text itself and its readers."[41]

This study explores the readings produced by that interaction. While a book is an object, reading is an activity. This activity is not tantamount to going to a field, the book, to dig for buried treasure, although some readers do approach books this way. Reading is more like a dialogue between two partners. I look now at the theories pertaining to each of these partners.

---

discussion as three forms of spatio-temporal mimesis, including the world the author and reader have in common and bring to the text, the world of the text, and the world of the reader as impacted by the text. Marguerat and Bourquin, *How to Read*, 141–45; see also Ricoeur, *Time and Narrative*.

41. Bauckham, *Scripture and Authority Today*, 21. Cf. Powell, *Narrative Criticism*, 17–18; Eco, *The Limits of Interpretation*.

The Reader

The critical theories clustering around Abrams'/Barton's category of reader are often broadly referred to as reader-response criticism. Reader-response criticism comes in many forms. Some forms minimize the interplay between reader and text, building theoretical castles around the reader that veritably guard against the encroachment of the text.[42] Such theories provide little space for the text-reader dialogue. Other reader-response theories, such as Wolfgang Iser's phenomenology of reading, foreground the co-working of the reader and text in a manner more helpful to this study. Iser argues that the "meaning" of the text is not "an object to be defined, but . . . an effect to be experienced."[43] The act of interpreting a text includes the reader's experience of the text: how the text affects the reader is part of the meaning of the text. Iser's emphasis is useful for my examination of the dynamic occurring between Luke and the child reader, although Iser limits his own discussion to the strategies embedded in the text and does not discuss real readers.[44]

Reader-response criticism includes experimental models which investigate the responses of real readers and which develop reading theories based on a synthesis of these responses. These theories tend to focus on the psychological roots of the readers' responses.[45] My research project is pragmatically aligned with this model, since it investigates the readings of real readers. However, while my analysis takes into account the pertinent cognitive and emotive responses of the child readers, it is not limited to the psychology of reading. Instead, I attempt to maintain a broad perspective on the sources of reading diversity, referring at times to psychological categories but just as often to socio-cultural influences and theological leanings. These sources of diversity, which originate with the child readers, are consistently balanced against the directives of the text. The focus of this study is upon the readings produced by the text-reader interaction, not upon readers *per se*.

Robert M. Fowler, in his seminal work on reader-response criticism and the Gospel of Mark, characterizes reading as an act of communication between the author, text, and reader, based on the communication model of the linguist Jakobson.[46] This model provides space for the interplay between text and reader. Fowler uses this model to analyze the Markan textual strategies that guide reader-response, but like Iser, he looks only at the text's role

---

42. For example: Fish, *Is There a Text in This Class?*; Holland, *Five Readers Reading*.

43. Iser, *The Act of Reading*, 9–10.

44. Ibid., x.

45. For example: Holland, *Five Readers Reading*; Gerrig, *Experiencing Narrative Worlds*.

46. Fowler, *Let the Reader Understand*, 54–55.

in the act of communication and appears to assume that all readers respond in a similar way to the text's guidance.

A more developed approach to the contribution of the reader may be found in Darr's reader-orientated study of Luke-Acts. Darr describes reading as a dialogical process that produces meaning through both "the rhetorical patterning of the text" and "the repertoire of cultural knowledge a reader brings to the text."[47] Although Darr's concern is with the "first" readers of Luke, his discussion makes some progress towards articulating the contribution of both the reader and the text to the act of reading. The attribution of meaning should neither ignore nor silence one of the partners in the dialogue. To do so is to reduce meaning to either a subjective experience or an inert set of concepts, respectively.

The Text

While reader-response theories comprise a class of literary criticism that foregrounds the reader, many other forms of literary criticism cluster around Abrams'/Barton's text category and seek to elucidate the world of the text. This category may be sub-divided into theories concerned with particular literary genres. Since Luke is a narrative, the forms of literary criticism relevant to this study are those concerned with narrative. These are generally referred to under the umbrella of "narratology." Jonathan Culler defines narratology as simply the "theory of narrative" and indicates that it focuses upon the fundamental components of narrative such as plot and narration.[48] Narratology, in its modern form, traces its roots to structuralism but has grown to encompass the aesthetic aspects of narrative as well: it is concerned with both narrative techniques and narrative effects.[49]

I limit my use of narratology to those concepts which pertain to readings of biblical narrative. Much of the vocabulary and many of the categories of narratology derive from the analysis of modern fiction.[50] My study, on the other hand, requires a broader understanding of narrative which respects Luke's status as an ancient, biblical narrative. Therefore I cannot utilize, without qualification, the vocabulary and categories of narratology. The exception, of course, may be discussions which focus on Luke's parables, but even these parables, while fiction-like, are certainly not modern.

47. Darr, *Character Building*, 17.
48. Culler, *Literary Theory*, 83.
49. Ibid., 83.
50. Genette, for example, develops his categories through his discussion of Proust's *A la recherche du temps perdu*. Genette, *Narrative Discourse*, 27–32.

Within the field of biblical studies, the term that is often used to describe the narratological analysis of Bible stories is "narrative criticism."[51] Narrative criticism analyses biblical narrative in its final form and treats the narrative as a whole unit. It takes into account both the story and discourse levels of narrative. For story, it analyses the role of key elements such as characters, plot, and settings, while for discourse it is concerned with the "devices intrinsic to the process of storytelling."[52] Its aim is to analyze the devices in the text that guide the reader and thereby place limits on interpretation. Some of these devices include perspective, voice, and patterns of organization like repetition.[53] These elements and devices provide a useful starting point for an examination of how Luke as a text guides children's interpretation.

Narratology has its own views of the reader. In narratology, the reader is usually *in* the text, a part of the narrative construction. The result of this construal of the reader has been theoretical constructs such as the implied reader[54] and the model reader.[55] Powell defends these constructs as necessary for understanding the narrative,[56] since for him the act of communication between text and reader transpires within the text itself, through the implied author, the narrative, and the implied reader. He treats "the real reader as extrinsic" to this communication act.[57] My study, in contrast, treats real readers as intrinsic to the reading transaction. Nonetheless, the theoretical constructions of the reader provide useful clues to the directives that the text uses in its dialogue with the reader.

The real reader in narrative criticism is in fact the critic, who may attempt to maintain a critical distance from the strategies of the text but is nonetheless their interpretive mediator. No text-centered criticism is purely an expression of the characteristics of the text. Since the textual critic is her or himself a reader, the world of the critic invariably intersects with the world of the text and shapes the resultant interpretation.[58]

---

51. The term, according to Powell, was coined by David Rhoads in his literary analysis of the Gospel of Mark. See Powell, *Narrative Criticism*, 6; also Rhoads and Michie, *Mark as Story*.

52. Powell, *Narrative Criticism*, 23.

53. See ibid., 32–33, for a delineation of different types of patterns found in biblical narrative. Powell's discussion cites Bauer, *The Structure of Matthew's Gospel*.

54. For example: Chatman, *Story and Discourse*; Iser, *The Implied Reader*.

55. Eco, *Six Walks*.

56. Powell, *Narrative Criticism*, 7.

57. Ibid., 19–20.

58. Fowler makes a similar point in his assertion that critics discuss their own experience of the text, whatever their chosen form of textual criticism. This often produces,

A useful concept drawn from the theoretical construction of the reader is that of reader competencies: embedded in narratives are expectations about what the reader brings to the act of reading. Marguerat and Bourquin provide a helpful list of some of these competencies, one of which is personal knowledge. A narrative assumes a certain set of knowledge on the part of its reader.[59] Reader competencies may develop and this development is crucial to the text-reader dialogue. The reader, for instance, accumulates knowledge about the narrative through the narrative, and this experience may elicit in the reader a quest for further knowledge.[60]

It may seem odd to refer to the text as being in dialogue since the text can only repeat the same thing over and over. Unlike the reader, the text's part of the conversation does not alter. As we have seen, Luke may be described as multivalent, so that how it is interpreted depends at least partially on the position of the reader. Building on this, if, as Eco suggests, a text produces the reader it needs, that is, a reader who is competent to read it,[61] then part of the strategic discourse of a narrative may be to shape its reader, with the result that the text may be heard differently whenever the reader returns to it. A text may thus be said to be in dialogue.

In order to employ a critical framework that accounts for the contributions of both the text and the readers, this study utilizes the relevant critical theories from Abrams'/Barton's text and reader categories, particularly narrative criticism and Iser's phenomenology of reading. Both of these critical approaches, however, deal with theoretical readers rather than real readers. In order to add real readers into the equation, my study draws on a concept from the literary critic and author, C. S. Lewis, the next subject in this discussion.

An Experiential Epistemology

Based on the discussion so far, reading a narrative may be described as an activity in which the reader engages with the text by interacting with its contents guided by its discourse. Reading thereby produces an experience of, or even with, the text. By reading Luke, the reader encounters the world of

---

for example, similar readings of the Gospel of Mark due to the textual strategies of Mark. See Fowler, *Let the Reader Understand*, 15.

59. Marguerat and Bourquin, *How to Read*, 130–31. See also the discussion in Culler, *Structuralist Poetics*, 113–30.

60. Ibid., 144–45.

61. Cited in ibid., 134. See also Eco, "Lector in Fabula," in *The Role of the Reader*, 200–260.

Luke. Lewis, in his essay "Meditation in a Toolshed," argues that such inside-experience is a key way of knowing the thing experienced.[62] In a striking analysis of how the knowing subject engages with the world around her or him, Lewis distinguishes between two different approaches to knowing: looking *at* versus looking *along*.

In order to explicate the differences between these approaches, Lewis describes his own experience of standing in a dark tool shed with a single beam of sunlight shining in over the top of the shed door. Looking *at* this beam allows examination of the light and consideration of the nature of the beam; it also throws some small light on the contents of the shed. Looking *along* the beam, in contrast, reveals the leaves dancing in the wind outside of the shed as well as the distant but brilliant sun. When the light is utilized, awareness of the beam itself is forgotten along with the dark shed. In Lewis's analogy, each position represents a different stance relative to the thing under discussion and Lewis argues that both of these stances are necessary for its understanding, but they produce very different results.[63] However, his central argument is for the importance of inside-experience, of looking *along*, for knowing.

Lewis's discussion is, of course, about epistemology. The idea that experience may be epistemic is upheld by the philosophers, George Lakoff and Mark Johnson. Their position goes beyond that of Lewis, whose discussion is essentially anecdotal. They argue that all human conceptuality is grounded in experience, with metaphors providing a means of conceiving of abstract ideas in terms of more concrete realities.[64] Lakoff and Johnson believe that experience of the primary world is fundamental to human understanding and even state that "we *understand* the world through our *interactions* with it."[65] Their assertion could be extrapolated to the understanding of a narrative world.

This discussion about epistemology has considerable bearing on the reading of narrative. Sandra Schneiders suggests that all forms of hermeneutics are based on some type of "global theory of what it means to understand . . . [that is], there is some ontological epistemological theory operative, at least implicitly, in all interpretive processes."[66] To interpret is to seek to know the thing interpreted. How someone interprets a text is

---

62. Lewis, "Meditation in a Toolshed," 50–54. The essay was originally published as an article in *The Coventry Evening Telegraph*, 1945.
63. Ibid., 53.
64. Lakoff and Johnson, *Metaphors*, 59.
65. Ibid., 194; italics in the original.
66. Schneiders, "The Gospels and the Reader," 104.

an expression of that person's philosophy of how to know that text. How real child readers interpret Luke may be an expression of their view of how to know Luke. They may seek to achieve understanding through certain processes and measure their understanding by certain criteria. This study aims to uncover those processes and criteria.

It is worth emphasizing that the knower is part of the experience of knowing. The scientist and philosopher, Michael Polanyi, argues that all knowing is in fact personal and begins with the knower.[67] Epistemology therefore implicates the knower. While Polanyi is concerned with the field of science, his point is also relevant to readings of a text. What a real reader knows about a text inevitably depends at least in part upon the situation and experience of the reader. How a reader seeks to know a text inevitably expresses the reader's view of how this knowing may be attained.

Returning to Lewis, his concern is with experience as an epistemological conduit in general, while my concern is with reading and I will limit my discussion to the implications of Lewis's epistemological framework for readings of the Gospel of Luke. Lewis's distinction may be articulated as the difference between analyzing a text and experiencing it. Looking *at* a text entails treating the text as an object of analysis. This is the common approach of theories belonging to Abrams'/Barton's text category. The reader seeks to know by adopting a seemingly detached position relative to the text. The resultant readings are nonetheless influenced by the context of the reader—Lewis's metaphoric shed—and will reflect that context in some way.

Looking *along* the text, on the other hand, entails involvement in the world created by the text and its epistemological method may be described as experiential. This reader seeks to know through immersion. The reader sees through the text, perceiving another world beyond her or his context, while simultaneously remaining in the context of the metaphoric shed. Here again, the reader's engagement with the text invariably reflects her or his context, but in this case through an overt interface of the worlds of the reader and the text.

It is important to clarify, at this point, the type of experience under discussion. The shed, in Lewis's analogy, represents the personal experience and context which the reader brings *to* the text. For experiential epistemology, this context is part of the interpretive process but not the focus. Looking *along* the text produces experience *of* the narrative world. It is this inside-experience of the text which is the focus of experiential epistemology. Iser describes this effect: "processing a text is bound to result in changes within the recipient, and these changes are not a matter of grammatical rules, but

---

67. Polanyi, *Personal Knowledge,* vii–viii, and in his other works.

of experience."[68] Immersion in the narrative world generates an experience with the text that in turn becomes part of the reader's experience. The reader may then bring this experience to the text in later readings, so that subsequent readings may be influenced by earlier readings.

In contrast, within biblical studies the discussion of the role of experience often focuses upon the contribution of the reader's context. In the field of practical theology, an aim of interpretation is often to address the reader's context: some practical theologians interpret the biblical text by focusing on the interface between the text and life experience. Zoë Bennett, for instance, advocates pursuing connections between the "text of the Bible and the text of life" as the key interpretive practice for practical theologians.[69] John Vincent models a hermeneutic that compares the "gospel experiences" in the world of the New Testament directly to experiences that "are like them today."[70] Any experience which the reader may have *of* the text is leapt over in favor of the experience which the reader brings *to* the text. Such interpretation has the benefit of making the contribution of the reader's context explicit. But it has the drawback of limiting the impact of the narrative world to its points of contact with the reader's context. A dialogue may be present, but the context dominates the discussion.

My focus, instead, is upon *reading as a way of experiencing the world of the text*. To make this clearer, I next explore some examples of readings of Luke that may be classified according to Lewis's two approaches to knowing: looking *at* and looking *along*.

Looking **at** *Luke*

The looking *at* approach aptly sums up the position often adopted by the biblical critic, a reading stance which positions the reader firmly outside of the narrative world. Kevin J. Vanhoozer also draws upon Lewis's essay "Meditation in a Toolshed" to argue that the biblical criticism of modernity and postmodernity tend to look *at* the biblical text and to look *at* interpretations of the biblical text, respectively. Such approaches, according to Vanhoozer, may reduce discussion of the text to the theories of the critic.[71] Fowler, comparatively, describes the critic's approach as belonging to the "objectifying pole" of the critic-reader spectrum, and the reader's approach

---

68. Iser, *The Act of Reading*, 32.
69. Bennett, *Using the Bible in Practical Theology*, 11, 40, 134.
70. Vincent, "How We Got Here," 12.
71. Vanhoozer, *First Theology*, 18–19, 36–37.

as belonging to the "subjectifying pole."[72] Following Fowler, Lewis's two approaches could be classified as objective versus subjective stances relative to the text, yet this is to ignore the subjectivity which the critic invariably brings to her or his reading, the subjectivity of the critic's context. The contexts of scholars are furnished with a vast array of semantic, socio-cultural, and historical-critical tools which enable them to dissect particular aspects of the text while keeping the world of the text at a distance. Their mere choice of tools betrays their stance relative to the text.

Fowler not only attributes too much neutrality to the position of the critic, but also underestimates the critical engagement of the reader. He assumes that non-critics do not analyze their reading and may fall prey to an uncritical internalization of the text.[73] But this too ignores the presence of the reader's context and the invariable critique which that context and personal experience may bring to any reading. Iser helpfully points out that since reading is not a one-way process, it does not produce "a direct 'internalization'" of the ideas of the text.[74] Reading is an interactive process to which both parties contribute. Green adds that to be addressed by a text like Luke, the reader must de-center her or his interests.[75] This approach may open the reader to influence by the text, but that influence is always relative to the reader's context.

Another issue is that the looking *at* approach may lead to a minimal focus on the narrative world. Frei cogently demonstrates how one looking *at* approach, historical-criticism, turned the interpretation of biblical narrative into the pursuit of referents external to the text.[76] Michael Legaspi, in his discussion of eighteenth-century historical critics, makes an assertion comparable to Frei's but using terminology which echoes Lewis: such biblical scholars, instead of "looking *through* the Bible in order to understand *the truth about the world* . . . looked directly at the text, endeavoring to find new, ever more satisfactory frames of cultural and historical reference by which to understand *the meaning of the text*."[77] Historical-criticism changes the interpretive focus from the story world to the world which produced the text.

An example of the effect of the historical-critical approach is evident in Howard Marshall's discussion of the Luke 15:8–10 parable of the Lost Coin. Initially, Marshall considers the historical and linguistic development

---

72. Fowler, *Let the Reader Understand*, 29. Fowler builds his discussion upon Steiner, "Critic/Reader," 423–52.

73. Ibid., 28.

74. Iser, *The Act of Reading*, 107.

75. Green, *Theology*, 130.

76. Frei, *Eclipse*, 9, 12, 16, 50, 281.

77. Legaspi, *The Death of Scripture*, 26; italics in the original.

of this parable, particularly in relation to the Luke 15:4–7 parable of the Lost Sheep.[78] Then he works his way through the three verses of the parable, stating what he deems to be the main point of each verse but focusing his attention on their historical antecedents. For verse 8, for instance, most of his discussion is concerned with the value of a drachma, including its devaluation in the ancient world. By way of addressing the narrative, he asserts that if such a coin "is lost, great efforts are made to find it."[79] He follows-up this statement by drawing a parallel between the actions listed in this verse and those listed in a comparable rabbinic parable. He concludes by delineating the idiosyncrasies of first-century architecture as a way of explaining the woman's fervent efforts.[80] The result is the smothering of the story under a barrage of historical and semantic details.

Narrative critics may also plant their feet firmly in the looking *at* camp. This may be seen in McComiskey's approach to the parables in Luke 15. His structuralist reading highlights the chapter's internal parallel structure, and its use of repetition and of the literary device of echo. He explicates it all on a handy table displaying the thematic resonance between Luke 15 and other parts of the Gospel. Since his aim is to investigate authorial intention for the literary correspondences within the whole Gospel, the parables function for him primarily as examples of these correspondences, and he pays only minimal attention to their content.[81]

Advocacy readings, by definition, foreground a particular ideological position relative to the text. They too handle the text as an object of analysis, for they look *at* the text relative to their advocated ideology. Such approaches establish boundaries within which the text-reader dialogue may operate, boundaries determined by the ideological frame. The resultant readings tend to be abstractions about the text relative to the critic's advocated position.

To take a feminist position as an example, Turid Karlsen Seim asserts that feminism "aims at uncovering power structures that keep women in place as 'the other' and overcoming marginalization of women and any

---

78. Marshall, *Gospel of Luke*, 602–3.

79. Ibid., 603.

80. Ibid.

81. McComiskey, *Lukan Theology*, 50–51. His aim in this section is to evaluate Tannehill's work, *The Narrative Unity of Luke Acts*. McComiskey is particularly concerned with the accuracy of Tannehill's discussion of literary correspondences in Luke-Acts. McComiskey uses his structuralist analysis to establish a platform for his pursuit of the Lukan author/redactor's intent for these correspondences. He therefore utilizes narrative critical tools to pursue a historical-critical aim. See *Lukan Theology*, 3.

cognition marked by androcentrism."[82] Such criticism approaches reading with one foot firmly anchored in the concerns of feminist ideology. The effects of this approach may be seen in Loretta Dornisch's reading of the Luke 15:8–10 parable of the Lost Coin. After briefly summarizing the parable's contents, the key questions this feminist critic asks are: What is the redactor indicating by placing this "woman's story" in parallel with a "non-woman's story," the parable of the Lost Sheep? Does the redactor reveal a particular position on women? Or are both parables retained due to the influence of real women on the redactor's writing?[83] Dornisch's hermeneutical method is governed by a feminist response to redaction criticism.[84] Ironically, it bypasses the strong model provided by the parable's female protagonist, who essentially represents God.

Looking *along* Luke

The looking *along* stance, in contrast, approaches the text from within the framework of the narrative world. The reader's viewpoint is one of looking *along* the path down which the narrative points, following its directives and, at times, responding to its concrete elements. Since experience is holistic, these responses may be cognitive, emotive, and sensory. Even when such an approach leads to abstractions about the text, these are rooted in the narrative constituents. Readers adopting this stance may step back and assess the narrative, but they do so from the position of inside-experience.

This reading position depends upon the reader heeding the guidance of the text. Bauckham, in his discussion of the Gospels as a form of ancient testimony, points out that testimony is a means of knowing: the account of another person, whether oral or written, has an epistemological function.[85] Although Bauckham's discussion is concerned with the Gospels as historical documents, his point about epistemology bears some relevance to the relationship forged between the reader and the text. A written narrative is a type of testimony. The reader comes to know Luke's narrative world through her or his reliance upon the account of its narrator.

Such reliance does not exclude critique. Bauckham indicates that knowing through testimony "entails a fundamental attitude of trust, but

---

82. Seim, "Feminist Criticism," 43.

83. Dornisch, *A Woman Reads the Gospel of Luke*, 175.

84. Spencer discusses a variety of other feminist readings of this parable, ranging from outright rejection "as a tale spun by a man for men" to embracing it as a model of feminist interpretive practice. See Spencer, *Salty Wives*, 40–54.

85. Bauckham, *Eyewitnesses*, 475–77.

not necessarily uncritical trust."[86] The reader trusts the narrator to present the narrative world, but the narrator's role equates to guidance not control, leaving the reader free to critique what is presented. Bauckham emphasizes that trust is fundamental to knowing, while critical evaluation is "feasible only as a secondary activity."[87] Trust need not be naïve, but it is crucial for gaining inside-experience. Maxwell helpfully adds that a reader's involvement in a story means that she or he "will be less likely to make superficial judgements and will be more likely to appreciate the complexity of the characters' situations."[88] Experiencing the narrative world positions the reader to critique it from within.

An example of the looking *along* approach may be seen in a reading of the Luke 15 parable of the Lost Sheep that was generated by a community of rural readers. These readers were part of a study, conducted by Louise Lawrence, of how contemporary communities read passages in Luke relative to their contexts. This group of adults entered the world of the parable and pondered the logic of the shepherd leaving ninety-nine sheep unprotected while he searched for one sheep.[89] They interpreted the story's wilderness setting as "a place that represented harshness and danger" and queried the shepherd's conduct. In order to account for this conduct, they attributed a motive to the shepherd, believing that he followed "the maxim that in order to gain something of worth, you have to let go of something dear to you."[90] This reading developed out of the readers' empathy with the shepherd's dilemma.

Examples of experiential reading may also be found within the world of biblical scholarship. Green specifically encourages readers "to adopt a perspective from within the narrative" so that they may "participate" in Luke's "vision of partnership" with God.[91] In his discussion of the Luke 15:8–10 parable of the Lost Coin, Green foregrounds the emotion that the parable elicits at its climax: he highlights the celebration that accompanies the discovery of the lost coin, and characterizes the story as a "parable of joy."[92] He also takes into account the hearer's/reader's potential response: "the enhanced portrayal of the woman's efforts as she attempts to locate what has been lost might also provoke reflection on the initiative taken by

---

86. Ibid., 478.
87. Ibid.
88. Maxwell, *Hearing Between the Lines*, 135.
89. Lawrence, *The Word in Place*, 65.
90. Ibid.
91. Green, *Theology*, 130.
92. Green, *Luke*, 576.

God in human recovery."[93] In Green's reading, the reader's experience of the narrative world serves as the basis for theological reflection.

Lewis did not develop his analogy any further, providing little more than a theoretical skeleton upon which further ideas need to form in order to give it flesh. The findings of this study provide some of that flesh relative to the act of reading. The defining characteristic of the looking *along* approach is that it entails an experience of the narrative world. As we will see, the child readers made sense of Luke's narrative world by engaging with that world. This approach to knowing the text aligns well with my proposed classification of Luke as participatory literature.

Summary

This chapter has shown that Luke is a narrative whose plot and theological worldview coalesce to form a narrative world. Luke invites its readers to participate in its narrative world. Narrative criticism provides guidance for assessing how Luke directs this participation, while reader-response theory highlights the role of the reader anticipated by the text. Both of these critical frameworks are useful for analyzing the children's readings of Luke, but they have the drawback of treating the reader as a theoretical construct.

Real readers' approaches to narrative are only minimally discussed in the literature, perhaps because the individuality of readers suggests unmanageable diversity. If my study is to assess how children actually read the Gospel of Luke, then the reading strategies of real readers must be taken into account. Lewis's category of looking *along*, or inside-experience, provides this study with a theoretical framework that allows for the contribution of both real readers and the text to the reading dialogue. This framework treats the reading transaction as an experience of the text. It is epistemological: the readers come to know the text through their transactions with it. An important question for this study, then, is what constitutes this transaction? I turn next to a discussion of the type of real readers represented by this study, children.

---

93. Ibid.

Chapter 3

The Child Reader

Kit: "I know that Luke's a very important book. And I'm starting to enjoy it a lot, so I would look forward to reading it every night."

Specifying the Literature

Having examined some of the most pertinent literature concerned with reading the Gospel of Luke, I now discuss literature pertaining to the other main subject in this study: the child reader. The literature concerned with children as readers is vast and I begin by narrowing the focus of this discussion.

It is useful to clarify, from the outset, the types of literature which are not directly relevant to this study and which therefore have little or no role in my discussion. Since this study is not concerned with the acquisition of the skill of reading, I do not examine the literature related to this subject area. My study is not driven by pedagogical questions about teaching the Bible to children, which means that literature with such didactic aims is not included. Instead, my concern is with literature that addresses how children interpret texts. Again, much of this literature is pedagogical, seeking to guide the adult's input into the child's interpretive process, and therefore not central to this discussion.

The focus of this chapter is upon those studies which address the developmental aspects of children's interpretation including the cognitive and literary processes that contribute to that interpretation. These studies tend to derive from the fields of developmental psychology and children's literature theory. A number of the childhood development theories are foundational to the studies of child readers' transactions with narrative and I begin this chapter by briefly discussing these theories. The body of literature concerned with developmental theory is, again, vast and I concern myself only with those aspects of it which are directly relevant to children as readers. The second half of this chapter looks more closely at the literary studies concerned with children's interpretation of narrative.

Childhood Development

Even a small amount of digging in the field of childhood development rapidly uncovers the names of three theorists whose work is fundamental to the growth of this field: Piaget, Kohlberg, and Erikson. All of these researchers devised theories of development that are constructed around progressive stages. Based on the findings of their empirical work, they theorized that children go through a series of stages as they progress to adulthood, and each stage must be passed through before the next stage may be reached. In the cases of Kohlberg and Erikson, these stages extend into adulthood. Each of these researchers has been heavily criticized and their theories significantly modified by the work of subsequent researchers.[1] Nonetheless, because of the foundational status of their work, I look briefly at the theory of each, concentrating upon those aspects which pertain to this study. I then consider the application of stage theory to faith development, a developmental area that pertains directly to children's engagement with the Bible. I conclude this section with a discussion of the criticisms of stage theory.

The Stage Theorists

Jean Piaget researched the cognitive development of children and formulated a theory that seeks to delineate the mental processes that enable children to think about their world. The final two stages in his theory, "concrete operational" and "formal operational," pertain, respectively, to seven- to twelve-year-olds and to individuals twelve years and older. These two stages overlap the age range of the participants in my study and are thus relevant to this research. In the concrete operations stage, children "require concrete objects and events to support their mental operations."[2] They think about and understand the world through the medium of tangible objects and

---

1. Developmental stage theories have been critiqued by other developmentalists for their methodological flaws, and by sociologists and feminists for their inflexible stratification and hierarchical approach to individuals. See, for example, Burman, *Deconstructing Developmental Psychology*; James and Prout, *Constructing and Reconstructing Childhood*.
2. Schaffer, *Child Psychology*, 177.

events; and personal experience is fundamental to this thinking.[3] Children reach the formal operations stage when these concrete objects and events are no longer necessary for their mental processes, when, instead, they can think using "hypothetical and abstract notions" and reason about "things they have never directly experienced."[4]

Piaget's delineation of the tools used in childhood reasoning may have implications for how a child engages with narrative. What a reader knows about a text may depend at least in part on those aspects of the text which the reader mentally processes, whether its concrete elements or its more abstract concepts. Readers in the concrete operations stage may be particularly drawn to the plot of a story, for instance, since it consists of tangible actions and characters. The children's literature theorist, J. A. Appleyard, however, views Piagetian theory as an inappropriate tool for evaluating reading since the theory equates the development of scientific thinking with cognitive maturity, and excludes, or labels as immature, the imaginative thinking that may be stimulated by stories.[5]

Such imaginative thinking is incorporated into Piagetian theory by Margaret Donaldson, who follows in the Piagetian tradition but counters the rigidity of the Piagetian stages.[6] She points out that even young children are capable of interpreting what they read, a process that demands some form of thinking about absent realities. She adds that written texts may promote a reflective thinking process that not only leads to interpretation, but also enhances the child reader's cognitive development.[7] Much of this reflective thinking makes use of concrete forms.

This reflective thinking through reading aligns with Piaget's position, both because of his insistence upon the contribution of concrete forms to thinking, and because he believes that a child's cognition develops through activity.[8] Children gain understanding through interaction with their world rather than through a passive accumulation of knowledge. This interaction

---

3. Piaget found, for instance, that children in this stage did not distinguish their thoughts about objects from the objects themselves. See Piaget, *The Child's Conception of the World*, 49–54.

4. Schaffer, *Child Psychology*, 181.

5. Appleyard, *Becoming a Reader*, 10–11.

6. Donaldson acknowledges her debt to Piaget before systematically pointing out a series of flaws in his methodology and conclusions. She re-interprets his theory for the sake of overcoming what she deems to be some key weaknesses in the British education system that may be attributable to Piagetian thinking. See Donaldson, *Children's Minds*, 95.

7. Ibid., 98–99.

8. Smith et al., *Understanding Children's Development*, 444.

is mutual: the child acts on her or his context and the context acts upon the child.[9] That is, children's understanding develops experientially.

In his discussion of Piaget, Schaffer clarifies that whenever individuals, whether adults or children, "encounter some new experience, [they] immediately try to make sense of it by relating it to other experiences . . . thereby giving the unknown meaning by relating it to the known."[10] The implications of this for reading are multiple. Since reading is an activity, it may contribute to the reader's developing experience, a developmental implication that coheres with the epistemological one discussed in the previous chapter. A reader may approach a narrative world like that of Luke by evaluating it relative to her or his general cognitive schema of reality, but based on Piagetian theory, this process may be two-way. While the reader's cognitive schema is invariably rooted in experience of the primary world, it may also be shaped by the reader's encounter with the world of Luke.

Another stage theorist, Lawrence Kohlberg, conducted a longitudinal study of moral reasoning that led him to posit six stages that individuals pass through as they develop moral judgement. His stage theory is built on that of Piaget, and Kohlberg believes that moral reasoning is dependent upon the development of cognitive reasoning.[11] The six stages are grouped into three pairs, with each pair representing a moral level. The level most relevant to this study is that of "conventional morality," which reflects the moral reasoning of the average adolescent. A person with conventional morality has internalized the rules of society and abides by them primarily because they are society's rules.[12] The two stages in this level, "stage 3 interpersonal" and "stage 4 social conscience," differ primarily in the point of view taken by the individual when making her or his moral judgements. A stage 3 moral reasoner thinks in terms of the self in relation to others while a stage 4 moral reasoner thinks in terms of upholding the overall system.[13]

According to Kohlberg, the development of moral reasoning is dependent upon social stimulation. In his study, he found that participation in a social group created opportunities for an individual "to take the social perspectives of others," which in turn fostered the development of moral reasoning.[14] This finding raises the question of the role of reading in moral development. Since reading a narrative often positions the reader to take

9. Schaffer, *Child Psychology*, 164, 166.
10. Ibid., 242–43.
11. Kohlberg, "Moral Stages and Moralization," 32.
12. Ibid., 33.
13. Ibid., 34–35.
14. Ibid., 39, 50.

the perspective of a character or the narratee, it has the potential to impact moral reasoning. What is more, Kohlberg connects moral conduct to moral reasoning, asserting that behavior follows in the wake of reasoning.[15] Thus a change in reasoning, including a change elicited through a narrative, could at least theoretically have an impact upon conduct. Alignment with a character's perspective in Luke, for instance, may stimulate a reader's ethical assessment of the situation faced by that character.

The third developmentalist, Erik Erikson, built his stage theory on the psychoanalytic work of Sigmund Freud, allowing him to combine the affective and cognitive dimensions of human development, in contrast to Piaget and Kohlberg who concentrate upon the cognitive dimension. While Freud anchors his discussion in human sexuality, Erikson seeks to delineate the psychosocial development of personal identity. He sets out eight stages of development, with the fifth stage, "Identity versus Role Confusion," corresponding to the teenage years and beginning at approximately eleven years,[16] the youngest age represented in my study. In this stage, the adolescent develops "a sense of self as a unique individual."[17] Working out distinctive personality traits is of paramount concern to individuals in this stage.

Erikson's theory stresses the contribution of social context to an individual's personal development. He describes individuals in his fifth stage as having the tendency to "over identify" with "heroes" whom they may encounter in "cliques or crowds" or other settings. Adolescents may "fall in love" with such heroes; this love is not primarily sexual but rather functions as a catalyst for young teens to work out their identity.[18] This hero attraction may include a search for people or ideas "to have *faith* in," whether peers or adults who will provide imaginative scope for the adolescent's aspirations.[19] While Erikson's focus is upon social roles, this orientation towards heroes could be also directed at narrative heroes who may potentially function as models for young readers.

Faith Development

Building on the work of the stage theorists, James W. Fowler in his classic text, *Stages of Faith*, joins the discussion by postulating the development of

---

15. Ibid., 32.
16. Erikson, *Childhood and Society*, 252–53.
17. Schaffer, *Child Psychology*, 316.
18. Erikson, *Childhood and Society*, 253–54.
19. Erikson, *Identity*, 128–29; italics in the original.

faith in six stages across the human life span.[20] Fowler's definition of faith is broad and encompasses a variety of religious permutations. He holds that all people have a faith and equates this faith with the search for meaning in life. In line with the other stage theorists' view of development, he asserts that faith development depends upon "the interchange between an active, innovative subject and a dynamic, changing environment."[21] If the Bible is a part of the child's environment, reading it may potentially serve as stimulant to personal faith development.

The age range of the readers in my study overlaps Fowler's stages 2 and 3, "mythic-literal faith" and "synthetic-conventional faith" respectively. Mythic-literal faith is specifically expressed and understood through stories. For children in this stage, narrative functions as a way of "finding and giving coherence to experience."[22] They use stories both to make sense of their beliefs and context, and to express what they think, while the story itself is part of the experience. Accordingly, the Lukan narrative may provide child readers with a framework for organizing and understanding their faith. The stage 3 adolescent, in comparison, adds the self into the developmental mix and Fowler believes that asking questions about God may be a part of the adolescent's formation. Faith develops when these youth encounter situations "that lead to critical reflection on their tacit value systems."[23] A text like Luke may therefore stimulate faith development by, among other things, challenging readers to re-think their value systems and faith traditions.

A number of studies have picked up from where Fowler left off. Anne Phillips conducted empirical research on the faith and spirituality of eleven- to thirteen-year-old churched girls. One of her key findings was the presence of the girls' spiritual awareness of God and their ability to theologize about their faith.[24] The age range Phillips investigates is comparable to the one in this study and highlights this age group's potential ability to read Luke with a spiritual and theological orientation.

Mark A. Pike adds that reading, in general, has a spiritual dimension. Child readers, for instance, "do not learn to read and *then* form a worldview; they do so *while* they are reading."[25] Within the classroom, interpretation has been secularized and young readers, including those from a church

---

20. Fowler, *Stages of Faith*.
21. Ibid., 100.
22. Ibid., 149; original italics removed.
23. Ibid., 162.
24. Phillips, *The Faith of Girls*, 103–5.
25. Pike, "Transactional Reading," 83; italics in the original.

tradition, are not encouraged "to connect their faith with their reading."[26] Pike points out that consumerism and popular culture currently function as some of the chief forms of childhood socialization. These products of secular culture have "replaced written biblical revelation" as the tools children use to interpret life.[27] Due to the life stage of the child readers in this study, my research invariably juxtaposes the Gospel of Luke with a teenage social context creating a scenario that opens the door to critique of both the text and that context.

Critiquing Stage Theories

The stage theorists have been critiqued repeatedly, from a variety of quarters. To begin with, some of the methods undergirding their theories are problematic. As Burman indicates, a number of the theorists used only male participants for their empirical work, while others studied only those with pathologies, making the applicability of their findings across genders and other social groups suspect.[28] Kohlberg's theory, for example, derives from a twelve-year longitudinal study of fifty men,[29] and Erikson's theory is based primarily on his clinical experiences with disturbed youth.[30]

The theorists' developmental frameworks are also problematic, since they often treat Western values as the pinnacle of development. Kohlberg values independent thought and the highest level of moral reasoning in his theory pertains to those who make judgements "in terms of self-chosen principles."[31] Similarly, Piaget values scientific reasoning and evaluates children's cognitive progress in terms of their development of logic and systematic thinking.[32]

Due to his high view of scientific reasoning, Piaget did not take into account the potentially wide range of influences upon childhood development. Although Piaget emphasizes the importance of interaction with the environment to cognitive development, his conception of this environment is generally limited to objects. Another developmentalist, Lev Vygotsky, counters that cognitive development is also a social process. Therefore the

26. Ibid., 90.
27. Ibid., 85.
28. Burman, *Deconstructing Developmental Psychology*, 5.
29. Kohlberg, "Moral Stages and Moralization," 42–43.
30. Smith et al., *Understanding Children's Development*, 684.
31. Kohlberg, "Moral Stages and Moralization," 33.
32. For a description of Piaget's aims, see Smith et al., *Understanding Children's Development*, 442–43.

"child-in-context" rather than the "child-in-vacuum" "should be regarded as the basic unit of analysis in our thinking about children."[33] Vygotsky's position dovetails with the epistemological argument of Lewis that the knowing subject always proceeds *in situ*. The child's context is not an optional extra.

A key weakness with the division of childhood development into progressive stages is the hierarchical assumption undergirding the concept of progression.[34] In the developmental theories, the lower stages represent periods of immaturity to be left behind as progress is made to more advanced stages. This perspective on development implies that children and adolescents, since they are at lower stages, have less to contribute to their social world. Their voices are silenced and they are placed in an educational holding pattern until they are deemed fit to join in the adult dialogue and social matrix. Conceiving of the stages as progressive implicitly devalues the child's contribution. My study seeks, in contrast, to value the child participants' readings of Luke. Their readings may differ from those of adults, but that does not make them inconsequential.

Children Reading Narrative

Having looked at some of the prominent theories of childhood development, the natural progression is to look next at developmental theories of reading. Two prominent studies in the field of children's literature explore children's engagement with narrative from a developmental point of view. In this section, I first discuss these studies, focusing on the findings that are relevant to children's readings of biblical narrative. After that, I discuss research that pertains to children's transactions with stories, beginning with studies concerned with the cognitive processes undergirding this transaction and then looking at studies that target the relevant literary processes.

Developmental Theories of Reading

In his important empirical study, *The Child's Concept of Story: Ages Two to Seventeen*, Arthur N. Applebee investigates the development phases in children's reading and story-telling strategies.[35] Methodologically, he enabled samples of children in different age groups to interact with similar narra-

---

33. Schaffer, *Child Psychology*, 194–95, 216; original italics removed.

34. Phillips discusses the general problems with this hierarchical perspective; see Phillips, *The Faith of Girls*, 24–27.

35. Applebee, *The Child's Concept of Story*, 2.

tives and story-telling scenarios. He analyzed the responses within each age cohort and compared the responses across cohorts, focusing on the differences between the cohorts. Applebee used Piaget's stages of cognitive development as the theoretical framework for his research,[36] which provides his discussion with a clear structure but also limits it to Piagetian categories.

One of Applebee's age cohorts is "young adolescents," which he defines as twelve- to fifteen-year-olds, aligning with Piaget's formal operations stage. However, Applebee's actual participants were a group of thirteen-year-olds whose responses he treats as representative of the entire age range,[37] an approach which he does not justify and which may be deemed empirically weak. Having acknowledged this shortcoming in his method, I focus on Applebee's discussion of this cohort because its age range is comparable to the age range used in my study.

Applebee found that the young adolescents' discussion of a story shifted from "retelling" the story, the key strategy of slightly younger children, towards an analysis of the story.[38] This cohort sought out the patterns of purpose in the sampled stories, including the cause and effect of the plot, the motives driving the characters, and the stories' unifying logic.[39] These findings suggest that Luke's plot and worldview, as discussed in chapter 2, may be of particular interest to this age group.

While the older adolescents in Applebee's study, aged over fifteen years, often drew on abstract categories to discuss or tell a story, the young adolescent cohort articulated their understanding of a story using concrete examples and categories, aligning with Piaget's view that children reason by using concrete forms. This younger group frequently made sense of a story through analogies. To explain a story, they exemplified it so that their interpretation was "tied to one or another specific situation rather than moving to a generalization."[40]

If this finding is relevant to this age group's reading of biblical narrative, then the young adolescent tendency will not be to discuss biblical narrative using abstract concepts. Instead, their interpretive strategies may include comparing the contents of a Bible story to personal experiences or events in their world. Applebee believes that the young adolescents' use of analogies reveals in these youth an awareness that the situations in the stories might have relevance beyond the boundaries of the narrative world. The

---

36. Ibid., 88–89.
37. Ibid., 110, 123–25, 150.
38. Ibid., 108, 119.
39. Ibid., 109, 115, 118.
40. Ibid., 115.

same could be true of child readers' approach to Luke: they may expect its stories to resonate with their world.

A key finding of Applebee's study is that as children grow older, they do not discard their old approaches to story in favor of new ones. Instead they build their new approaches on the foundation of their old approaches.[41] This integration of strategies provides children with an increasingly complex repertoire to draw on in their handling of stories. This finding contrasts with that of the stage theorists, who view earlier stages as periods of development to be discarded as the child progresses to higher stages.

Applebee's description of increasing complexity in reading validates child readers' forms of interaction with biblical narrative as appropriate to their developmental stage. It also raises questions for the view that there may be only one appropriate approach to reading the Bible. A child's reading strategy may be the one that reaps interpretations that are most appropriate for her or his view of the world. If a reading at a more complex stage builds on a reading at a less complex stage, it does not invalidate the earlier reading strategy but rather grows out of it and may even be said to depend upon it.

While Applebee's research focuses on the broad category of children's interaction with stories, the other key researcher in this field, Appleyard, concentrates his empirical investigation on one part of this interaction, the act of reading narrative. In his ground-breaking work, *Becoming a Reader: The Experience of Fiction from Childhood to Adulthood*, Appleyard sets out a "developmental view of reading," which he defines as "a somewhat regular sequence of attitudes readers go through as they mature that affects how they experience stories."[42] Appleyard's central thesis is that the way readers attribute meaning to a narrative changes as they develop. His methodology included qualitative interviews and the analysis of relevant texts. Although his study primarily targets fiction, much of his discussion is pertinent to engagement with narrative in general.

Building upon reader-response theory as well as Erikson's psychosocial theory of development, Appleyard assumes as his starting point the "transaction that occurs between reader and text" and examines "the changes in the reader that shape that transaction."[43] He believes that any reading of a narrative is "an event that has roots both in the text and in the personality and history that the reader brings to the reading."[44] For Appleyard, reading entails "*accommodating* our minds to the shape of the world that literature

---

41. Ibid., 114, 125.
42. Appleyard, *Becoming a Reader*, 2, 8.
43. Ibid., 3, 9.
44. Ibid., 9.

opens up to us."[45] How readers make that accommodation reveals their particular reading stage, or, to use Appleyard's term, their reading "role."

Appleyard's theory posits five different roles that readers assume in the course of their development, beginning with very young children and continuing into adulthood. Each of these roles represents a "cluster of responses, a set of attitudes and intentions" that readers utilize with texts.[46] Corroborating Applebee's findings, Appleyard found that each role lays a foundation for the subsequent roles. The reading roles are not abandoned as the reader matures but rather coalesce to form an increasingly complex tool kit any part of which the reader may employ in her or his interaction with a story.[47] The age of the participants in my study overlaps two of Appleyard's reading roles: the Reader as Hero or Heroine, the role assumed by school-aged children, approximately six to twelve years; and the Reader as Thinker, the role assumed by adolescents, approximately thirteen to eighteen years. I look at each of these in turn.

In the Reader as Hero or Heroine role, readers "imagine themselves as heroes and heroines of romances that are unconscious analogues of their own lives."[48] They approach narrative as a type of adventure story in which the central character faces and overcomes some form of struggle. Following the plight of a hero archetype serves a double function for the reader: "to give concrete form to threatening evil and then to assure that it will be defeated."[49] Children in this role read in order to gather and organize information about the world, and to explore their own developing inner world.[50] Applying Appleyard's findings to children's readings of Luke, readers in this role may be attracted to the conflict in Luke's narrative and they may focus on the plights of its central characters, particularly Jesus.

Unfortunately, much of Appleyard's discussion of the Reader as Hero or Heroine role derives from his analysis of the literature targeting this age group rather than from research with real readers.[51] This is a real limitation in his methodology. It is difficult to determine from his study the extent to which children in this age group assume this role because it is the primary option provided for them in this literature (a literature written, published, and often purchased for them by adults), and the extent to which this lit-

---

45. Ibid., 42; italics in the original.
46. Ibid., 14, 19.
47. Ibid., 15.
48. Ibid., 60.
49. Ibid., 63.
50. Ibid., 59.
51. Ibid., 60–64.

erature is produced as a way of meeting the narrative orientation of this age group.

Appleyard handles the Reader as Thinker role differently, developing this role based on a series of interviews which he conducted with adolescent readers. This reader seeks role models as well as "insights into the meaning of life, values, and beliefs worthy of commitment."[52] Appleyard notes the adolescent reader's penchant for total immersion in a narrative world, stating that this experience "often goes together with intense emotional reaction to the story."[53] He warns that if adolescents are not enabled to develop as readers at this level, but propelled instead towards a detached analysis that keeps the story at a distance, then there is a risk of undermining this crucial stage of reading development and depriving adolescents of reading skills that will enable them to use books as tools for dealing "with the world of ideas and values."[54] This warning no doubt extends to adolescents' readings of the Bible.

Adolescent readings of biblical narrative may, then, be personal and comprised of affective responses and evaluations of a story relative to real-life situations. This reading role may be described as generating a *reading experience*, a description that supports the use of Lewis's experiential epistemology for analyzing the readings at the heart of my study. But there is a drawback. Most of Appleyard's interviewees for this age group were aged 15 years or older, so his description of this role most likely reflects the tendencies of readers who are slightly older than the child participants in my study. The age range for my study represents the transition age between this role and the previous role and is significantly under-represented in Appleyard's study.

Appleyard helpfully notes that his proposed reading roles are not merely the product of developmental stages; rather, they "describe an education in the mainstream culture's values as much as they do an evolution of innate human capacities."[55] The roles that readers assume in their engagement with narrative may be, at least in part, socially constructed and may vary across cultures and for types of literature. This social construction of reading roles raises some questions for this study. For instance, are there alternative, socially constructed reading roles that pertain to child readers of the Bible? What kind of reading role may enable child readers to interact with Bible stories in terms that make sense to them?

52. Ibid., 14.
53. Ibid., 101.
54. Ibid., 116.
55. Ibid., 15.

The Cognitive Process

Whether or not the way a child reader engages with narrative is partially socially constructed, this engagement is also a mental act and therefore clearly dependent upon cognitive functioning. I turn now to research into the cognitive processes involved in reading narrative. Here I look at three studies, two of which included child participants.

In the first study, *Experiencing Narrative Worlds: On the Psychological Activities of Reading*, Richard J. Gerrig seeks to explicate the human experience of narrative through an analysis of the cognitive processes that enable that experience.[56] His research is based on readers' reports of their experiences of narrative combined with the findings of other empirical studies. Gerrig's thesis is that the cognitive processes used for reading narrative are the same as those used for daily life.[57] He uses two metaphors to characterize these processes: the reader being *transported* by a narrative, and the reader *performing* the narrative. Each metaphor signifies a "domain of experience" for the reader.[58]

In reference to the transport metaphor, Gerrig believes that narrative experientially transports the reader out of her or his situation and into the narrative world. He highlights a number of cognitive processes that make this transport, or immersion, "virtually inevitable."[59] For instance, the narrative deploys the reader's working memory through its control of the reader's attention. Immersion in a narrative world intensifies the experience of that world.[60] Gerrig's description of narrative transportation coheres with Lewis's idea of looking *along*, as discussed in chapter 2. The reader comes to know a narrative world through inside-experience of that world.

Gerrig's second metaphor aligns with a view of reading as a dialogical act. Gerrig argues that the task of being a reader is much like the task of being an actor, since "readers must use their own experiences" to construct the narrative world and to "give substance to the psychological lives of characters."[61] Individual readers may interpret the same narrative differently, but these interpretive differences are comparable to the different ways that actors interpret the same dramatic role. This metaphor affirms the mutual contributions of both the reader and the text to the act of reading,

---

56. Gerrig, *Experiencing Narrative Worlds*, 1.
57. Ibid., 238.
58. Ibid., 2; italics in the original.
59. Ibid., 238.
60. Ibid., 66–67.
61. Ibid., 17.

and in the case of this study, the contributions of both the child reader and the Gospel of Luke to readings of Luke.

In a separate study, Paul Harris researched the benefits of imaginative thinking in human development. Part of his empirical work included looking at the responses of real readers to stories.[62] Harris found that adult readers process a story by constructing in their imaginations, "a mental model of the narrative situation being described." This mental model is seen from "a particular spatio-temporal locus" and is updated as the plot unfolds.[63] Similar research with children showed that "when children reproduced a simple story, they imposed a situation model with a consistent perspective on the story events, in much the same way as adults."[64]

Harris' findings suggest that the creation of a mental model of a narrative world may be a standard feature of engagement with narrative. That a spatio-temporal perspective is fundamental to this model suggests that the reader assumes a particular point of view relative to the narrative. This mental alignment with a viewpoint affirms Lewis's experiential epistemology: looking *along* a narrative world could be described, in cognitive terms, as developing a mental perspective on the key features and events of that world. This viewpoint is not static but rather develops in line with the narrative trajectory.

Keith Oatley takes Harris' findings a stage further in his research into the cognitive functions of child readers in their interaction with narrative. Although Oatley studies the role of fiction in childhood development, he concedes that it may not be fiction itself as a genre, but its narrative form that is the source of his key findings. Oatley's central thesis is that children use mental models of the primary world to work out how that world works and children respond similarly to narrative worlds: narrative presents readers with another type of world to investigate. The reader responds to the narrative world with a mental simulation of that world which helps the reader "to see how the parts fit together in combination."[65]

An important corollary for Oatley is that a reader's schema of the narrative world is constantly developing as the reader seeks to make sense of that world. This development occurs through the act of reading. Oatley's research builds on a number of other cognitive studies which show that filling in the gaps of a story involves active, rather than passive, mental

---

62. Harris, *The Work of the Imagination*.
63. Ibid., 192.
64. Ibid., 193.
65. Oatley, *Such Stuff as Dreams*, 17.

engagement with the narrative world.[66] His investigation also takes into account Iser's thesis that gap-filling is an act of the imagination.[67] Oatley's own research with child readers suggests that narrative gaps that cause readers to "construct their own inferences about what characters [are] thinking and feeling" lead to better comprehension of the text.[68] The result of active participation is a better understanding of the narrative world. When children read Luke, then, interaction with Luke's narrative world may enhance their understanding of that world.

Oatley investigates the persuasive force of narrative by building on previous studies of immersion in the narrative world, including the study by Gerrig. These studies showed that the greater the immersion, the greater the likelihood that the text will impact the reader's belief system and emotive state.[69] One study, by Green, found that it was the narrative form of a story that enhanced immersion, and that affixing the label of either fact or fiction to the story seemed to have "no effect on the extent of transportation" experienced by the reader.[70] Oatley's research supports this finding and adds that a text is more persuasive when read experientially, as opposed to when it is handled as an object of analysis. These studies suggest that presenting Bible stories *as* stories may enable a text like Luke to function as a more robust interlocutor for a child rather than, for instance, presenting Bible stories as moral illustrations or the instantiation of a theological concept.

Empathy, a reading strategy that is particularly relevant to this study, is also examined by Oatley. He found that child readers often make mental models of key characters in a story. This model-making produces empathy which enables the readers not only to engage with the characters but also to make sense of the text. Oatley's discussion builds on a concept which cognitive psychologists call the theory-of-the-mind. This theory holds that children as young as four years hypothesize about what other people, including characters, are thinking and why they conduct themselves in the way that they do.[71] Readers may approach a character by seeking to understand that character's viewpoint, and this alignment with viewpoint in turn allows the

---

66. Ibid., 58–62, 163. The studies include, among others: Bartlett, *Remembering*; Peskin and Astington, "Metacognitive Language," 253–73.

67. Oatley, *Such Stuff as Dreams*, 128; see also my discussion in chapter 2 under "In Search of a Theory."

68. Ibid., 163.

69. Ibid., 172. The studies include, among others: Green and Brock, "The Role of Transportation," 702–21; Tsai et al., "Learning What Feelings to Desire," 17–30.

70. Oatley, *Such Stuff as Dreams*, 172. See also Green, "Transportation into Narrative Worlds," 247–66.

71. Ibid., 115, 119.

readers to see from inside the story. This finding highlights the potential contribution of empathy to a child reader's ability to grapple with Luke. If empathy with a character is ignored or controlled, the reader's engagement with the story may be diminished.

Another approach to reading narrative that Oatley investigates is that of mental picturing, or visualization. His investigation builds on studies by Andy Clark that found that the brain has two mental processors: one that is language-based and sequential; and one that is association-based and intuitive.[72] In the text-reader dialogue, the reader has to take in "a language-based story" and "translate it into terms of intuition and experience, in an inner mental enactment."[73] The mental processing of a narrative begins in the verbal processor but spills over into the mental models and visual images that enable the reader to process through association. Oatley thus provides a cognitive reason for mental visualization: the images of the imagination go beyond language to enable reasoning that is associative and intuitive. Applying this finding to children reading Luke, the readers' use of the imagination may actually be fundamental to how they think about the text.

The Literary Process

Much of this discussion so far has been driven by the analysis of mental processes. Although children's reading of narrative is clearly dependent upon mental activity, it should not be reduced to a cognitive act. To do so would be to mechanize reading and to exclude holistic engagement with a narrative. A balance may be brought to the discussion by considering the literary aspects of children's engagement with narrative. This topic has been the subject of research in the fields of children's literature theory and education. I discuss some of the most pertinent studies here.

The educator, Donald Fry, conducted a qualitative study of six children's perspectives on reading and concluded that child readers particularly engage with stories when the stories are presented as "forms to be experienced" and not as tools for expounding ideas.[74] Fry found that one of the key values of reading narrative was the extension of the reader's experience, for a narrative is not only about experience, it creates an experience.[75] This

---

72. Ibid., 76–77. See also: Clark, "Language, Embodiment, and the Cognitive Niche," 370–74; Clark, "Material Symbols," 291–307.

73. Oatley, *Such Stuff as Dreams*, 77.

74. Fry, *Children Talk about Books*, 38.

75. Ibid., 107.

finding upholds my use of Lewis's experiential epistemology as a theoretical framework for analyzing the readings generated by this study.

In her treatise, *How Texts Teach What Readers Learn,* Margaret Meek also stresses the centrality of experience to the text-reader dialogue and adds that narrative texts are the best guides for teaching children how to read stories.[76] One of Meek's key points is that engaging with narrative shows children that reading is a "process of discovery" and "not a program of instruction" instituted by adults.[77] Reducing reading to functional lessons about the mechanics of a story robs the story of its central power, the reading experience. Comparatively, Luke may provide child readers with a distinct experience of its world that cannot be replicated through any form of discussion *about* the contents of the text.

According to Meek, one insight that child readers may glean from reading narrative is the role of intertextuality in the creation of meaning. Meek points out that oral tradition plays an important part in children's reading and that children may enter the "intertext of literature, oral and written, very early."[78] This point has particular relevance for this study since a number of the stories in Luke's Gospel, such as the stories of Jesus' birth and death, the parable of the Good Samaritan, and the story of Zacchaeus, have a place in the oral and visual tradition of many British children due to these stories' virtually ubiquitous presence in the National Curriculum, church festivals, Sunday School material, and the media surrounding Christmas. Meek holds that such knowledge provides the child reader with an inter-text to build upon in her or his reading. Even knowledge acquired from the diluted, cultural renditions of biblical narrative will impact children's experience of the Bible.

In her landmark study, *Powerful Magic: Learning from Children's Responses to Fantasy Literature,* Nina Mikkelsen outlines the characteristics of children's engagement with fantasy narrative. Mikkelsen conducted a qualitative investigation into how and why child readers become "involved in a book."[79] Much of her empirical work focused upon the cross-fertilization of the world of the text with the world of the reader, and it revealed that child readers use narrative "to make sense of the world." She concludes that this is a two-way process: child readers "shape literature in terms of their own worlds and reshape their worlds in new and different ways after reading

---

76. Meek, *How Texts Teach.*
77. Ibid., 19–20.
78. Ibid., 22.
79. Mikkelsen, *Powerful Magic,* 3, 14.

books that evoke their deep engagement."[80] For such a process to occur, children need to be free to engage holistically with a text.

Mikkelsen describes holistic engagement as living through a story via "associations, feelings, attitudes, and ideas."[81] Her discussion echoes that of Fry and Meek, with an added emphasis upon the mutual shaping that takes place between the reader and the text. This mutual shaping harks back to the developmental theorists with their emphasis upon the child's active engagement with her or his context as a stimulus for development. It may be the case, then, that when child readers interact holistically with Luke, this mutual shaping may be part of their reading transaction.

One of Mikkelsen's key critical frameworks is her "field of literacies," which is essentially a list of eight different ways that child readers may engage with a text.[82] This field is of Mikkelsen's own devising and allows her to categorize the responses she observed in her child readers. Each literacy originates conceptually from another theorist. Mikkelsen's category of "aesthetic literacy," for instance, derives from the discussion of aesthetic reading by Rosenblatt.[83] The eight literacies, taken together, reveal the complexity of children's interactions with narrative and serve as a useful set of tools for analyzing their readings. Some of the literacies that prove particularly useful for analyzing the children's readings of Luke include aesthetic literacy which refers to the child reader's use of the imagination, and personal/empathetic literacy which considers how the child connects with characters in a text.

Mikkelsen's key contribution is to elucidate the complexity involved in a child's reading of narrative. Much of her discussion consists of detailed analyses of real children's readings of various texts, which she executes through an application of the literacies. She asserts repeatedly that her eight categories overlap and are interdependent, but she does not develop an organizing principle that explains how they might cohere.[84] She does helpfully conclude, however, that the "emotional content of a book is its primary value for child readers" and possibly the doorway into all of the other approaches to reading.[85] In my analysis of the children's readings of Luke, I take the next step and propose that experience of the narrative world lies at the heart of the children's reading strategies.

---

80. Ibid., 171, 176.
81. Ibid., 55, 69; citing Rosenblatt, *The Reader, The Text, The Poem*, 25.
82. Ibid., 3–4.
83. Ibid., 3, 55, 70. See also Rosenblatt, *The Reader, The Text, The Poem*, 22–47.
84. Ibid., 6–7, 35, 107.
85. Ibid., 177.

The literary theorist, Maria Tatar, investigates the value of children reading stories and argues that narrative is an important means of opening up new worlds to child readers. Her study draws on adult readers' memories of their childhood reading experiences as well as her own close readings of a number of children's texts. The result is a helpful discussion of some of the impetuses behind children's reading. Tatar characterizes child readers as "enchanted hunters" who explore new worlds when they engage with a story.[86] Such reading is not passive, but rather a type of intellectual game that employs both the reader's mind and senses.

Tatar emphasizes the role of the imagination in this exploration, adding literary support to the findings of Harris and Oatley. According to Tatar, the child reader engages with the narrative world in a veritable "*pas de deux* with words."[87] The imagination is central to the efficacy of reading for it contributes to the child's ability to witness narrative events and to grapple with the characters. For child readers to generate their own interpretations of Luke, then, they need space to explore actively and imaginatively Luke's narrative world.

Summary

The aim of this chapter has been to consider some of the key literature concerned with children as readers. The discussion of the stage theories showed that children tend to engage actively with their contexts as a part of their developmental process, so that experience enhances development. This finding supports the use of an experiential model for this study's analysis. The stage theories, however, have a fundamental weakness relative to this study: they imply that the contribution of child readers is immature, a position which could devalue the children's readings of Luke.

This weakness is countered by the studies conducted by Applebee and Appleyard which found that, although children's reading develops through stages, each stage represents a set of skills to be gained. A reader does not outgrow these skills, but builds upon them and may draw upon them in her or his subsequent interaction with stories even as an adult. These researchers, along with Piaget, indicate that a child's transaction with a narrative may be orientated towards the text's concrete elements. My discussion of the cognitive processes of reading identified some of the factors that contribute to interpretation, including immersion, empathy, and the imagination. I take each of these factors into account in my analysis of the children's

86. Tatar, *Enchanted Hunters*, 27.
87. Ibid., 132.

readings. The mental models that children construct of the narrative world align well with the epistemological approach of looking *along* a narrative.

Finally, the literary theorists emphasize that children extend their experience by reading, and that the process of interacting with a narrative enhances children's ability to interpret narratives. In my study then, the children's direct encounters with Luke may provide reading experiences that shape their interpretation of the biblical world. Mikkelsen's research specifies that if this experience is holistic, it may shape not only the reader's interpretation of the text, but also the reader. Having established some of these key features of children reading narrative, I look next at studies of how readers interact with the Bible.

Chapter 4

Perspectives on Children Reading the Bible

Stephanie: "Luke made more sense than normal, cause normally we just read tiny little bits, and you don't know how Jesus got to this place, and why he's doing this. If you read the whole thing, then you can know everything that happens."

This chapter addresses two related topics. The first, and briefer of the two, is drawn from the field of the Bible and practical theology, and focuses on studies of how ordinary people engage with the Bible. This discussion provides a foundation for the second, more in-depth topic: literature concerned with children's engagement with the Bible. The aim throughout is to bring to light findings that are relevant to this study and to identify gaps in the literature that the empirical work may potentially address.

Real Readers of the Bible

The studies of ordinary, non-theologically trained readers' engagement with the Bible tend to target adults. Nonetheless their concern with how real readers approach the text is relevant to my research since children may be classified as a sub-group of these readers. There has not been much empirical research in this field, even among adults, but it is a growing area.

A notable quantitative study was conducted by Andrew Village, who investigated the influences impinging upon ordinary readers in their interpretation of the Bible.[1] Village defines "ordinary readers" as people who have not been exposed "to a particular way of reading the Bible: the way of the academy." A basic premise of his study is that theological scholarship

---

1. Village, *The Bible and Lay People*.

tends to separate readers from the text, preventing the Bible from impacting their lives.[2] His study aims to demonstrate "how the church actually uses the Bible, rather than how it ought to" according to the academy,[3] an aim that is comparable to the aim of my study.

Methodologically, Village's study tested "a range of interpretative possibilities in relation to a range of extra-biblical variables that might have some predictive capabilities."[4] Village used only one passage, Mark 9:14–29, the story of Jesus Healing an Epileptic Boy, limiting some of his findings to the particularities of this passage, as he is well aware.[5] Among other things, he found that, although neither age nor gender appeared to predict his participants' interpretation of the passage, education and church tradition did have significant predictive capability. Literal interpretation was strongly affiliated with less education and with the Evangelical church tradition.[6] Village defines "literal" as "the belief that events in the Bible happened as described"; that is, they occurred as depicted in the text and these depictions are of historical events.[7] The child readers in my study have considerably less education than many of Village's participants, potentially aligning them with this group of interpreters and their literal reading strategy.

In another study, Andrew Rogers used an ethnographic methodology to compare how two Evangelical churches engaged with the Bible.[8] His analysis also probes how hermeneutics is learned in a church context.[9] Rogers constructs a helpful hermeneutical phenomenology delineating the views of the Bible held by the congregations, the chief Bible-related practices, and the resulting hermeneutical virtues that may develop in a congregation. His study highlights the ecclesiological influences upon biblical interpretation. Although Rogers's study does not include children,[10] his research foregrounds influences that may well impact child members of a congregation and underscores that the church is a key environment where a child's expectations about the Bible are shaped.

---

2. Ibid., 1–2, 91. It is worth noting that by "academy" Village seems primarily to be referring to those who approach the biblical text with a historical-critical interpretive framework.

3. Ibid., 51, 163.

4. Ibid., 159.

5. Ibid., 95.

6. Ibid., 68.

7. Ibid., 57.

8. Rogers, *Congregational Hermeneutics*, 19.

9. Ibid., 22–24.

10. Ibid., 4n7.

Contextual Bible Study

Perhaps the largest group of recent studies of real readers' engagement with the Bible comes out of the Contextual Bible Study movement. Contextual Bible Study is a method that seeks to enable ordinary people and marginalized groups in particular to interact with the biblical text on their own terms.[11] According to one advocate of this movement, John Riches, its study method uses questions which target the interface between the Bible and the readers' context, so that the readers' context orientates theological reflection upon the Bible.[12] That is, the readers' context is part of the interpretive equation. Close readings of the Bible are central to the method since such readings make the text accessible to those who are unfamiliar with it.[13]

The roots of Contextual Bible Study are in liberation theology, which often asks how to use Bible reading as a means of liberation. Yet many of the movement's concerns are relevant to any group of real readers. Gerald West, an initiator of the movement, seeks to avoid both a "romantic listening to" readers that idealizes their ideas, and an arrogant "speaking for" that rationalizes their contributions relative to the church or the academy.[14] The movement recognizes that the concerns, experiences, and needs of ordinary readers invariably shape their reading, and the aim of the study method is not to discover "right" readings but rather "lines of connection" between the text and the world of the reader.[15] West argues that the resultant pre-critical readings should not be labelled as either "better" or "worse" than critical readings, although they may help scholars to recover readings that have been lost through critical scholarship.[16]

Some of West's points are pertinent to the present study. The need to respect the children's readings without idealizing them is an important criterion for my study. West makes a strong case for the value of the readings of the poor since the biblical text is aimed at the poor as much as at the educated, and perhaps a similar argument could be made for the readings of children as the voice of those who exemplify how to "enter the kingdom." What is lost when the child's voice is silenced? Interestingly, Christopher Rowland and Jonathan Roberts, who also argue for context-orientated Bible study, take Jesus' view of children as a model for allowing readers who may

---

11. Riches, *Contextual Bible Study*, 3.
12. Ibid., 5.
13. Ibid., 40–42.
14. West, *The Academy of the Poor*, 37.
15. Ibid., 58, 77, 155; original italics removed.
16. Ibid., 90, 93.

be deemed as "not worthy" to have a voice in interpreting the text.[17] These two scholars use children only as an analogy for the uneducated and poor, but their discussion leaves open the possibility that the voice of the child may be one of those that is silenced by the hegemony of scholarly voices.

Another useful exploration of the effects of Contextual Bible Study comes from Lawrence, who conducted an ethnographic study using four passages in Luke with five different communities in the UK. Her aim was to use these passages as a means of encouraging her participants to challenge "non-place" discourse within their contexts, in favor of an affirming and even transformative "place-making" discourse. The latter discourse grew out of the participants' interaction with the passages.[18] The text-context interface was central to the discussion method she used with the groups.

Lawrence's groups responded to the juxtaposition of text and context by using reading strategies which she divided into three categories: allegory, parable, and midrash.[19] Her participants used allegory to map cultural elements onto a passage, so that their readings spoke "directly to the contexts and challenges" of the readers' situation. The groups used "parables" when they cast one concept alongside of another in order to produce new understanding.[20] Midrash refers to a mode of interpretation that fills in gaps and poses questions about the Bible relative to contemporary culture.[21] Each of these reading strategies could potentially be used by child readers. As discussed in the previous chapter, Applebee found that children use analogy to understand narrative, an approach that may overlap Lawrence's parable category, while Oatley's research showed that filling gaps was part of a child's reading process.[22]

An important difference between the Contextual Bible Study movement and my research is that while the former is orientated towards readings relative to particular contexts, this study provides space for the child readers to engage with Luke relative to their contexts but does not direct them to do so. Therefore, any interface of the text and the reader's context in the children's readings may be deemed a product of the children's reading strategies. Such context-orientated reading will be taken into account in my analysis of the children's readings.

17. Rowland and Roberts, *The Bible for Sinners*, 58.
18. Lawrence, *The Word in Place*, xvii.
19. Ibid., 128.
20. Ibid., 129.
21. Ibid., 130.
22. Applebee, *The Child's Concept of Story*, 115; Oatley, *Such Stuff as Dreams*, 163; see also my discussion in chapter 3 under "Children Reading Narrative."

Having considered these studies of ordinary readers in general, I focus next on the chief concern of this chapter, studies of children interacting with the Bible.

Children and the Bible

One of the first things that becomes evident when investigating the literature on how children read the Bible is how little of it there is. A search on the British Education Index database using "children" and "Bible" as the keywords leads to only five titles published since the year 1975. While a similar search on the theological database, ATLA, gives over six hundred results, more than five hundred of these date from the sixteenth through nineteenth centuries and are either treatises concerned with the spiritual formation of children or references to children's bibles. I exclude these from this discussion and concentrate upon the fewer than 100 remaining results.

In the remaining literature, the focus varies from children's direct engagement with the Bible, to contemporary concerns about Christian education, to sociological influences. An ample supply of this literature is didactic and concerned with methods for teaching either particular biblical passages or views of the Bible to children.[23] Since this concern is outside the parameters of this study, I exclude most of this literature from the discussion, except for a few pertinent empirical studies. Another portion of the literature delineates the research of social phenomena pertaining to children's engagement with the Bible. Leslie J. Francis, for instance, investigates the demographics of young teens who read the Bible.[24] Pamela Caudill Ovwigho and Arnold Cole use extensive surveys to analyze statistically the connection between Bible reading and moral conduct among children,[25] as well as teens and adults.[26] Again, this literature falls outside the parameters of this study.

23. For example: Birnie, "Is Teaching the Bible Too Dangerous a Task for Schools?"; Hartin, "The Bible, The Child, and Education"; Smith, "The Bible and Education."

24. Francis profiles the type of thirteen- to fifteen-year-olds who read the Bible and finds that only a small proportion of his participants read the Bible with any regularity. Those most likely to read the Bible are younger middle-class females who attend church regularly. Francis does not, however, compare this to the amount of general reading done by this age group: of those surveyed, how many regularly read any form of literature? What Francis's results show is that reading the Bible is strongly associated with church attendance. Francis, "Who Reads the Bible?"

25. Their key finding is a small but statistically significant correlation between high levels of Bible engagement and lower engagement in at-risk behaviour. Ovwigho and Cole, "Scriptural Engagement."

26. Cole and Ovwigho, "Bible Engagement and Social Behavior."

Only a small portion of the literature is concerned with how children interpret the Bible, and this literature is the focus of the following pages. The scarcity of this literature reflects the fact that only minimal research has been conducted in this area, much of it in the last fifty years. This literature falls into two categories: literature that reports the findings of empirical research; and theoretical discussions of the topic. I look at both types of literature, beginning with the empirical studies.

Reading Literally

Due to the paucity of research into children's interpretation of the Bible, the few studies that have been done have had a significant impact on the use of the Bible with children. One of the first of these was the empirical research conducted by Ronald Goldman in the mid-1960s which altered the course of religious education in the UK for the following two decades.[27] Goldman examined the religious thinking of six- to seventeen-year-olds by interviewing over two hundred participants about their readings of three short Bible stories. He used his findings to assess children's readiness for encountering the biblical text in particular, and for religious education in general. Goldman's theoretical framework was based on Piaget and he concluded that the Bible should be withheld from children until they reach the age of eleven or twelve, the beginning of the formal operations stage. Even then, he believes, they should only be introduced to the New Testament.[28] His conclusions fall prey to the hierarchical assumption built into Piaget's theory and he deems children's religious thinking to be not only immature but even inappropriate.

While a number of scholars follow Goldman's lead,[29] his research has also been widely critiqued.[30] Indeed, it has a number of glaring weaknesses. Perhaps the key weakness lies in his approach to analysis: he evaluates his children's readings against the standards of his own theological position.

27. Goldman, *Readiness for Religion*, and *Religious Thinking*.

28. Goldman's approach to the canon is decidedly Marcionite.

29. For example: Holm, "What Shall We Tell the Children," in a special themed issue of *Theology* on *The Use of the Bible Today*; Francis, "Research and the Development of Religious Thinking"; Peatling, *Religious Education in a Psychological Key*.

30. Religious educators continue to refer regularly to Goldman's work, if only to refute it. As late as 1998, scholars such as Kay and Wilkins, in "Reading for Readiness," 65–69, were calling for Goldman's ideas to be discredited and seeking to counter his impact on the religious education system in the UK. See also Ashton, "Readiness for Discarding"; Slee, "Goldman Yet Again"; Greer, "Thinking about the Bible"; McGrady, "Religious Thinking."

He defines as "appropriate" those readings that align with his theological belief that "mature" religious thinking is concerned solely with human development.[31] For example, Goldman asserts that mature interpretation develops as children gradually learn not to believe in miracles.[32] Regarding the "Crossing of the Red Sea," he states: "The most mature view expressed by pupils is that God does not interfere with nature but influences man internally or uses natural occurrences to help man in his distress."[33] His study's conclusions consistently reflect his theological bias.

Goldman's literary skills prove little better. His hermeneutic construes the biblical text as comprised of timeless truths, so that biblical narrative needs to be unraveled for the truths concealed within it. Goldman asserts that the "truths to be gleaned from most biblical stories are generally abstract, are of a propositional nature, and are dependent upon the capacity to see analogies from one situation to another and to understand the metaphors in which religious narratives abound."[34] He relegates the value of biblical narrative to the realm of the abstract and reduces the effect of story to little more than a pleasant way of communicating religious truths. Accordingly, his interview questions often ignored the Bible story's content. For instance, in reference to the adult Jesus' temptation by the devil, he asked his participants: "Did Jesus ever do wrong when he was a boy?"[35]

Goldman found that children and young teenagers tended to use a "literal" hermeneutic which he labelled "immature," and he advocates withholding the text from such readers.[36] By "literal" Goldman means thinking about the world of the text in concrete terms, a category he derives from Piaget but which he also, without justification, equates to historical fact, leading him to reject its interpretive viability for theological reasons.[37] His assertion that readers will outgrow "literal" reading as they progress through developmental stages is refuted by Village's findings which point to adults using this strategy.[38] Additionally, Applebee's and Appleyard's findings that

---

31. Goldman, *Religious Thinking*, 76, 107, 112–13. Goldman acknowledges his theological perspective and even admits that to conduct research from a different theological position, not only his criteria for analysis, "but the whole nature of the questions and the interview procedure would have to be radically changed," *Religious Thinking*, 49.

32. Ibid., 112.

33. Ibid., 113.

34. Ibid., 226.

35. Ibid., 257.

36. Ibid., 227.

37. Ibid., 20, 55–57, 70.

38. Village, *The Bible and Lay People*, 68.

the reading strategies of childhood become part of an adult's interpretive tool kit suggest that literal interpretation has a role to play in reading even in adulthood.

Goldman does not consider the possibility that interpreting a narrative world *as* a narrative world means taking into account the concrete elements of that world, such as its actions, characters, and setting. "Literal" in this latter sense entails using the elements of the narrative to make sense of the narrative, an approach used by many of Goldman's participants but overlooked by him.[39] In his discussion of patristic methods of reading the Bible, Dale Martin refers to this form of reading as pursuit of the "narrative sense" of the text,[40] suggesting that this reading strategy has a literary dimension.

Goldman's most useful finding for my study, ironically, rests here. The "immature" readings of Goldman's younger participants hint at reading strategies that I take into account in my analysis. For instance, another interview question Goldman asked with reference to the story of Jesus' temptation was: "When Jesus was a man was he specially different from all other men?"[41] In response, Goldman's middle age group, nine- to twelve-year-olds, repeatedly characterized Jesus as a unique miracle worker. Goldman classifies this view of Jesus as a step beyond the "crude" Christology of younger children who primarily viewed Jesus as a "devout man," but not yet achieving the "advanced" view of the older teenagers who articulated ideas about Jesus' "saviorhood and divinity."[42] This middle age group overlaps partially with the age range of the participants in my study and its view of Jesus raises a number of questions. What does the group's focus on Jesus' ability to perform miracles reflect about the way these children interpret narrative? What aspect of the story led them to think of Jesus in terms of his actions? Appleyard's role of the Reader as Hero or Heroine may be relevant here since heroes are often associated with the enactment of the extraordinary.

That the British religious education system was so deeply influenced by Goldman's research is indicative of how little empirical research has been done on children's readings of the Bible. As will be clear in the following discussion, studies subsequent to Goldman's tend either to follow his lead, or to define themselves against him. Goldman's study was extensive, if theologically limited, and therefore provided religious educators with a starting point for bringing together children and the Bible.

---

39. For examples, see his description of various children's readings in Goldman, *Religious Thinking*, 118, 123–24, 158–59.

40. Martin, *Pedagogy of the Bible*, 53.

41. Goldman, *Religious Thinking*, 157.

42. Ibid., 157, 160.

Measuring Biblical Interpretation

While Goldman used a particular theological lens to evaluate children's readings of the Bible, other studies have confined the actual production of the readings, the raw data, within the parameters of a particular interpretive framework. This effect is particularly evident in an empirical study conducted by Susan E. Loman and Leslie J. Francis.[43] These researchers developed their own quantitative research instrument for measuring how young teens read a Bible passage. They administered this research instrument through the religious education departments of eighteen British secondary schools to pupils in Years 7 and 9. A total of 3,412 pupils took part.

Their research instrument was a tick box, self-completion questionnaire with standardized close-ended responses. It assessed how its respondents read eighteen different New Testament passages. Unfortunately the researchers do not include a list of these passages in their article, making it impossible to compare directly the passages and the responses on the questionnaire. They do, however, delineate the response categories. Each New Testament passage, or quote, was accompanied by three possible responses each of which represented a different "interpretation" of the passage, including: a literal interpretation, a symbolic interpretation, and rejection of the text. The respondents were asked to tick the response "which *best* shows your views about the quote."[44]

The researchers used their study to test the theory, derived from Goldman, that young teenagers read the Bible literally and that this reading strategy is one that they will outgrow. They claim that their findings show how children's readings alter across age and gender. Although they recognize some of the weaknesses in Goldman's analysis, Loman and Francis' range of responses derives partially from his research.[45] They define the questionnaire responses very precisely. A "literal interpretation" "affirms that things actually happened as described in the Bible." Note that this definition equates literal to historical. A "rejection response" takes the opposite position, maintaining "that there is no truth in the biblical account" or "these events did not happen." The final type of interpretation, "symbolic," "affirms that the biblical account conveys a religious truth although not a historical

---

43. Loman and Francis, "The Loman Index."
44. Ibid., 136; italics in the original.
45. Ibid., 132.

truth."[46] These response options imposed a set of interpretive categories on their young participants, pre-determining the range of their interpretation.[47]

The fundamental limitation of Loman and Francis' study is the hermeneutical assumption framing their research. In quantitative research, the process of operationalizing a concept, that is, the process which these two researchers used to devise the responses in their questionnaire, is only valid if the statements being measured adequately reflect the concept being tested. Loman and Francis assumed that their conceptualization of biblical interpretation provided an adequate representation of young people's interpretive strategies. But in order to achieve a measurable definition of biblical interpretation, they chose one interpretive framework among many and failed to acknowledge the limitations of their choice.

Biblical interpretation spans a large range of approaches to the Bible, each of which has its own theological implications. Paula Gooder, for instance, discusses twenty-three different interpretive frameworks.[48] Marguerat and Bourquin add that every interpretation of the biblical text "defines itself by the questions that it addresses to the text."[49] Loman and Francis directed their participants to ask questions about the historicity and religious significance of the text. Their "literal" and "rejection" responses queried whether the passage represents a historical event, while the "symbolic" response queried the text's religious value. The researchers limited young teenagers' readings to the confines of a historically and symbolically orientated hermeneutic. Their "literal" has nothing to do with making narrative sense of the text using its concrete elements. As a result, what we know from their study is how the 3,412 respondents aligned themselves within the researchers' chosen and rather limiting interpretive framework.

In short, their conceptualization process was reductive so that their research instrument did not adequately represent biblical interpretation: their empirical method used as an inadequate form of knowledge representation.[50] Loman and Francis admit that "the construct 'biblical interpretation' is used elsewhere in a variety of different senses,"[51] but they do not explore whether these other "constructs" may be relevant to the reading strategies of the age group they investigate. If such strategies are to be identified, they

---

46. Ibid., 135, 136.
47. Ibid., 135.
48. Gooder, *Searching for Meaning*.
49. Marguerat and Bourquin, *How to Read*, 4.
50. See the discussion of knowledge representation in Rugg and Petre, *Research*, 161–62.
51. Loman and Francis, "The Loman Index," 132.

might most helpfully originate with the interpreters, that is, the child readers, rather than with the researchers. Wellington and Szczerbinski indicate that if a researcher is seeking to understand the perspectives of the people being studied, then a qualitative approach should be used.[52] My empirical research, accordingly, employs a heuristic qualitative methodology in order to discover, rather than direct, the participants' approaches to Luke. One of its results will be to cast doubt on the framework adopted by Loman and Francis.

Reading for Values and Morals

Another prominent empirical study, the Biblos Project, examined the use of biblical narrative in British secondary schools. This study, conducted by Terence Copley and the School of Education at the University of Exeter, consisted of an extensive program of mixed methods research. According to Copley, the study aimed to "investigate how biblical narrative might be taught in public schools in a society labelled variously post-Christian, postmodern, plural, and secular."[53] Despite its didactic orientation, the Biblos Project is relevant to my study because it assessed the relationship between children and biblical narrative.

The Biblos Project unveiled some of the key forms of biblical interpretation present in the world of secondary religious education. According to the first report of the Project, many religious education teachers use biblical narrative as a proof-text for the morals and values of secular society.[54] The third report, which records the results of a survey of 1,066 school pupils, indicates that children tend to follow the lead of their teachers and perceive the Bible as a source of truth and morality.[55] Narrowing interaction with the Bible down to questions about its truth-claims proved to be a potential means of alienating readers from the text.

---

52. Wellington and Szczerbinski, *Research Methods*, 11, 20.

53. Copley, "Young People," 256.

54. Copley, *Echo of Angels*. While the Biblos Project focuses on secondary schools, David Clines, based on his own informal research, makes a similar argument with reference to British culture in general. He asserts that British culture uses the Bible to support its views when these views happen to coincide, while rejecting what it does not want to hear. In particular, it jettisons the divine from the Bible, but to do so is no longer to have the Bible since the divine is its central concern. Clines asserts that "it is bad for the morals of the society to think that they can have Scripture's backing when it suits them—and not buy the whole package." See Clines, *The Bible and the Modern World*, 53–54.

55. Copley et al., *On the Side of the Angels*.

The third report included 98 follow-up interviews focusing on the participants' views of the "truth" and moral significance of the Bible.[56] The interviewees indicated that they respect the Bible for its moral values, but their belief that the Bible is concerned with how to behave leaves it with "an image problem"[57] that makes it unappealing. The participants who were most negative about the Bible were those who believed it not to be true, with the peak of this negativity coming around Year 9, or pupils aged thirteen to fourteen years.[58] In contrast, biblical literacy, including a more robust understanding of interpretation, generated positive attitudes towards the Bible.[59]

The Biblos Project also examined the religious education material concerned with biblical narrative and found that this material directs children towards "secular human values rather than issues about God."[60] This secularization of the Bible causes children to expect to learn only secular values from religious texts.[61] Copley concludes that secular discourse largely shapes children's readings of biblical narrative within the school environment. The general outcome of the UK's national religious education program, as far as children's interaction with biblical narrative is concerned, is a reading strategy that moralizes the text to prop up Western values.

The findings of the Biblos Project highlight some of the issues with using an externally imposed framework to delimit children's engagement with the Bible. Such frameworks hold the text at bay, allowing it neither to set the theological agenda nor to challenge the reader. When the biblical text is presented as a repository of morality, reading the Bible is reduced to the pursuit of appropriate behavior. Narratives like the Good Samaritan take precedence, since they align well with this hermeneutic; and narratives that have no obvious moral message, such as the Parable of the Tenants and the Vineyard, are sidelined.[62] Child readers never really engage with the Bible on their own terms, and may come to view the text as a religious artefact. They are left with a reading strategy that seeks validation for a particular set of concerns but not one that enables them to interrogate those concerns or the ideologies from which they arise. When these young readers begin

---

56. Copley et al., *The Speech of Angels*.
57. Ibid., 21.
58. Copley et al., *On the Side of the Angels*, 38, 49.
59. Ibid., 56.
60. Copley, "Young People," 257.
61. Ibid., 259.
62. See Luke 10:25–37 and 20:9–19, respectively. Notably, the Parable of the Good Samaritan is the most commonly used Bible story in the National Curriculum.

to question the morals of their adult gatekeepers, the Bible may be cast off along with the morals which it is deemed to inculcate. Such a reading model positions children to outgrow the text.

Not only does the moral reading model obscure potentially subversive values in the Bible, but it also prevents the reader from experiencing immersion in its narrative world. The power of story is derailed, as child readers learn to look *at* the text for its morals, rather than to experience the story. This raises the question, what happens when children approach a biblical narrative *as* narrative? My study seeks to answer that question.

Valuing the Child as an Interpreter

The studies discussed so far have all either imposed an interpretive framework on children's readings of the Bible, or, in the case of the Biblos Project, sought to uncover the frameworks at use in a particular institution. In contrast, Howard Worsley's research, the Bible Story Project, seeks to hear the voice of the child "speaking for him or herself as scripture is encountered."[63] The Bible Story Project consists of a series of qualitative studies of how children understand Bible passages.[64] One of Worsley's key premises is that the most appropriate approach to Bible stories for a child is one that originates with the child.[65] He views childhood as a spiritually open period of development and seeks a children's hermeneutic that reflects this openness.[66]

Worsley's first study investigated how nine- to ten-year-old children in two primary schools responded to two Bible stories. The stories were communicated using the method of Godly Play and the child participants were encouraged to respond creatively.[67] The second study consisted of interviews with six children, from three different developmental stages, about the creation accounts in Genesis 1–2. The interviews targeted what the participants believed the accounts meant, but were based on the children's previous experience of the accounts rather than on readings of the passage.[68]

In the final, larger study, Worsley investigated children's engagement with the Bible within the familiar environment of their homes. He set up

63. Worsley, "The Bible in Family Context," 117.
64. Worsley, "How Children Aged 9–10 Understand Bible Stories"; Worsley, "Insights from Children's Perspectives"; Worsley, *A Child Sees God*; Worsley, "The Bible in Family Context."
65. Worsley, *A Child Sees God,* 12–13.
66. Worsley, "How Children Aged 9–10 Understand Bible Stories," 205.
67. Ibid., 206.
68. Worsley, "Insights from Children's Perspectives," 249–59.

a three-way interaction between child participants, an adult reader, and a Bible story, which positioned the children as the interpreters. Forty-five children in twenty-three different family units participated in this study. The child participants, who ranged in age from three to twenty, engaged orally with selected Bible passages within the context of family reading sessions. The researcher provided the family units with twenty-one different NRSV Bible passages representing seven different categories of biblical narrative, and asked the participants to select seven texts, one from each category, for reading. The adult "co-researcher," usually a parent, read the selected passages out loud and let the child participants talk about them using open-ended discussion. Afterwards, the adult made notes on the session and these notes functioned as the raw data.[69]

A key finding in Worsley's studies is that the imagination plays a role in children's engagement with the Bible.[70] This finding aligns with Harris' and Oatley's findings that children use their imagination to interpret stories.[71] In Worsley's first and second studies, this finding may have been connected to his decisions to use Godly Play and to encourage the participants to give creative responses.[72] In his final study, Worsley connects the children's imagination to their spirituality. He believes that children's interactions with the Bible are characterized by a wonder that may lead to spiritual insights.[73] My study probes this finding and seeks to clarify further the role of the imagination in children's readings of the Bible.

It is worth noting that Worsley's view of children is decidedly romantic. He describes children's responses to the Bible as "natural and apparent," twice citing a Wordsworth poem to substantiate his position.[74] This view limits his analysis of his participants' responses. Much of the report of his larger study consists of excerpts from the transcripts. These excerpts highlight the child participants' insights, and, although Worsley provides comments on each excerpt, his comments usually take the form of explanation rather than critique.[75]

Worsley's methodology raises a few questions. He samples from a large age range, and to make the Bible stories accessible to the very young, his

---

69. Worsley, *A Child Sees God*, 118–19, 121.

70. Worsley, "How Children Aged 9–10 Understand Bible Stories," 213.

71. See my discussion in chapter 3.

72. Worsley, "Insights from Children's Perspectives," 257.

73. Worsley, *A Child Sees God*, 144, 147, 149.

74. Ibid., 13–14, and Worsley, "The Bible in Family Context," 122–23. Worsley is citing William Wordsworth, *Ode on Intimations of Immortality from Recollections of Early Childhood*.

75. For example, Worsley, *A Child Sees God*, 84–87.

methods in all three parts of his project depend upon oral encounters with the text. Such encounters necessitate an adult mediator and Worsley notes that these mediators at times influenced the children's engagement.[76] The transcripts of his larger study, for instance, show that the adult readers occasionally provided directive input in the story-telling sessions.[77] However, Worsley's intention is to examine children's responses to Bible stories and not children's unmediated encounters with the text. My study takes a different angle and seeks to investigate a more unmediated encounter: what happens when a child reads biblical narrative.

What the Bible Might Do to the Child

I turn now to the theoretical literature concerned with children and the Bible. A significant portion of this literature addresses the potential results of the encounter between the child and the text. One branch of this literature debates how the Bible might influence its young interlocutors, and a common concern is the issue of exposing children to stories that, as John and Marianne Meye Thompson state, "fall short of virtually every moralist's canon."[78] The Thompsons point out that such stories are often censored or silenced altogether by the adults who guide children's engagement with the Bible, even while children encounter similar or stronger tales on television and the internet.[79] The Thompsons counter that these stories may benefit children if the adult gatekeepers drew connections between the stories and the demands of real life.

Francis Landy, in his article on the ethics of allowing children to read the Bible, adds that the aim of children's Bible reading should be to explore the problems of the primary world.[80] He describes the biblical world as one in which good and evil are entangled, an entanglement that speaks to the human condition. The biblical world helps children to think about the conflict between good and evil, and reveals that this conflict is both external and internal to human beings.[81] Landy's argument makes space for child

---

76. Worsley, "The Bible in Family Context," 123, 126

77. For example, Worsley, *A Child Sees God*, 70–71, 116–17, 125.

78. Thompson and Thompson, "Teaching the Bible to Your Children," 297. This is reminiscent of Karl Barth's assertion: "Large parts of the Bible are almost useless to the school in its moral curriculum." Barth, "The Strange New World Within the Bible," 38.

79. For a full discussion of this phenomenon as it pertains to children's Bibles, see Bottigheimer, *The Bible for Children*; Bottigheimer, "The Bible for Children."

80. Landy, "Do We Want Our Children to Read This Book?," 160.

81. Ibid., 164.

readers to adopt Appleyard's Reader as Hero or Heroine reading role. It also points to the gap between the use of the Bible as a moral repository and the child reader's interest in narrative that is characterized by conflict.

In her book, *The Children of Israel: Reading the Bible for the Sake of our Children*, Danna Nolan Fewell similarly argues that children profit from being exposed to the flaws of human existence that are portrayed in the Bible. Her argument rests on the juxtaposition of her view of the Bible as a text shot through with moral ambivalence with her view of children as subject to a morally corrupt world. She jettisons any treatment of the text as a repository for morality, asserting that sanitizing the text leaves it insipid and irrelevant.[82] Instead, Fewell argues, children need to encounter the moral and theological difficulties of the Bible in order to be able to "grapple with their own development as moral beings."[83] Fewell believes that such interaction may provide children with insight into the human condition.

Fewell takes this position a step further in her discussion of child characters in the Bible. She believes that the stories of these characters explore triumph in the face of adversity and model how children "can be not only heroes of their own lives, but redeemers of their own communities (even saviors of the world!)."[84] The Bible provides children with models who may inspire them to counter the problems they face and even to become leaders who may make a difference in their personal contexts. Like Landy, Fewell's discussion validates the child approaching the Bible through the Reader as Hero or Heroine role and, going a step further, even extrapolating aspects of that role to her or his personal context.

Both Landy and Fewell address the impact of the "difficult" parts of the Bible on the child reader, and their arguments are marshalled in defense of that impact. Fewell nonetheless prefers to withhold the Bible from younger children until they are aware of "the complexities of life."[85] Her position highlights a tension at work in this debate: either the Bible is given to children in all of its complexity, or the Bible is adapted and presented to children in a tamed form by the institutions which defang it.[86] This tension hinges upon a particular view of children held by those in the debate: children as passive interpreters relative to the text. My study takes a more robust view of children's interpretive capacity and treats the text-reader dialogue as two-way.

---

82. Fewell, *The Children of Israel*, 108–9.
83. Ibid., 107.
84. Ibid., 112.
85. Ibid., 109.
86. As Bottigheimer makes clear, in her *The Bible for Children*, 51.

What the Child Might Make of the Bible

A different branch of the theoretical literature reflects upon the child's potential construal of the Bible; that is, what might child readers make of the text? While the Thompsons, Landy, and Fewell all seek to prevent the text from being sequestered from children, Hugh Pyper turns the discussion on its head and contends that the Bible may in fact be seen as a book suitable for children, or, in his words, as a "children's book."[87] Much of his discussion stems from his own experience as a child reader of the Bible and he emphasizes how this reading unleashed his imagination. He found that stories such as Jesus Walking on the Water (John 6:16–21) "gave a glimpse of another world, or, more accurately, a transfigured version of the world we live in." As a child, he protested against adult attempts to explain the historical possibilities of this story for his "acceptance or rejection of it was not concerned with plausibility, but with believability."[88] This view suggests that the narrative world, rather than external referents, may be the key interest for the child reader and what the child expects is for the narrative world to be viable.

In his discussion of the Gospels, Petri Merenlahti proposes that a child may provide a useful instantiation of Eco's model reader.[89] Children are like model readers because they want the whole story and they receive much of the information necessary for comprehension of the story from the story itself.[90] This view dovetails with Meek's assertion that children learn about how a narrative works by reading it.[91] Yet Merenlahti concedes that a child's lack of awareness of the complexity of the Gospels may prevent the child from fully inhabiting the role of a model reader. Since the Gospels assume certain literary and historical knowledge on the reader's part, the child reader may have larger narrative gaps to fill than an adult.[92] The adult imposition of interpretive frameworks upon children's encounters with the Bible, as discussed earlier in this chapter, may well be an attempt to prevent children from filling in these gaps "incorrectly," that is, in ways that do not align with the adult gatekeepers' interpretive concerns.

Daniel A. Csanyi discusses the child as an interpreter and emphasizes the use children make of the Bible's concrete elements. He believes that

---

87. Pyper, "What the Bible Can Do to a Child."

88. Ibid., 148.

89. Merenlahti, "Reading as a Little Child," 142, 146. Merenlahti references Eco, *Six Walks*, 8–9.

90. Ibid., 142, 146.

91. Meek, *How Texts Teach*, 19–20; see my discussion in chapter 3.

92. Merenlahti, "Reading as a Little Child," 146.

biblical narrative provides "stepping-stone images" that lay a foundation for the child's understanding of God.[93] According to Csanyi, children may use such images to make sense of their beliefs as well as to determine their place in their tradition. Bible stories provide children with a concrete way of thinking about the biblical world in relation to their world, and as a result may help them to shape their identity.[94] This orientation towards the text's concrete elements aligns with the literal reading strategy highlighted earlier in this chapter.

This literal approach echoes Lakoff and Johnson's argument, discussed in chapter 2, that abstract concepts are grasped through concrete experience.[95] The centrality of narrative to the Bible prevents Christianity from being distilled into a set of abstract concepts. Arthur J. Rowe adds that while children appear to depend upon context to understand a story, biblical stories in turn provide contexts for understanding concepts.[96] A reading strategy that treats stories as mere containers to be opened up for the conceptual nuggets inside may not only undermine children's enjoyment, but also truncate their understanding of the narrative.

What the child makes of the Bible depends upon the interpretive process she or he uses with it. Pike thinks that in secondary schools the Bible has the status of a sacred text which can cause a "reverential attitude among readers."[97] This attitude leads to passivity as teenagers expect those already skilled in the text to communicate its sacred or moral meanings to them. Pike argues that, instead, active engagement with the Bible should be encouraged and personal interpretation should be legitimated.[98] Such an approach may foster children's "aesthetic, imaginative, and creative experience," and nurture their spirituality.[99]

Rosemary Cox rejects directive interpretive strategies for similar reasons.[100] She asserts that in the church, biblical material "has been presented in a 'closed' or 'given' way, pointing out the 'moral' or 'message' of the Bible passage."[101] This shuts down children's interaction with the Bible, teaching them to seek a "right" answer when, in fact, children tend to "make meaning

---

93. Csanyi, "Faith Development," 523.
94. Ibid., 521.
95. Lakoff and Johnson, *Metaphors*, 59.
96. Rowe, "Children's Thinking and the Bible," 27.
97. Pike, "Belief as an Obstacle," 161.
98. Ibid., 161.
99. Pike, "The Most Wanted Text in the West," 38.
100. Cox, *Using the Bible*, 15.
101. Cox, "Using the Bible with Children," 42.

in a 'storied' way."[102] Cox's position, along with the arguments of Csanyi, Rowe, and Pike, highlights the potential value of giving child readers the opportunity to engage freely with biblical narrative using their own reading strategies.

Experiencing the Bible

Much of the theoretical literature discussed so far focuses upon the outcome of the text-reader dialogue. My final category of literature is concerned, instead, with the nature of the actual dialogue: what might the dialogue look like? The most prominent discussion here is that of Roger and Gertrude Gobbel who propose an experiential model of interaction between the child and the Bible.[103] Gobbel and Gobbel argue that "Goldman's conclusion should be reversed" and children should be given unfettered access to the Bible so that, through this experience, they may gain an understanding of the text that is "significant and useful to them."[104]

While Gobbel and Gobbel emphasize the importance of experience, their driving argument is not epistemological but developmental. Their reading model is grounded in Piaget's developmental theory, although their conversation partners are the heirs and critics of Piaget rather than Piaget himself. They argue that a child's understanding of the Bible, even though different from an adult's understanding, is still "valid and adequate" since children's interpretations are part of their developmental process and will develop as they develop.[105] They view children as "active participants" in the construction of meaning for their own worlds,[106] and assert that the Bible could contribute to that construction process. Otherwise, they believe, the Bible's transformative power is exchanged in favor of religious lessons.

At the heart of the authors' discussion is their analogy of the Bible as a playground, which they use to explicate their model. Children learn to use various types of playground equipment by experiencing that equipment. Thus, "pictures, descriptions, and stories may assist the child to know *about* the slide, but the child *knows* neither the slide *nor* what he or she can do with it" until she or he visits a playground.[107] Similarly, the Bible offers children a variety of literary forms and children should be given opportunities

---

102. Cox, *Using the Bible*, 8–9, 18.
103. Gobbel and Gobbel, *The Bible: A Child's Playground*.
104. Ibid., ix, 8.
105. Ibid., 7, 9.
106. Ibid., 32.
107. Ibid., 45; italics in the original.

"to engage, act upon, and interact directly with the Bible *as they are able*" in order to "experience, know, and achieve understanding of it."[108] Here their discussion slips into the realm of experiential epistemology, and their emphasis on the advantages of development through experience dovetails with Lewis's commendation of inside-experience.

Gobbel and Gobbel assert that adult concern with children's understanding of the Bible consistently takes adult understanding as its reference point, but with child readers, a different reference point is needed: "the children themselves."[109] Like adults, children may read the Bible with reference to their own lives. If adult points of reference are consistently imposed upon children's reading, the biblical contents may be rendered personally irrelevant. Accordingly, my study uses an interview method that enables the participants to discuss the Gospel of Luke relative to their own social and developmental situations, rather than with reference to an adult agenda.

The Gobbels do not describe what children might *do* on the biblical playground, although they do assert that children may interpret the Bible using "the same abilities and experiences" with which they interpret their own world.[110] At this point, they suggest methods that adults may use for enabling children to interact with the Bible, for instance open-ended questions, drama, and associative conversations.[111] This tactical move reveals the key drawback in Gobbel and Gobbel's theory: it is not substantiated by empirical evidence. Their valuing of experience derives from their application of developmental theory to children's interpretation of the Bible. My study embraces the Gobbels' argument then picks up where they left off and examines what child readers do in their encounters with Luke.

A number of other scholars ponder what a child's dialogue with the Bible may look like. Karl Nipkow also urges that young readers be given direct experience of the Bible,[112] and suggests that such an approach may incorporate open conversation with the text, affective responses, and imaginative reading.[113] Nipkow's suggestions provide a helpful guide to potential reading strategies that children may use with the Bible. Patricia Van Ness adds that a child's interaction with the Bible may be holistic, incorporating the child's "mind, body, emotions, spirit, and community."[114] Cox points out

---

108. Ibid., 47; italics in the original.
109. Ibid., 55.
110. Ibid., 141.
111. Ibid., 123–34, 143–49.
112. Nipkow, "Elementary Encounters," 164.
113. Ibid., 165.
114. Van Ness, *Transforming Bible Study*, 45. Landy makes a similar point in, "Do

that a holistic approach is not common in either church or school because "Piaget's emphasis on cognitive skills has denied a place to the imagination and the feelings"[115] in children's engagement with the Bible, a point that echoes Donaldson's critique of Piaget.[116] All of this literature has a noticeable gap: it is primarily theoretical. My study seeks to fill that gap by evaluating children's readings of Luke, taking into account the cognitive, emotive, imaginative, and personal aspects of those readings.

The Need for Further Study

This survey of the literature addressing real readers' engagement with the Bible has revealed a number of issues. Within the field of practical theology, only a few qualitative empirical studies have been conducted on how individual readers interpret the Bible. My study partially redresses that situation through the examination of the readings of one group of ordinary, albeit young readers. In the literature concerned with children and the Bible, many of the empirical investigations utilized interpretive grids which delimited the text-reader transaction. The literature suggests that the primary institutions that bring together the child and the Bible, school and church, do the same. The theoretical literature, although sometimes displaying a greater vision for children's interpretive capacity, provides primarily anecdotal evidence for its conceptions of children's readings.

All of the literature concerned with children reading the Bible may be classified according to its treatment of the text-reader dialogue. The studies that impose boundaries on children's readings do not trust the dialogue. The literature that highlights the child's potential interpretive insights focuses on the reader half of the dialogue and potentially side-lines the text. The literature that concentrates upon the impact that each partner in the dialogue may have upon the other partner is outcome-orientated and thus concerned with what occurs after the dialogue. Finally, some of the literature considers what type of dialogue may be efficacious and recommends an experiential approach to children's interaction with the Bible. My study aligns most closely with this latter literature.

It is also clear that the model of interpretation that the adult gatekeeper brings to the child-text interaction shapes the outcome of that interaction. Robert Alter states that reading "any body of literature involves a specialized mode of perception in which every culture trains its members from

We Want Our Children to Read This Book?," 165.
   115. Cox, "Using the Bible with Children," 46.
   116. See my discussion in chapter 3 under "Childhood Development."

childhood."[117] This survey suggests that children are being taught interpretive methods which may run counter to the way a narrative like Luke works. Talbert notes that in Luke "the overall picture of Jesus is a theological rather than a strictly historical entity,"[118] but interpretive frameworks like those of Loman and Francis provide space primarily for the latter. Such frameworks fit Appleyard's description of socially constructed reading roles.[119] But what are the consequences of these constructions?

It may be argued that the ethical teaching in Luke is part of the worldview of the text and thus part of the logic that makes the text coherent. But separating the morals of the text from their narrative framework, a tactic used by schools and noted by the Biblos Project, invariably cuts their ethical significance down to the size of a predictable platitude. In his book on biblical exegesis, Peter J. Leithart traces the development of contemporary hermeneutics and argues that a "modernist, post-Kantian hermeneutic" treats biblical narrative as a husk to be discarded for the timeless ethical substance embedded within it.[120] Leithart believes that this hermeneutical method often characterizes the interpretive practice of the contemporary church. A similar argument could be made for the use of the Bible with children.

Treating biblical narrative as a repository of morality or a receptacle from which Christian truths and religious symbols may be derived is tantamount to treating it as an object. Lewis, in his discussion of how readers handle literature, states that a text can be either received or used: "When we 'receive' it we exert our senses and imagination and various other powers... When we 'use' it we treat it as assistance for our own activities."[121] To treat a narrative as an object is to use it. Good reading, counters Lewis, results from receiving the book on its own terms. The narrative power of Luke may be lost to child readers if adult gatekeepers limit the terms upon which the story may be encountered.

Some of the literature discussed in this chapter seems to ignore direct engagement with the Bible, particularly where children are concerned. In contrast, the literature on children as readers, as discussed in the previous chapter, suggests that children read by adopting roles that enable them to live through a narrative. They are active participants who engage holistically

---

117. Alter, *The Art of Biblical Narrative*, 62.
118. Talbert, *Literary Patterns*, 112.
119. Appleyard, *Becoming a Reader*, 15
120. Leithart, *Deep Exegesis*, 29, 36.
121. Lewis, *An Experiment in Criticism*, 88. Lewis's approach is applied directly to biblical texts by Wright, "An Experiment in Biblical Criticism."

with the narrative world, an engagement that may include their imagination and empathy. Of the empirical investigations discussed here, only Worsley takes into account the role of the imagination in children's encounters with the Bible.

Such participation may entail looking *along* the story line to see what the narrative brings into view. Both the literature on children as readers and a number of the empirical studies in this chapter point to a literal interpretation strategy that focuses on the concrete elements of the story world. But the empirical studies examined in this chapter equate this strategy to an extrapolation from the narrative world to the primary world and do not pause to consider that the interpretation of a narrative world necessarily engages with the narrative's concrete elements. If child readers construct mental models of a narrative world, these models will necessarily take literally the concrete elements of the narrative world in order to make sense of that world.

It may be that how children read is not completely at odds with the invitation extended to readers by the Gospel of Luke. The literature in this chapter suggests that the potential alliance between children as readers and biblical narrative as participatory literature has largely been neglected. Instead, adults appear to make assumptions about what children may or even should glean from their interaction with the Bible without first asking what actually happens in that interaction. Meanwhile, children read narrative with a set of tools whose potential implementation with the Bible remains unexplored.

Finding A Way Forward

What is needed is an investigation that frees children to interact with biblical narrative *as* narrative. Although it is impossible to examine the actual moment of interaction, it is possible to discuss that interaction with the child and to analyze the readings that result from it. Such a study must take a heuristic approach that seeks to uncover the key features of the readings and the reading strategies used by the participants, whether consciously or unconsciously, rather than seeking to direct those strategies through moral or theological concerns. This is the empirical investigation that I undertake: I seek to understand how one group of children read biblical narrative.

The features of the children's readings will invariably be shaped by the readers' expectations, which in turn will depend upon their developmental phases and personal contexts. Pennington states, of readers of the Gospels in general, that they inevitably read "the text with different degrees of understanding and depth based on their own knowledge, experiences, maturity, and skills as readers."[122] No child reader will come to the Bible free of already formed opinions, concerns, ideas from peers, or adult influences. They will not read the Bible with a *tabula rasa*: any child who is old enough to read is old enough to have had their understanding and views molded, to some extent, by their context and experience. The key here is that the child is free to choose for her or himself what parts of that context and experience to employ when interacting with the Bible.

It is likewise impossible for an adult researcher to analyze the text-reader interaction completely free of a theoretical perspective on that interaction. My theoretical model reflects that described by Gobbel and Gobbel: I seek to enable the child reader to function as an independent interpreter of Luke. But my study also seeks to go beyond the Gobbels and to examine the components of that interaction. I have already made clear my view of the need for the text and reader to be treated as equal partners in their dialogue. Since Luke is a narrative, this study approaches the children's readings from a narratological perspective, seeking to understand which aspects of the narrative guides the readers. I assume that the readers use interpretive strategies, even if these are unconscious, and part of my aim is to identify those strategies by probing the ways in which the readers engage with the narrative world. Finally, my study critiques the children's readings, particularly through cross-comparisons between the children's readings and other readings of the same biblical passage.

This chapter concludes the review of the literature most pertinent to this study. In the next two chapters, I describe the methodology used in the empirical research. That discussion explains the methods I used to generate the children's readings.

---

122. Pennington, *Reading the Gospels Wisely*, 117–18.

Part Two

The Investigation of the Children's Readings of Luke

Chapter 5

Research Methodology: The Set-Up

Jeremy: This [translation of Luke] "says, 'Children's version.' I thought that it might be a bit too simplistic."

Introduction to the Empirical Research[1]

The backbone of this study is its empirical research into the transaction that takes place between child readers and the Gospel of Luke. This transaction occurred when children read the text, and the evidence of this transaction was the children's readings of the text. These readings are the data of this study. The central actions at the heart of the empirical research were straightforward, at least on the surface: to provide child readers with a copy of the Gospel of Luke to read and then to discuss their readings with them. However, as the following two chapters show, executing these actions involved considerable planning and careful implementation.

The aim of these chapters is to provide a thorough discussion of the development and execution of the study's empirical methodology. This chapter delineates how the research was set-up and the following chapter explains the actual execution of the research. In this chapter, I look first at the reasons behind my choice of research methodology, then discuss the issues surrounding research with children, before outlining the various preparatory steps leading up to the investigation.

---

1. Three of the key documents produced for the empirical research are available in the appendices of this book. All of the documents produced for the empirical research may be viewed at www.melodyrbriggs.com

Qualitative Research

Although reading a text is usually a private act, discussing that reading is a social act. My empirical research is built upon discussions with child readers, and so I turned to the field of social science for a research strategy. As we have seen in the previous chapter, only a few theories about children's readings of biblical narrative exist, and none of them are comprehensive. Since I needed to generate theories, I chose a qualitative research methodology. Qualitative research "emphasizes an inductive approach" to data.[2] An inductive approach is defined by its relationship to theory: it uses data to generate theories.[3] Qualitative research therefore provided my study with a methodology for theorizing about the children's readings.

Qualitative research is concerned primarily with meaning and words, rather than for instance causes or numbers. It seeks the meaning that participants attribute to an experience through an inductive exploration of that experience.[4] Rather than endeavoring to make statements about the general population, it addresses "research questions that require explanation or understanding" of particular phenomena.[5] These phenomena may include the participant's beliefs, values, understanding, and actions, all of which may shape how a child interprets a biblical text. A qualitative research strategy interprets these phenomena in order to understand the topic under investigation. In the case of this study, it enabled me to analyze the various facets of the children's readings of Luke in order to construct theories about those readings.

The main research instrument in a qualitative study is the researcher, who works closely with the participants in order to understand the topic under investigation from their perspective.[6] One of the consequent weaknesses of such research is its subjectivity. The results are based on the researcher's understanding of the participants' accounts of their experience. The type of relationship that the researcher forms with the participants also invariably shapes the results. These criticisms are valid for this study and have been taken into account in my analysis of the findings.

Yet a personal perspective is fundamental to the production of data in a qualitative study. A child's reading of a biblical text, or indeed of any text,

---

2. Bryman, *Social Research Methods*, 22.

3. A deductive approach, in contrast, begins with an existing theory and generates data in order to test that theory. Quantitative research uses a deductive approach to data.

4. Creswell, *Qualitative Inquiry*, 39.

5. Snape and Spencer, "Foundations," 5.

6. Ibid., 4.

is necessarily an articulation of the perspective of the reader. As John Creswell points out, qualitative research is the approach used when researchers want "to empower individuals to share their stories" and seek to "hear their voices."[7] This personalization does not rule out the possibility of similarities between the children's readings.[8] But it does mean that my study takes the child readers' perspectives as its frame of reference. One of the aims of my research is to describe and interpret the participants' readings in their own terms.

Since a qualitative research strategy looks in-depth at the experience of its participants, it generally produces small-scale studies that generate data "which are very detailed, information rich, and extensive."[9] A qualitative study essentially holds a microscope up to its topic, analyzing as many of the details as possible. Consequently a narrow, clearly defined research area is necessary for a qualitative study to be effective. The specific parameters for my study are delineated below, in my discussion of the study's sample.

The need for narrow parameters highlights one of the limitations of a qualitative research strategy: it is not possible to generalize from the results. An in-depth look at one area means that only that area can be discussed and the conclusions drawn will not necessarily transfer to other areas. Therefore the results of my study cannot be said to be representative of all children's readings of the Gospel of Luke. However the aim of my study is not to generalize to a broader population. Rather the aim is, borrowing Alan Bryman's phrase, "to generalize to theory."[10] The theories resulting from my study may in turn facilitate future investigations of children's readings of biblical narrative.

Qualitative research is normally used to investigate naturally occurring social phenomena. In contrast, my study constructed an unnatural situation: child participants reading the Gospel of Luke in order to be interviewed. The production of the children's readings was dependent upon researcher-initiated circumstances. This is not to imply that the participants would have never read Luke on their own initiative. A number of them had already read other books of the Bible prior to being recruited as participants, so reading Luke at some future point was certainly a possibility. Their readings of Luke for this study were nevertheless products of the research

---

7. Creswell, *Qualitative Inquiry*, 40.

8. My analysis chapters demonstrate that this is indeed the case: various trends can be identified in the children's readings.

9. Snape and Spencer, "Foundations," 5.

10. Bryman, *Social Research Methods*, 391.

itself. This is not particularly a weakness for my study, however, since the study's focus is not social but hermeneutical phenomena.

As Dawn Snape and Liz Spencer point out, qualitative research is actually "an overarching category" that covers "a wide range of approaches and methods."[11] The hermeneutical questions at the heart of my study narrowed the range of potential qualitative methods that I could use for the empirical work. I needed to select methods that were not dependent upon natural social processes and sociological questions to be effective. Not all qualitative methods assume the presence of naturally occurring social phenomena, and the method that I chose was individual interviews since such interviews could produce data that had the children's readings at their center. To interpret this data, I chose to use grounded theory, a method of analysis that allowed me to focus on the readings as readings. Finally, I used focus groups, another qualitative method, to validate the results. I discuss the details of each of these methods later in this chapter and the next. But first it is important to consider some of the implications of working with child participants.

Researching Children

This study views child readers as the best informants about their transaction with Luke, and, in line with the general move within the field of social research towards consulting children,[12] aims to hear the voice of the child. This aim directly affected how the study was conducted. Priscilla Alderson and Virginia Morrow indicate that the researcher's view of children has ethical implications in any study in which children participate.[13] Children are people and, to be ethically valid, a study involving children must value their perspective. Respecting the viewpoint and valuing the experience of the child participants in my study was fundamental both to hearing what they said and to interpreting what they meant.

For this reason the child interviewees were and are referred to as "readers," both during the empirical phase of the research and throughout this written account of the study. This label affixes their role to the central act they performed for the study: the reading of a text. Using this label foregrounds the validity of their perspective as people engaging with a text and situates them as consultants for the project. The label stresses the children's

---

11. Snape and Spencer, "Foundations," 2.

12. See, for example, Alderson and Morrow, *Ethics*, 10–11; Greig et al., *Doing Research with Children*, 157; Greene and Hill, "Researching Children's Experience," 1.

13. Alderson and Morrow, *Ethics*, 23.

agency as readers who have something of value to communicate. As will be seen in the following chapters, their voice is central to the study's findings so that the results are at least partially child-led.

Valuing a child participant's perspective and experience does not equate to treating her or him like an adult. While children are, in the words of Shelia Greene and Malcolm Hill, "complete social actors,"[14] their conduct is a product of their age, ability, and social roles. Although the methods I used required only minimal adaptation in order to be appropriate for the young participants, I needed to take into account a number of factors in order to conduct research with the children. These included: protecting the children especially through obtaining informed consent and preserving confidentiality; the power dynamic between the children and myself, the adult researcher; and taking the participants' developmental phase into account. I look at each of these in turn.

Consent and Confidentiality

Protecting child participants is essential to good research with children. My very first step in the empirical phase of the study was to obtain external approval for the project to ensure that it was in line with accepted standards of good practice with children. The study was authorized by the University of Sheffield and received ethical approval from the University of Sheffield's Research Ethics Committee. I also underwent a Criminal Records Bureau check. These assessments brought the research methods under the scrutiny of external bodies and provided the study with a line of accountability. The empirical work began after these assessments took place.

To maintain good practice, this study used two forms of participant protection: the readers were fully informed of and agreed to any risks that could be incurred through participation in the study; and their identity was protected. I look first at informed consent. Obtaining informed consent from the participants is one of the chief ethical requirements in any form of social research. Alderson and Morrow define informed consent as "the legal means of transferring responsibility for risk-taking from the researcher to the participant." Consent may only be viewed as "informed" if "the risks are explained and understood."[15]

In order to enable participants to be informed, the risks must first be identified. The empirical work in my study was not physically dangerous nor was its focus a topic that would necessarily lead to the discussion of

14. Greene and Hill, "Researching Children's Experience," 8.
15. Alderson and Morrow, *Ethics*, 35.

painful past experiences. There were, nonetheless, a number of inconveniences incurred by the readers. These included a loss of time since they had both to read the Gospel of Luke and to take part in an interview. There was also minor intrusion on their personal lives as they discussed their personal responses to Luke.[16] Finally, their interaction with their parents about their reading of Luke was limited prior to the interview. I address each of these "risks" in more detail below.

I sought informed consent from both the readers and the adults responsible for them. Since the participants were children, consent for their participation needed to include both parties. The study's participants were young teens who were capable of understanding the purpose and methods of the research project. Therefore, they had a right to know "exactly what their role in the research" was.[17] Seeking informed consent from the children showed them respect and gave them control over their participation.

After gaining access to a potential child participant, as delineated below under "Access," I met with her or him and at least one parent for a brief research information and consent session. This session normally took place in the child's home and rarely lasted more than thirty minutes. At that meeting, I gave information sheets about the study to both the child and the parent.[18]

Both the layout and the language of the child's information sheet were designed to provide the reader with a clear understanding of the project. The information sheet was divided into clearly defined sections that helped the reader to identify its main topics. The entire sheet was presented as an invitation to participate in the research, used short sentences, and made requests rather than demands of the child. It was written in the second person and the active voice, making the information personable and the reader's role clear. The information sheet clearly set out the commitment the participants had to make in order to be involved in the study: reading the Gospel of Luke and then being interviewed about their reading. Thus from the outset, both the participants and their parents were clearly informed of the potential time commitment required for the child's participation.

---

16. Nesbitt, in her study, "Researching 8 to 13-year-olds' Perspectives," finds that the researcher's sensitivity is the most important factor in researching this age group's experience of religion. She finds this sensitivity necessary due to her investigation of topics deemed "sacred" by a variety of religious faiths, and due to her inclusion of groups that are considered controversial. My study, in contrast, investigates the reading strategies used with a religious book. Since the latter may lead to personal topics, this could be deemed a risk and was handled accordingly.

17. Greig et al., *Doing Research with Children*, 176.

18. The University of Sheffield's Research Ethics Committee's evaluation of this study included approval of these information sheets and the consent forms.

During the information and consent sessions, I discussed the research with the potential participants and answered their questions. Included in this discussion was an oral listing of two or three sample questions from the interview script. I did not write these questions down and present them to the potential interviewees because I did not want them to prepare in advance for the interview. The purposes for orally listing a few questions were to give the participants an idea of the kinds of questions that they would be asked and to demonstrate that responding to the questions would involve expressing personal opinions. Hence, the participants knew what types of questions to expect in the interview prior to signing the consent form.

I also asked the potential participants and their parents not to discuss the participants' reading of Luke until after the interview. The reason for this was to minimize adult input into the children's interpretations of Luke. I wanted the interviews to be an articulation of the reader's transaction with Luke, not a channeling of adult ideas gleaned from a discussion with a parent. Although I articulated this request as part of the information and consent session, it was not recorded in writing and at least two participants and their parents did not follow this request. In both cases, the parents concerned later confessed that they had briefly discussed their child's reading of Luke with the child prior to the interview.[19]

As indicated above, protecting the identity of the participant is the other main form of protection used in this study. The information sheets promise that the interviewer will maintain participant confidentiality. The consent forms that the participants, their parents, and I signed specifically commit me, as the researcher, to confidentiality. To implement this confidentiality, I asked each reader to choose a code name and I used this name on all of the interview documents as well as throughout the interview itself. This commitment to confidentiality freed the participants, at least in theory, to say what they liked during the interview. Choosing their own code name gave the readers some control over how they are represented in the study. Whenever I refer to a participant anywhere in this study, the name used is always this code name.

To further protect the identity of the participants, no one except the researcher was allowed access to the audio recordings of the interviewees. Although only the code names were used in these recordings, this extra precaution precluded someone identifying a participant by her or his voice.

---

19. I have taken into account the potential influence of these two discussions on the children involved. If these two cases are in any way representative, then a number of other parents may have similarly discussed Luke with their child prior to the interview and not informed me.

I also removed from the written transcripts any names, places, or organizations that could lead to the identification of an interviewee.

At the conclusion of the information and consent session, those who agreed to participate signed the two consent forms, one for the child and one for the parent. These forms assert that participation is voluntary and that the participant may withdraw from the study at any time without supplying a reason. So even those who signed the forms had the option of later terminating their participation. None of the children were interviewed until this information and consent session had occurred and the consent forms had been signed.

Power Dynamics

Another issue in conducting research with children is the unequal power distribution between children and adults.[20] Indeed a "power asymmetry" exists in all interviews, whatever the age difference between the interviewer and the interviewee.[21] As the interviewer, I was the initiator of the interview event and the agent of the interview dialogue, while the interviewees functioned primarily in the role of respondents. On a number of occasions, an interviewee reversed these roles by asking me questions. But even then, such questions were generally driven by a desire to acquire knowledge from me, thus placing me in a position of authority.[22]

The fact that I was an adult interviewing young teenagers exacerbated this power asymmetry. Age is one of the "characteristics on which our culture builds generalized and exacting differentiations of role."[23] Both the participants and I entered the interview dialogue with already established social roles based on our ages, including expected forms of "appropriate behavior" and of communication[24] which implicitly guided our interaction. This age differential invariably influenced the readings and the data were interpreted knowing that the responses the readers gave to me, an adult, may not have been the same as the responses they would have given to their peers. As discussed in the next chapter, the peer-based focus groups helped to redress this imbalance.

---

20. Hill, "Ethical Considerations," 63; Holmes, *Fieldwork with Children*, 5; Eder and Fingerson, "Interviewing Children and Adolescents," 182.

21. Kvale, *Doing Interviews*, 14.

22. For instance, Elaine asked me to explain Jesus' assertion in Luke 12:49.

23. Benny et al., "Age and Sex in the Interview," 35.

24. Ibid.

Pertti Alasuutari indicates that all interviewees interpret "what is going on" in an interview and respond accordingly.[25] Interviewees often orientate themselves in an interview "by applying the frame of a familiar situation that best applies to the situation."[26] In my study, the interviewees were all school pupils whose main experiences of discussing literature were with teachers at school. Many were also regular church attendees and their primary experiences of discussing the Bible were with adult Sunday School and youth leaders. Although I functioned as neither the teacher nor the youth leader for any of the participants, I was an adult asking questions of child readers and the central content of the interview was the discussion of a written biblical text. Therefore the situation may have evoked these two familiar contexts for the interviewees.

In order to mitigate against the interviewees perceiving me in the role of a teacher or church worker, I emphasized that the interviews were not connected to school or church and that there were no right or wrong answers to the questions. This was articulated during the information and consent sessions and repeated at the beginning of each interview as part of the interview briefing. I emphasized that I was not looking for particular answers but wanted to know what the readers thought of Luke. As their interviews progressed, a number of the interviewees visibly relaxed and became more animated and engaged in the conversation. This was possibly due to realizing that the interview really was about what they thought and not an examination of what they remembered. Although I was the one asking the questions, it was the interviewees who did most of the talking, and I made a point of letting them know that their opinions were valuable.

The interview location was also chosen to redress the power imbalance. As John Rich aptly puts it, the interview begins as soon as the child "sees the building in which the interview is to take place."[27] Since surroundings influence how a child interprets an interview situation, I sought an interview location that would, as much as possible, signal a more equal relationship between the interviewee and the interviewer. I eliminated from the beginning the possibility of meeting in a school or church because I did not want the readers to associate the interview with either institution. Chris Robinson and Mary Kellett warn that "school is a context where the adult-child power imbalance is particularly acute."[28] Helen Westcott and Karen Littleton add that if the interview location is any type of educational setting,

25. Alasuutari, *Researching Culture*, 90.
26. Ibid., 90–91.
27. Rich, *Interviewing Children and Adolescents*, 58.
28. Robinson and Kellett, "Power," 91.

the child's responses will be influenced by that educational context since children have particular expectations about what is required of them in that context.[29] I did not want the venue to impose this type of expectation on the participants.

The location of the interviews varied initially as I explored the most viable venues, but it quickly became apparent that the readers were most comfortable in a café setting. As a result, I conducted most of the interviews in a local, spacious café. A café is normally the setting for informal chats and this venue had the potential of adding a layer of informality to the interviewees' interpretation of the situation.[30] Donna Eder and Laura Fingerson assert that a natural context should be chosen when interviewing children[31] while Hill adds that neutral territory is often desirable.[32] For this age group, cafés function as a place for meeting with their peers as well as the site of family outings. Meeting me in a café provided the readers with a sense of independence and allowed them to respond as individuals in a setting that was not associated with school, church, or even directly with home.

There were some limitations to this venue. Since we met in a public space, the readers could become self-conscious if an acquaintance came into the cafe.[33] Likewise the readers may have altered or limited their responses if they were concerned about being overheard. This was unlikely, however, due to the high noise level in the café. This noise level resulted at times in miss-hearings in the interviews, a few of which did not become evident until the transcription stage. Although the noise level slowed down the transcription process, the audio equipment was good quality and very little data were lost due to noise interference.

Age and Ability

Children, of course, vary significantly dependent on their developmental phase. The participants in this study were young teenagers and the empirical research was adapted to this age group. As discussed in chapter 3, this age group has a number of distinct characteristics regarding not only their

---

29. Westcott and Littleton, "Exploring Meaning in Interviews with Children," 148–49.

30. This was certainly evident when interviewees such as Abby teased me and others, such as Percy, told me jokes.

31. Eder and Fingerson, "Interviewing Children and Adolescents," 183.

32. Hill, "Ethical Considerations," 72.

33. In fact, this only happened twice and there was no clear evidence of a change in openness on the part of the interviewee on either occasion.

cognitive ability, but also their moral and emotional development. The discussion in that chapter will not be repeated here but I will note the relevant adaptations made to the study.

Teenagers are developmentally in the transition from childhood to adulthood, and the participants were just at the beginning of that transition. Alan France describes this phase as "a critical stage in the formation of identities and rationale thought and behavior."[34] This transitional phase was one of the reasons for choosing this age group as participants. The early teen years are the most common age range at which children leave the church,[35] indicating, among other things, this age group's development of independent thought and identity relative to their church tradition. Investigating the readings of this age group had the potential, at least, of discovering the child readers' insights just at the point when they began to wrestle for themselves with the meaning of the Bible.

Although the participants were starting the transition into adulthood, they were still fundamentally children. Therefore one of the potential issues was maintaining their interest and attention during the interview. Whenever possible, I kept the length of the interview to less than one hour. Greig, Taylor, and MacKay advocate making the interview process fun when working with children.[36] Choosing to interview in the informal atmosphere of a café associated the interview with a pleasant outing, as did the provision of hot drinks.

I also emphasized the value of the readers' participation by treating each one as a research consultant. In her study of young people's social attitudes, Helen Roberts reports that the youth involved "enjoyed being asked their opinions."[37] In line with my study's aim of giving the child readers a voice, I approached each reader as an informant who was providing information to which I would not otherwise have access. France describes youths as "competent and reliable witnesses to their own lives."[38] In this case, the readers were the experts witnessing to their interpretation of Luke, while I was the learner seeking to understand their readings.

Interviews revolve around questions and questioning children effectively depends upon making appropriate adaptations to their developmental abilities. All questioning of children "involves the cognitive abilities of

---

34. France, "Young People," 176.
35. See Brierley, *Reaching and Keeping Tweenagers*.
36. Greig et al., *Doing Research with Children*, 92.
37. Roberts, "Listening to Children," 269.
38. France, "Young People," 177.

language, thought, and memory."[39] Although young adolescents have an understanding of time, order of recall, and memory recall comparable to adults,[40] it was still essential to use clear, unambiguous questions and an age-appropriate vocabulary in the interviews. Each interview question was phrased in a way that promoted open dialogue. The phrasing of the interview questions is discussed in the next chapter under "Interview Script."

Even if a young teenager understands a question, this does not mean that she or he will respond openly. I needed to build a good rapport with each participant. In order both to build rapport and to show respect for the child, Alderson and Morrow advocate sitting at eye level with the interviewee, maintaining good eye contact, and letting the participant hear her or his voice on the audio recorder.[41] I conducted the interviews at a table or on a sofa where sitting at eye level and maintaining eye contact was not difficult. At the beginning of each interview, I tested the recording equipment by asking the reader to state her or his code name into the audio recorder and then playing this back. This allowed the participant to handle the audio recorder, to see how it worked, and to hear the sound of her or his voice. It also alleviated some of the curiosity about the recording device that may have otherwise distracted the participant during the interview.

Walter Parker warns that young adolescents may "withhold personal information from adults" due to the increasing influence of peer identification.[42] On occasion the interviews led me to the opposite conclusion from Parker's. Rather than withholding information, a number of the readers openly discussed aspects of their personal lives. The interview script included a question about the impact of reading Luke on the reader's life and this sometimes led to the reader articulating personal convictions about her or his misconduct.[43]

Another issue in questioning children is their penchant for giving answers to win adult approval.[44] The questions used in the interviews mitigated against this, at least in part, since they were constructed to elicit the interviewees' opinions and experiences rather than "correct" answers. Notably the interviewees regularly gave responses that clearly were not intended to gain my approval. For instance, when I asked Stephanie if she would ever

39. Greig et al., *Doing Research with Children*, 93.
40. Ibid., 91.
41. Alderson and Morrow, *Ethics*, 52–53.
42. Parker, "Interviewing Children," 21.
43. Jack, for instance, told me about how he "cheated" when he cleaned his room, hiding his possessions in corners rather than putting them away.
44. Greene and Hill, "Researching Children's Experience," 9.

read Luke again, she responded: "Probably not. I might read it [again] if I was really bored." A few of the readers commented on Jesus' anger and described him in terms that certainly would not receive approbation in the average church context.

Finally, children "can respond differently to questions depending on whether they are asked in a one-to-one or peer group situation."[45] This issue was dealt with by using the same children in the one-to-one interviews and the interviewee focus groups. Although the individual interviews and these focus groups did not use the same questions, they covered similar material. This is discussed in the next chapter under "Focus Groups." I look now at the set-up phase of the interviews.

Preparing for the Interviews

The most fundamental empirical step in this study was to generate the children's readings of the Gospel of Luke. To do this, I needed to decide whose readings I was going to investigate. To be precise, I needed to work out the profile of the readers and determine how to access those readers. I also needed to work out the specific text the children were going to read. I discuss each of these in turn.

The Profile of the Participants

Since qualitative research involves the in-depth exploration of a small and clearly demarcated research field, my study needed to work with a reasonably uniform group of participants. To select the participants, I used purposive sampling, a sampling method which seeks participants who "have particular features or characteristics which will enable detailed exploration and understanding of the central theme which is being investigated."[46] This sampling method has the advantage of establishing a clear connection between the sample and the research questions. Accordingly, I developed a participant profile that was pertinent to the investigation and then purposely sampled for readers who fit this profile.

The profile used in the study was children who: are in the British National Curriculum Key Stage 3 and thus eleven to fourteen years old; attend the target comprehensive school; are affiliated with some form of church

---

45. Greig et al., *Doing Research with Children*, 93.
46. Ritchie et al., "Designing and Selecting Samples," 78.

tradition; and view themselves as readers. Each of these parameters provided limits to the study. I discuss the reason for each of these parameters in turn.

Sampling from only Key Stage 3 provided a coherent age and educational grouping. Other reasons behind the choice of this particular age range were discussed above under "Age and Ability." Drawing on readers from the same school allowed some control over the variable of educational input, since all of the children would be receiving instruction in religious education from the same group of teachers. Using readers from the same school also provided a pragmatic limit to the number of children available to participate. The target comprehensive school was chosen primarily for its accessibility to the researcher. It is a large school located on the edge of a university city. About 65 percent of its pupils are middleclass, with the remaining 35% coming from working class families living in villages in the catchment area of the school. Although social background was not part of the sample profile, the overall reader demographic was representative of the school's social class make-up.

A particular focus of my study is upon children who can be described as churched. This is a broad category and the profile parameter included any tradition that fit within mainstream Christianity. The readers themselves designated their chosen church tradition or affiliation on their reader profile. Eric J. Sharpe argues that when defining "religion" the "only tenable criterion is that of the firm conviction *on the believer's part*."[47] Allowing the participants to define their faith position preserved their personal experience and meaning, both of which were fundamental to the concerns of this study.[48] Through this self-definition, the readers expressed their personal alignment with a faith tradition.

The final profile parameter, children who view themselves as readers, was partially a product of the target school. Due to its location near a university, this school both attracts and produces pupils who are academically orientated and its ethos encourages reading. Although not all of the participants were avid readers, all of them were willing readers. For this study, I define "willing readers" as those who voluntarily read at least six books each academic year. The evidence for this was provided by the reader profiles, which included a question about how many books each participant read

---

47. Sharpe, *Understanding Religion*, 48; italics in the original.

48. Note that sociologists such as Thompson, *Understanding Social Work*, counter that external criteria, and not just personal self-definition, are necessary for observers to understand the social influence of religious faith upon a participant. However, this position was less relevant to my study, since my central questions are hermeneutical and not sociological.

in the previous year. This particular parameter was, of course, conducive to a study that involved reading a text while at the same time exclusive of children who do not read voluntarily.

Although the resulting profile is fairly homogeneous, it still incorporates a number of variables, including sex, age, and church tradition. These are discussed in the next chapter under "Demographics." From this point onwards, when I refer to a child's reading, I mean specifically a reading that emerged from this particular sample and do not intend any form of generalization beyond this sample.

It is also worth noting that although this project used grounded theory for its analysis, it did not use the sampling method of grounded theory, theoretical sampling, to modify the participant profile, primarily for pragmatic reasons. Theoretical sampling uses an iterative approach, so that the researcher alternates between sampling and theoretical reflection that may lead to adjustments in the sample profile. Due to time restraints, there was not sufficient time to return repeatedly to the field to sample participants with different profiles. The child participants grew older and continued to develop throughout the course of the project, making it imperative to conduct the empirical research, culminating in its final focus groups, in as short a time period as possible.

Snowball Sampling

Purposive sampling determined the parameters of the study population to be investigated. Generating a sample that fit these parameters required the application of a sampling technique. I needed a sampling technique that provided direct contact with potential participants. Since I was already acquainted with a number of potential readers who fit the participant profile, I chose the technique of snowball sampling. Snowball sampling involves asking participants to identify other potential participants.[49] I initially interviewed readers whom I knew and who fit the profile, and, at the end of each interview, asked each reader to suggest other potential participants. I continued this procedure throughout the interview phase of the research, with the result that the final interview sample contains a large number of readers whom I had never met and to whom I would otherwise not have had access.

This sampling technique tapped directly into the readers' social world. Neither the target school nor any of the local churches were involved in generating the sample or promoting the research in any way. Rather the

49. May, *Social Research*, 119.

readers themselves provided contact with the network of potential participants. This had the advantage of producing a cohesive sample and paved the way for the use of peer-based focus groups at the end of the study. It also gave the readers a further voice in the research process as they helped to identify participants.

Snowball sampling has some disadvantages. The diversity of the sample is limited to the contacts available through the participants. If the participants are too similar, the resultant data may "reflect a particular perspective and thereby omit the voices and opinions of others who are not part of a network of friends and acquaintances."[50] While this is certainly a concern for this study, the target population for the sample was small to begin with. The number of eleven- to fourteen-year-olds attending the target school and also having some sort of church affiliation was not large. I achieved some diversity in the sample by diversifying the initial interviewees: I initially drew on participants from all three of the relevant year groups in the school and from different churches. These readers, in turn, often identified potential participants who were either in their own year group or attended their church. As a result, at least three different age cohorts and a variety of social networks are represented in the interview sample. The sample was further diversified through the focus groups which represented a cross-section of the whole school population.

Another issue with snowball sampling is that it depends upon the researcher having appropriate contacts to initiate the sampling process. I had a network of relationships within both the school and local churches to draw on for the sampling process and it is important to note that the investigation was in part shaped by the relationships that I had with some of these children. Drawing on these relationships meant that I was already acquainted with the initial children in the sample. In total, I was already known to just over one-third of the interviewees and no doubt many of these children were willing to participate because I was familiar to them.

My established relationships with these participants may well have influenced the study's findings but it is impossible to pinpoint the exact nature of that influence. The participants whom I knew may have discussed Luke with me more freely than they would have with a stranger. Alternatively, they may have held back in the interviews since I was, in many cases, an acquaintance of their parents. The resultant data may reflect these different forms of engagement. The control for this issue was the interview script which ensured a consistent focus of discussion throughout the interviews regardless of the interviewees' familiarity with me. The potential influence

---

50. Ibid., 119–20.

of these established relationships on the findings is also balanced by the findings of the interviews with the participants who had no previous contact with me.

Access to the Participants

Working out a viable sampling technique was not the only step in recruiting the participants. I also needed to gain access to them through an accepted contact method. Since the participants were young teenagers, this meant accessing them through the adults whose formal permission was necessary for the research to proceed. Such permission is necessary partially because of the legal status of children as dependents and partially as a means of protecting children.[51] In the case of this study, the adult gatekeepers were the children's parents. I also informed the head teacher of the target school about the interviews, but this was an act of courtesy rather than one of necessity.

Access to the readers proceeded through a number of steps. Initially I made contact with the parent of a potential reader to ask permission to ask the child to be a participant. If the parent agreed, then I approached the child to ask if she or he would consider participating.[52] These contacts with both the parent and the child were always done personally, either face-to-face or via a telephone call. If both parent and child agreed to consider participation, I arranged for the information and consent meeting with the reader and at least one parent, as described above under "Consent and Confidentiality."

At the information and consent meetings, those children who consented to participating received a copy of the Gospel of Luke and a copy of the reader profile. They were instructed to begin reading Luke as soon as they were ready, as well as to complete the reader profile and to bring it along with them to the interview. The information sheet which I gave out at the meeting contained my contact details and the reader used these details to contact me when she or he finished reading Luke. The interview was then arranged for a day and time as soon as possible after the child finished reading Luke in order to enhance the reader's ability to recall details about her or his reading. I discuss the interviewing method in the following chapter.

---

51. Hill, "Ethical Considerations," 70.

52. On occasion the parent preferred to ask the child her or himself. When this happened, I did not have direct contact with the reader until the information and consent meeting.

Choosing the Text

I conclude this chapter by describing how I selected the version of Luke that I used in the study. My first criterion was to be able to give the readers a copy of Luke as a separate text: I wanted to present the readers with one book to read, not an entire Bible. This approach enabled the readers to view Luke as one unified text rather than a disconnected set of stories that they could dip in and out of at random, following a model they may have already encountered in church or a school classroom, as discussed in chapter 4.[53] This criterion eliminated a number of translations that were not available as individual Gospels.

After determining which translations were available as individual books, I investigated the accessibility of their language. The Lukan prologue particularly influenced my choice since I knew that the opening lines would shape the reader's first impression of, and possibly attitude to the whole book, as well as being crucial to the child's willingness to continue reading. I particularly did not want a participant to think that Luke was too difficult for her or him even to attempt to read.

I eliminated the translations that began:

- "Inasmuch as many have undertaken to compile a narrative..." (ESV).
- "Most honorable Theophilus: Many people have written accounts about the events that took place among us. They used as their source material the reports circulating..." (NLT).
- "Many have undertaken to draw up an account of the things that have been fulfilled among us, just as they were handed down to us by those who from the first were eye witnesses and servants of the word" (TNIV).

The opening lines of these translations use a vocabulary that suggest that Luke is a document from a bygone era. This vocabulary could signal that the text should be treated as a source of historical information, much like a text book. The translations' formal language, although not beyond the reach of many of the interviewees, distances the reader from the text.

---

53. I was thus signalling to the readers that reading Luke would be akin to reading other forms of narrative and not, for example, a text book. This decision had a pragmatic and literary goal: to enable the children to read Luke as a continuous text. It was not a deliberate attempt to encourage the reading strategy advocated by Benjamin Jowett: to "interpret the Scripture like any other book." See Jowett, "On the Interpretation of Scripture," 377. Jowett's assertion reflects a particular theological position on the nature of the Bible. In this study, my decision may have had theological implications, but its aim was not to advocate Jowett's or any other theological position.

As Gordon D. Fee and Mark L. Strauss point out, all translation is interpretation and a translation is "successful only when its readers (or hearers) actually get the message."[54] Idiomatic translations seek to use natural English and are "particularly helpful for new Bible readers, who are unfamiliar with the traditional Bible language."[55] Such translations tend to be reader-orientated. Included among them are the Good News Bible and the New Century Version, and I eventually narrowed the choice of translation down to these two versions. They begin, respectively:

- "Dear Theophilus: Many people have done their best to write a report of the things that have taken place among us" (GNB).
- "To Theophilus: Many have tried to give a history of the things that happened among us" (NCV).

The final choice between these two translations was made by the first six children who went through the information and consent sessions. At these sessions, I gave these readers a copy of both translations and asked them to choose just one to read. Included in their interviews was a question about how they made this choice. Their responses to this question functioned as a method for selecting the translation and their most pertinent comments are recorded here rather than in the analysis chapters of this study.

All six readers chose to read the Good News Bible. Although their choice was influenced by a variety of factors, the main influence was the presentation of the two books.[56] The GNB had a purple cover and its brightness proved an attraction. Sophie M. said: "For a book as old as this, I thought it was a pretty modern cover." The New Century Version's front cover, in contrast, was dominated by a cartoon of the Luke 5:17–26 story of the Healing the Paralyzed Man. It included a blurb which claimed that the NCV was "the version children can read and understand." Interestingly, this presentation of the text led the participants to avoid the NCV. Jeremy explained:

> Part of it was looking at this one {indicates NCV}. It says, "Children's version." I thought that it might be a bit too simplistic. Also on the back I noticed it said, "Ideal for 6 to 12" . . . I thought

---

54. Fee and Strauss, *How to Choose a Translation*, 40.

55. Ibid., 29.

56. Often referred to as the peritext. For a discussion of peritext as a message produced through the text's presentation, see Genette, *Paratexts*.

it might mean it's just a bit too, well it's a bit easy, too easy for what I'm looking for.[57]

Both its cover illustration and blurb led to a perception of the NCV as juvenile and targeting a readership that was too young for a group of young teens who perceived themselves as moving towards adulthood.

The neutrality of the GNB cover relayed minimal signals about its contents while the NCV cover implied that the booklet did not contain the actual biblical text but was a children's bible. Kit preferred the GNB because it "looked more like a challenge." The readers wanted, in the words of Sophie M., "to get as close to the real thing as possible." As young teens, the readers' perceived themselves as ready for the real Bible rather than an adaptation.

None of these six participants read a portion of the books in order to make their decision. Of course the whole point was that they were making a decision about what to read *prior* to beginning to read, and so, for this decision, appearance was paramount. Just one of the six interviewees made his choice based on any of the contents of the two books. Even for this reader, James S., it was the footnotes, and thus also a presentation factor, that swayed him: "I liked this one {indicates GNB} cause there were some little explanations on what other versions of the Gospel might have. Those on the bottom" {indicates footnotes}. Again this reader chose to read what he perceived to be the more adult-orientated translation. After these initial interviews, I gave the remainder of the interviewees a copy of only the GNB. Thus the final selection of the text was made by the readers themselves.

Summary

This chapter has examined the background decisions and preparatory steps of the empirical work. My study aims to keep the voice of the child participants at the center of its findings. In order to enhance the child readers' involvement, their developmental phase was taken into account and a central part of this chapter is its consideration of the issues surrounding working with children. These include protecting the children and maintaining confidentiality, balancing the power dynamic between the researcher and the participants, and utilizing methods that are appropriate to the participants' ages and ability.

I chose to engage in qualitative research because it provided a methodology for theorizing about the children's readings of Luke. This methodology

---

57. In this and all subsequent readings, the notations in { } brackets indicate the reader's body language or other forms of non-verbal response.

gave depth to the investigation while also limiting the range of its results. This chapter outlined the set-up phase of this investigation, including the parameters established for the participant profile, the sampling methods used to select participants, and the selection of the GNB translation of Luke as the key text.

Chapter 6

Research Methodology: The Empirical Work

Percy: I thought the interview "was relaxed, conversational."

Having established in the previous chapter the preparatory steps for the investigation, I turn now to the actual execution of the empirical work. This chapter begins with a discussion of the interview method, then describes the method of data analysis. Finally, I explain how I validated the results using two types of focus groups. This latter discussion includes some of the results of the investigation.

The Interviews

Interviewing is a research method that seeks to reconstruct the phenomena under investigation through re-processing and re-telling.[1] It takes place after the event and the data are generated through the participant's reflection on her or his experience. The aim of the interviews in my study was to enable the interviewees to reflect on and describe how they interpreted Luke. A reader's transaction with a text is usually an individual experience, sanctioning the use of individual interviews. Jane Ritchie points out that the process of interview reflection reveals the meaning that the participant attaches to the phenomena under discussion,[2] a particularly relevant target for a study framed by hermeneutical concerns.

In this section, I discuss how I selected the interview method, outline the actual interview event, describe the interview script, and explain the transcription process. I provide details of the demographics of the readers.

1. Ritchie, "Qualitative Methods," 36.
2. Ibid.

Semi-Structured Interviews

My study needed an interview method that kept the discussion focused on the participants' readings of Luke while enabling open dialogue. I chose to use the semi-structured interview method which, by definition, follows an established set of questions while allowing flexibility in the coverage of those questions.[3] A fundamental aim of this method is to enable participants to convey their understanding "from their own perspective and in their own words."[4] Semi-structured interviews provided space for the readers' interpretive strategies to emerge.

This interview method has a number of strengths. As Eleanor Nesbitt indicates, semi-structured interviews "allow greater flexibility than fully structured ones, while also facilitating comparison."[5] The interviews followed an interview script comprised of open-ended questions. The flexibility of this method allowed me both to ask unscripted follow-up questions in order to probe a reader's response, and to alter the order of the questions when a reader initiated a relevant discussion prior to a scripted question being asked. The method also permitted the interviewee to interject points of discussion. Using an established set of questions meant that the responses of the interviewees could be compared, enhancing the analysis of the data.

Semi-structured interviews are appropriate for working with children. Alderson recommends this method because it provides space for the child's input into the interview discussion,[6] so that the interview resembles a conversation. At the same time, this method, in contrast to unstructured interviews, provides questions to stimulate conversation with the result that the child does not feel pressure to think of things to talk about. The structure also helps to keep the interview conversation on topic, which can be an issue with young interviewees.

Nonetheless semi-structured interviews have a few weaknesses. During interviews with readers who were either thorough in their responses or natural conversationalists, it was difficult at times to know when to stop a response and move the discussion on to a different question. The openness of the method meant that certain questions could be discussed at length leaving little time for other questions. Having a set of questions to cover meant that I, as the interviewer, had to maintain some control over the pace of the interview.

3. Wellington and Szczerbinski, *Research Methods*, 83.
4. Kvale, *Doing Interviews*, 11.
5. Nesbitt, "Researching 8 to 13-year-olds' Perspectives," 143.
6. Alderson, "Ethics," 100.

Conducting the Interviews

At the beginning of each interview, I went through the reader profile with the interviewee to learn and begin using her or his code name, and to learn a little more about the participant. Next, I went through the interview briefing with the interviewee. According to Steiner Kvale, an interview should be introduced by a briefing "in which the interviewer defines the situation" for the participant, briefly reiterates "the purpose of the interview," explains the use of the audio equipment, and asks if the participant has any questions.[7] The interview briefing for this study was essentially a synopsis of the information about the interview that I had communicated during the information and consent session. Its repetition just prior to the interview reminded the reader of the relevant points from that session.

After the interview briefing, the interview began. Each interview was audio-recorded on a small digital recorder. At the conclusion of each interview, I turned off the recorder and debriefed the interviewee. The debriefings gave the readers a chance to ask questions that would not be recorded and to give feedback on their personal experience of the interview. At this point, many readers made further, unsolicited comments about their reading of Luke. One reader described the interview as boring, but most indicated that it had felt like a conversation and others even said that they had enjoyed it. This latter response may have been induced by a desire to please me, but the fact that some of the readers continued, at their own initiative, to discuss Luke with me was evidence of the sincerity of their responses.[8]

Afterwards I wrote up field notes on the interview, including information about the interviewee's overall response to the interview session and any new insights that I derived from that interview. Any unsolicited comments were also noted down.

The Interview Script

The interview script consisted of open-ended questions which enabled the interviewees to discuss their readings of Luke from a variety of angles. To formulate the questions, I used Aidan Chambers's "Tell Me" approach to discussing books with children.[9] This procedure is designed to stimulate children to talk about their reading and to enable the adult listener "to hear

---

7. Kvale, *Doing Interviews*, 55.

8. In the case of John, the conversation continued until I parted from him almost fifteen minutes later.

9. Chambers, *Tell Me*.

about the reader's experience."[10] It encourages discussion by beginning many of its queries with the phrase "tell me." According to Chambers, this phrase "suggests a desire for collaboration, indicating that the [person asking] really does want to know what the reader thinks, and . . . it anticipates conversational dialogue rather than an interrogation."[11] In the field of developmental psychology, the "tell me about" approach is referred to as "a free description procedure."[12] The procedure provided space for the interviewees to discuss Luke freely and openly. Seven of the questions on the interview script, including the first three questions, began specifically with the phrase "tell me" (see Appendix A for a copy of the interview script).

Chambers divides question types into three categories: basic, general, and special questions.[13] I look at each of these in turn. The basic questions are introductory and allow readers to share their responses to the book in the same way that they might talk about a book in everyday conversation.[14] The opening section of the interview script included all four of Chambers's suggested basic questions (questions 2, 3, 5, and 6). To Chambers's basic questions, I added two others: question 1 allowed the readers to begin the interview by stating their overall reaction to Luke; and question 4 allowed for the possibility of a reader not finishing Luke[15] while also probing what the reader found compelling about the text. Since these six opening questions are opinion-based, they established from the outset that the interview was not an oral exam but a discussion of the reader's views. Asking these basic questions helped to put the reader at ease at the beginning of the interview.

Chambers's general questions are those that can be asked of any text. They encourage the reader to make comparisons and explain her or his reading of a book. I adapted five of Chambers's suggested general questions and included these in the interview script (questions 9, 11, 19, 20, and 21). Special questions are those that are specifically tailored to the book under discussion. Here I adapted two of Chambers's model questions (questions 12, 14a, and 14b),[16] and designed others specifically for the Gospel of Luke (questions 10, 13, 14c, 14d, 15, 16, and 17).

10. Ibid., 45.
11. Ibid., 49.
12. Schaffer, *Introducing Child Psychology*, 260.
13. Chambers, *Tell Me*, 87–89.
14. Ibid., 16–17.
15. In fact, all of the interviewees finished reading Luke, although some of them more thoroughly than others.
16. See Chambers, *Tell Me*, 87–91, for his list of suggested questions.

For the interviews to be effective, the scripted questions needed to pertain to the phenomena under investigation. My adaptation of Chambers's questions and construction of other questions was therefore guided by the study's working question, as stated in chapter 1: *what are the key features and strategies that characterize children's readings of the Gospel of Luke?* This broad, heuristic question breaks down into two sub-categories for investigation: the main features of the readings and the strategies that produce the readings. Most of the interview questions link to at least one these sub-categories. These links are shown in Table 1.

TABLE 1

Relationship between the Research Areas
and the Interview Questions

Research Areas	Interview Questions*
Working questions	
Features: the traits that mark out the readings	1, 2, 3, 4, 7, 9, 10, 14, 15, 20, 21
Strategies: the methods the readers use to interpret the text	5, 6, 10, 11, 12, 13, 16, 17 18, 19
Subsidiary questions	
What role does the reader's imagination play in the readings?	11, 12, 13
What role do the reader's emotions play in the readings?	8
In what ways do the readers approach Luke as a narrative?	7, 18

*The numbers refer to the question numbers on the interview script.

To these two sub-categories, I added a number of subsidiary areas which arose out of the literature review. In order to ascertain if the readings derived from holistic engagement with Luke, I constructed questions about the imagination (questions 11, 12, and 13) and about the readers' affective responses (question 8). In order to determine if the readers approached Luke as a narrative, I added questions 7 and 18. The links between the scripted questions and these subsidiary areas are also shown in Table 1. It should be noted, however, that most of the interview questions generated data pertaining to more than one of the research areas. For instance, while question 18 generated discussion of Luke as a narrative, it also probed reading strategies.

Modifying the Interview Script

The final interview script was twenty-two questions long. This final form reflected the criteria listed above but was also a product of the actual interviews. The script underwent a few changes during the course of the interviews, partially because I determined which questions worked by asking the questions. For instance, in order to find out if a reader took on the role of any of the characters, I initially asked, "If the story were a play, which part would you like to play?" I soon discovered that this led to ruminations on the reader's personal experiences of dramatic performances; that is, the question elicited responses that were more about the reader than about the reader's transaction with Luke. One reader, for instance, responded that he would like to be a donkey since he preferred animal roles. So I altered that question to make it more direct, simply asking: "Did you imagine yourself as any of the characters?" (question 12b in the interview script).

I also honed the interview script by using theoretical sampling. In theoretical sampling, developing theories are tested through subsequent data collection.[17] My analysis of the initial interviews led me to reflect theoretically on some of the study's areas of investigation. Based on this reflection, I modified some of the interview questions and thus altered the type of data being collected, in order to flesh out my emerging theories. For instance, it became apparent in some of the early interviews that the readers' imaginations played a significant role in their readings of Luke. Consequently, I probed this area more thoroughly in later interviews and thereby more fully developed this particular theoretical area.[18]

In the early interviews, some of the most interesting readings emerged through the discussion of a passage in Luke. These discussions generated rich and varied data about the contents of Luke and the interviewees' reading strategies. The initial interview script initiated discussion of two passages, and one of these was near the end of the interview. I moved that question to an earlier part of the script (question 10 in the interview script) and added a question about a third passage (question 13).

The interview process led me to reduce the number of questions. Although the original interview script was 20 questions long, some of its questions had sub-questions which functioned as related but separate questions. In the initial interviews, reader interest and freshness sometimes began to wane if the interview lasted for an hour. Consequently, I eliminated a number of the sub-questions in order to reduce the length of the interview.

17. Charmaz, *Constructing Grounded Theory*, 96.
18. I discuss this more thoroughly in chapter 8.

Unscripted Questions

The scripted interview questions functioned as topics around which the interview conversations took place. Tom Wengraf points out that a semi-structured interview requires the interviewer to improvise responses to the interviewees' answers to the scripted questions.[19] I usually followed up the scripted questions with unscripted questions. Kvale discusses the various types of unscripted follow-up questions.[20] To probe responses, I repeatedly employed what Kvale refers to as general invitations, using phrases such as "tell me about that" to encourage a reader to explain what she or he meant. In order to clarify a response, I asked, "Am I hearing you say . . . ?" followed by a summary of my understanding of the interviewee's response. I used prompts such as "right" and "okay" in order to indicate that I was paying attention to the interviewee without, in the words of Nesbitt, "steering the child with more explicit cues."[21]

I also used the interview tactic of beginning a statement and then stopping to allow the interviewee to complete the sentence, in order to encourage the interviewee to elaborate on a point. This can be seen in the following exchange with Zak:

> **Interviewer:** Which characters didn't you like?
>
> **Zak:** It was obviously Judas. At first you're like, "How could he do such a thing?" Then he looks back on it and says, "Oh my gosh. I shouldn't have done that." So it evens it out a little bit. But it would probably be the Romans, Pharisees, and Judas.
>
> Interviewer: So anyone who was basically . . .
>
> **Zak:** Yeah, involved in getting Jesus killed.

Rather than formulating a new question to clarify Zak's response, which may have led him off in a different direction, I kept the dialogue going through an unfinished statement that followed naturally from his assertion. This statement led Zak to clarify the common attribute that caused him to dislike this particular group of characters. Without this probe, I would have known which characters the reader disliked, but not why.

---

19. Wengraf, *Qualitative Research Interviewing*, 5.
20. Kvale, *Doing Interviews*, 60–62.
21. Nesbitt, "Researching 8 to 13-year-olds' Perspectives," 146.

Transcription

Audio-recording the interviews freed me to focus upon the interviewee during the course of each interview. Although an audio-recorder has the benefit of being small and unobtrusive, its presence may have led some interviewees to adjust their responses to present themselves in a particular way for the recording.[22] The notes taken during an interview cannot represent everything an interviewee says, while an audio-recording captures everything articulated, including pauses, tone of voice, and laughter. Yet audio-recording also involves a frustrating loss of non-verbal data. What the participants said was a matter of not only their words, but also their body language and facial expressions, none of which were captured by the audio-recorder.

Some of this non-verbal data was preserved through minimal, non-intrusive note-taking during the interviews. I developed symbols for common non-verbal gestures which I jotted down on the reader's interview script. For instance, when a reader acted out a passage, I wrote the letter "A" next to the interview question which stimulated this enactment, and later inserted in the written transcript "acted out." In this way, I was able to retain some of the non-verbal expressions that constituted part of a reading.

I integrated this data into the written transcript as part of the transcription process. After each interview, I transcribed the audio-record into a written record. As Kvale indicates, the researcher needs to ask, what "is a useful transcription [method] for my research purposes?"[23] For my study, the purpose of transcription was to enable the analysis of the participants' readings. Therefore, I chose to transcribe those dimensions of the interviews that preserved the readings *as* readings: the readers' words, tone, and non-verbal language were paramount. Constructing a written record from the audio-record led to the further loss of data, particularly audio data such as voice tone, pace, emphasis, and length of pauses. Again, some of this information was retained through insertions in the written transcripts.

Demographics

Each participant filled out a reader profile which provided her or his demographic information. This profile covered four topics: basic demographic details, school and church background, reading interests, and information on how the participant read Luke. A fifth, optional section allowed the

---

22. Cf. Wellington and Szczerbinski, *Research Methods*, 87.
23. Kvale, *Doing Interviews*, 98.

reader to draw a picture of one part of Luke that particularly interested her or him. Eighteen of the readers completed this final section and their pictures were discussed in their interviews.

The reader profiles revealed that none of the readers had read the whole Gospel of Luke prior to beginning the interview process, although most of them indicated that they were familiar with some of Luke's contents, particularly a few of the parables and the birth and passion narratives. All of the readers indicated that they had heard passages from the Bible read aloud in either school or church, but only a few of them had read parts of the Bible on their own initiative.

A total of thirty-one interviews took place, including two pilot interviews with readers who did not fit all of the sample parameters.[24] An overview of the reader demographics can be found in Table 2 and a summary of this information can be found in Table 3. The readers are listed in Table 2 in the order in which they were interviewed. As Table 3 shows, the gender of the interviewees was almost evenly divided between females and males. The average age of the interviewees was thirteen years, one month.

Table 2

Reader Demographics

Code Name	Sex	Age	Tradition
1 Elaine	F	12.9	Free Church/Charismatic
2 Kit	M	12.0	Free Church/Charismatic
3 Rachel	F	13.10	Free Church/Charismatic
4 James S.	M	14.1	Methodist
5 Vanessa	F	12.11	Orthodox
6 Sophie A.	F	14.3	Roman Catholic
7 Fishy	M	11.11	Roman Catholic
8 Sophie M.	F	14.5	Anglican
9 Jeremy	M	14.0	Anglican
10 Jenny	F	14.6	Anglican
11 Jake	M	14.8	Anglican

24. One reader did not attend the target school and another had no church affiliation. However, the latter was involved in some of the local church youth activities.

Code Name	Sex	Age	Tradition
12 Zak	M	12.3	Pentecostal
13 Ebby	M	14.0	Pentecostal
14 Allie	F	12.3	Roman Catholic
15 Abby	F	13.10	Anglican/None
16 Trevor	M	14.10	Methodist
17 Percy	M	13.8	Pentecostal
18 James A.	M	13.1	Anglican
19 Hannah M.	F	12.10	Anglican
20 Jack	M	11.7	Pentecostal
21 Stephanie	F	12.8	Anglican
22 John	M	13.5	Free Church/Charismatic
23 Lucy	F	12.10	Free Church/Charismatic
24 Tarquin	M	12.7	Free Church
25 Boris	M	11.10	Anglican
26 Robyn	F	11.10	Anglican
27 BC	M	11.11	Methodist
28 Hannah C.	F	11.10	Anglican
29 Grace	F	12.6	Anglican
30 Lisa	F	14.3	Methodist
31 Michael	M	12.1	Free Church/Charismatic

The readers designated their church tradition on their reader profile. Using these self-designations, I established a number of categories within the church tradition demographic, including: Anglican, Free Church/Charismatic, Pentecostal, Roman Catholic, Methodist, and Orthodox. Some of the participants viewed themselves as belonging to more than one tradition and a number of others no longer attended church but had some type of church background. It should also be noted that a popular ecumenical church youth project exists in the target city, which has the effect of homogenizing its attendees' church influences. Twelve of the participants were attached to this youth project in some way.

Table 3
Summary of the Reader Demographics

Sex	Female: 15	Male: 16
Age	11 yrs: 6	13 yrs: 5
	12 yrs: 11	14 yrs: 9
Tradition	Anglican: 12	Pentecostal: 4
	Free Church: 7	Roman Catholic: 3
	Methodist: 4	Orthodox: 1

Since this was not a quantitative investigation, the demographics were not analyzed for correlations. However, the analysis chapters of this study occasionally refer to one of these demographics when it is pertinent in some way to a reading.

Analyzing the Data

Once an interview was transcribed into written form, it was ready for analysis, the next step in the empirical work. I began the analysis as soon as the first interview transcript was ready and the findings of the analysis fed back into the interview process, so that these two phases of the research proceeded in parallel and shaped each other. This iterative system was fundamental to the chosen method of analysis, grounded theory.

Grounded Theory

Since I took a heuristic approach to the children's readings, it was important to use a method of analysis that included procedures for generating theory. Grounded theory is an inductive method that by definition uses data generated by the research to construct theories about that data. It specifically aims to produce "an abstract theoretical understanding of the studied experience."[25] The studied experience, in this case, was the child readers' dialogue with Luke. Grounded theory enabled me to move from the raw data to theories about the reading strategies that produced the readings.

This method of analysis consists of "systematic, yet flexible guidelines for collecting and analyzing qualitative data to construct theories 'grounded'

---

25. Charmaz, *Constructing Grounded Theory*, 4.

in the data themselves."[26] Its operating guidelines are broad enough to be used in a variety of empirical scenarios, including the investigation of readers' transactions with a text. I employed three of these guidelines, including: theoretical sampling, coding, and writing memos. Earlier in this chapter, I discussed how I used theoretical sampling to modify the interview script so that the interview process helped to develop theories about the data. I now look at the role of the other two guidelines.

Coding

The thirty-one interviews resulted in over one thousand pages of written interview transcripts, field notes, and reader profiles. The first step in analyzing this raw data was to conceptualize it through a process called coding. Coding is a method of interpreting the data.[27] In coding, the data are broken down into succinct parts and each part is given a representative label or code which simultaneously summarizes and categorizes the data.[28] Although a variety of coding procedures exists, the procedures I used were those that are normally associated with grounded theory.

Grounded theory initially breaks data down into small segments through a procedure called line-by-line coding. This procedure involves working through the data systematically in order to define and interpret what is occurring in each segment. Every line, phrase, or statement in the data receives a code.[29] I initially analyzed all of the interview transcripts in hardcopy using line-by-line coding in order to capture the significance of each interview statement. To take an example from Jeremy's transcript: I asked Jeremy if he imagined any part of Luke and he responded, "I imagined [Jesus] sweeping through towns with lots of people around him. It helped me to envisage how things might have gone." Next to this statement, I wrote as a code, "imagining action to work out events."

Another common procedure in grounded theory is *in vivo* coding, which treats the words or phrases of the participants as the actual codes. Such coding enables the researcher to "represent [the participants] in their own terms."[30] I used *in vivo* coding whenever possible. This procedure preserved the readers' perspectives during the analysis process and gave them a voice in the resulting theories. Some of the headings and sub-headings

26. Ibid., 2.
27. Ibid., 45.
28. Ibid., 43.
29. Ibid., 46.
30. Eder and Fingerson, "Interviewing Children and Adolescents," 196–97.

in the following chapters are *in vivo* phrases. Again to provide an example, in her interview, Robyn said of reading a book, "It's like I'm watching it." For her, visualizing the contents of a book is fundamental to reading. Her statement became a code category under which I classified similar readings from other interviews and which eventually became a part of my theory of the role of the imagination in interpretation.[31]

The initial coding led to the construction of code categories that provided a framework for further analysis. This stage, known as focused coding, was done electronically. Each transcript and its codes were entered into the qualitative analysis software program, NVivo. This program enabled efficient cross-comparison of the transcripts and the codes. The most frequent and significant line-by-line codes were sorted into conceptual categories that, in turn, were organized into hierarchical trees that reflected the structure of the data.[32] Robyn's code eventually became part of the imagination tree. The inter-relationships within each tree and the relationships between the different trees were theorized, a process known as theoretical coding. These final coding steps were procedures for developing theories about the data. These theories provide the basis of the discussion in the following analysis chapters.

Memo Writing

A grounded theory procedure that is used alongside of coding is memo writing. Memos are written records of the researcher's "abstract thinking about the data."[33] They provide "an immediate illustration for an idea"[34] and function as a catalyst for analysis. In my study, memos served as a means of recording my reflections about the data as well as of interpreting the codes, sorting them into categories, and analyzing those categories.

I began memo writing while coding the first interview transcript and these early memos added focus to subsequent interviews. For instance, one of the early memos reflected on the link between Fishy's visualization of a passage in Luke and his interpretation of that passage. This led to further investigation of the role of the readers' imagination in working out the sense of the text. Writing memos enabled me to work at a more

---

31. Full discussion of this finding may be found in chapter 8 under "To Read is to Imagine."
32. Cf. Bazeley, *Qualitative Data Analysis with NVivo*, 100.
33. Strauss and Corbin, *Basics of Qualitative Research*, 198.
34. Glaser and Strauss, *The Discovery of Grounded Theory*, 108.

abstract level with the data and to make comparisons between different codes and code categories.

The memo writing accelerated during the focused coding stage. As a part of the NVivo coding procedure, I wrote a memo for each code category. In these memos, I recorded any theoretical insight or question that occurred during the coding. By the time this stage of coding was complete, I had a memo for each code category containing ideas and reflections from all thirty-one transcripts. These memos represented the incipient stage of theorizing about the categories. I compared the memos and thus the categories, and used these comparisons to structure the emerging theories. Through this method, for instance, it rapidly became apparent that the readers imagined the concrete elements of the text in order to make sense of the text, a finding that is discussed in chapter 8.

The Focus Groups

In this final section, I discuss how the theories that emerged from the interview stage of the research were tested by returning to the field to conduct focus groups. Focus groups are a method of data collection in which the participants engage as a group in a guided discussion about the research topic. This study used two types of focus groups: Interviewee Focus Groups and Respondent Validation Groups. Both types of focus groups were conducted during the same time period, in the final month of the empirical field work. I delineate the purposes of the focus groups and then discuss each type of group.

The Purposes of the Focus Groups

Rather than depending upon one method, semi-structured interviews, for developing theories about the children's readings, this study used three methods. The use of three methods is referred to as a triangulation of the investigation and the purpose of triangulation is often to cross-check findings.[35] Such cross-checking was the primary reason for the inclusion of focus groups in this study: the groups were specifically designed to test the interview findings. The data of such methods "cannot stand alone" but are interpretable through their link to the main project.[36] The data generated by the focus groups were contingent upon the interview findings.

35. Bryman, *Social Research Methods*, 379.
36. Morse, "Mixed Methods," 193.

Thus the key purpose of the focus groups was respondent validation of the interview findings. Respondent validation is "a process whereby a researcher provides the people on whom he or she has conducted research with an account of his or her findings."[37] If the participants agree with the researcher's account, usually by generating similar data, this agreement validates the original findings. Such validation cannot be dependent upon the participants theorizing about the data. The participants have neither the overview of the data nor the theoretical knowledge that the researcher brings to the task.[38] Accordingly, I presented the developing theories to the focus groups in the form of questions and statements, and asked them to respond. Their responses functioned as data that could be compared and incorporated into the theories.

The focus groups had several benefits relative to the child participants. The groups provided an alternative context in which to generate and test the empirical data. Alasuutari points out that "individual interviews and group discussions produce material of a different type and quality."[39] Children may give different answers to similar questions when interviewed individually and in groups. Using focus groups as a follow-up was a means of examining this potential source of variation in the participants' responses. The groups also kept the children's perspectives at the center of the findings, since the groups allowed me to check with the participants that the findings made sense to them.[40] Another advantage was that "the method acknowledges the participants as experts."[41] For both types of focus group, I emphasized that the contributions of the participants was paramount. In the first type of group, the participants introduced and led points of discussion, accentuating their expertise relative to the data.

The Interviewee Focus Groups

The first type of focus group brought together the readers who had previously been individually interviewed. I conducted two of these group sessions, which I refer to as an Interviewee Focus Group (IFG). Twenty-two of the original thirty-one readers participated in these IFGs. Like the interviews, the IFGs took place in the neutral territory of a local café. The period

---

37. Bryman, *Social Research Methods*, 377.
38. Barbour, *Doing Focus Groups*, 13.
39. Alasuutari, *Researching Culture*, 92.
40. Cf. Greene and Hill, "Researching Children's Experience," 12.
41. Hennessy and Heary, "Exploring Children's Views," 238. Hennessy and Heary are citing Levine and Zimmerman, "Using Qualitative Data."

of interviewing took almost two years and these focus groups occurred at the end of that two year period.

Since the readers attended the same school, most of them knew each other at least by sight; therefore, the sessions included participants who interacted with one another in other contexts. Rather than attempting to reduce this variable, I decided to use it to enhance participation and constructed the IFGs around the peer groupings of the pool of readers. Using peer groups provided the readers with a natural context for discussion, something Eder and Fingerson advocate when working with children.[42] The primary stratifying criterion for the groups was the readers' school year, because the readers' peer groups derived primarily from their year groupings in the target school. Of course, using peer groupings meant that already established personal relationships and group dynamics influenced the group discussions, and these influences were taken into account as part of the analysis. IFG1 was attended by 12 participants and comprised of the older readers, while IFG2 was attended by 10 participants and comprised primarily of the younger readers.

The IFGs were organized using what David Morgan refers to as a "less structured approach." The goal of such an approach is to "understand participants' thinking" so that the participants' "interests are dominant."[43] This meant conducting sessions in which the participants did much of the talking, and I developed a Discussion Guide using questions that were intended to stimulate discussion. The questions introduced particular topics but allowed the participants to lead the discussion of those topics. The Discussion Guide ensured that both sessions covered the same topics (see Appendix B for the IFG Discussion Guide). The power imbalance between child interviewees and the adult interviewer is at least partially redressed through this method.[44] The readers' interactions with one another were central to the sessions, and I functioned primarily as a facilitator. This dynamic meant that the interaction of peers generated some of the study's data, rather than just an adult-child interaction.

The IFG discussions centered around four topics. The first two topics targeted the interview findings: the participants' accounts of how they read Luke (question 1 on the Discussion Guide); and the researcher's theories about how the participants' read Luke (question 2). For the second question, I presented the theories to the participants in the form of codes. I wrote each

42. Eder and Fingerson, "Interviewing Children and Adolescents," 183.

43. Morgan, "Focus Group Interviewing," 147.

44. Cf. Eder and Fingerson, "Interviewing Children and Adolescents," 182, 183; Hennessy and Heary, "Exploring Children's Views," 237.

code on a separate card and attached the cards to a whiteboard, in no particular order. The participants then discussed the codes and re-arranged the order of the code cards based on priority, with their most common reading strategy at the top. The final two questions on the Discussion Guide, while less central to the findings, were important to the readers' participation: the impact of reading Luke on their engagement with the Bible (question 3); and the participants' experience of being involved in the interview process (question 4). The aims of these final questions were to enable the readers to discuss their personal experience of the research and to bring a sense of closure to their involvement.

The IFGs were audio recorded and later transcribed. I coded their transcripts in the same way as those of the individual interviews and used their code categories to modify the emerging theories. The result was a more nuanced understanding of the children's readings. Table 4 lists the codes discussed in the IFGs. These codes came directly out of the interview findings, but some were more prominent in the findings than others. I also encouraged the IFG participants to add codes. As Table 4 indicates, they added one code: they read Luke "as a story." They also eliminated one code, "by asking questions," which for them was too general. They subsumed two other codes, "by asking how I should act" and "by wondering how it works for a teenager," under the code "how does it relate to me?" which for them was the more pertinent issue. My analysis in the following chapters reflects this alteration in codes and code structure.[45]

---

45. See my discussion in chapter 10 under "How Does That Relate to Me?"

Table 4
IFG Codes Under Discussion

I read Luke . . . *codes presented by the researcher*	I read Luke . . . *participants' preferred codes and code order*
• as a conflict	• by imagining
• and found that Jesus is human too	• by puzzle-solving: *meaning-orientated reading*
• for the characters	• as a conflict: *plot-driven reading*
• by imagining	• for the characters
• by puzzle-solving	• by asking how does it relate to me? *the participants included under this code:* by wondering how it works for a teenager, and by asking how should I act?
• by asking questions	
• by asking how does it relate to me?	
• by asking how should I act?	
• by wondering how it works for a teenager	• as a story: *added by the participants*
• by comparing it to what I believe	• by comparing it to what I believe
	• and found that Jesus is human too

Overall, the IFG findings supported those of the interviews, firming up the theories while also highlighting the centrality of some of the codes. I discuss this in more detail at the end of this chapter.

The Respondent Validation Groups

The second type of focus group I refer to as a Respondent Validation Group (RVG) since its primary aim was to collect data that would verify the findings of the base study. The RVGs served as a means of testing whether or not a broader sample of participants produced data that were similar to the data generated by the interviews. The RVGs maintained some of the parameters of the initial participant profile, including the parameters of the target school and the target age range. The primary alteration was that of religious affiliation. The RVGs included participants from a variety of religious and non-religious backgrounds.

The RVGs were more formal than the IFGs and mixed qualitative and quantitative research methods. The RVG participants' primary form of response was through an anonymous questionnaire which allowed for a quantitative collation of results. Morse indicates that an adequate mixed method design uses one method to supplement another, in order "to collect data that would not otherwise be obtainable by using the main method."[46] The quantitative findings of the RVGs supplemented the qualitative findings of the interviews. The groups provided a cross-sampling of the population of the school and the quantitative method permitted the collection of data from a larger sample. The number of RVG participants was 162.

I conducted a total of six RVG sessions, all within the context of Religious Education lessons in the target school. Each session functioned as one lesson for six different classes, including two year 7 classes, two year 8 classes, and two year 9 classes. Although these sessions were not set up deliberately to include readers from the interviews, invariably a few interviewees were present in some of the sessions; however, most of the participants were not interviewees. The RVGs were conducted during the same month as the IFGs and concluded the two year empirical investigation.

Prior to conducting the RVGs, I gained additional ethical permission for this phase of the research since the sessions included a large number of new participants and took place within the context of a comprehensive school. Both the school and the University of Sheffield's Research Ethics Committee granted ethical approval for these groups, providing two forms of external accountability for this part of the empirical work.

At the beginning of each session, each participant was given a response sheet to work through during the course of the session. All of the participants in the same RVG received the same response sheet. However, four different forms of the response sheet were used across the six RVGs. The first section of all four response sheets was identical: it consisted of demographic questions while maintaining respondent anonymity. The other sections of the response sheets varied based on the Lukan passages selected for the session. The selected passages had frequently come up for discussion in the interviews. Each RVG consisted of discussion of two passages and the passages covered included: Luke 6:43–45, the Tree and its Fruit; Luke 10:38–42, Mary and Martha; Luke 15:1–7, the Parable of the Lost Sheep; and Luke 20:19–26, Taxes to Caesar. A sample of one of the response sheets may be found in Appendix C. The passages were distributed across the RVGs so that each year group looked at each passage once.

The four passages represented eight different codes that I targeted for validation, with two codes per passage. The codes and their representative passages are found in Table 5. However, some of the passages allowed for the testing of additional codes. Each RVG session was conducted using a power

---

46. Morse, "Mixed Methods," 191.

point with the relevant passages displayed on a power point slide. I read the passages out loud to the groups off of the slides, a method which enabled participants to read the passage with me or simply to hear the passage if their reading skills were prohibitive. All of the passages were taken directly from the GNB so that the participants in the RVGs encountered the same version of Luke as the interviewees.

TABLE 5
RVG Passages and Codes

RVG Passage	Code 1	Code 2
Mary & Martha	Character Empathy	Reading for Personal Meaning
Tree & Fruit	Reading by Imagining	Reading by Puzzle-Solving
Taxes to Caesar	Plot-Driven Reading	Jesus as the Hero
Lost Sheep	Teen Reading	Ethical Reading

Each passage was followed up with three to six questions which I delivered orally to the RVGs, but to which the participants responded individually on their response sheets. I structured these questions around a quantitative format, primarily as closed fixed response questions and Likert scales. Respondents were asked to circle their preferred response to each question. This type of question places participants in the role of respondents rather than informants,[47] so that the role played by the RVG participants was either to confirm or to refute the interview findings. The questions were worked through one at a time, as a group, so that each of the potential responses was clarified before each participant made her or his individual choice.

The RVGs included some qualitative features. I used a variety of response methods, in order to enhance participation.[48] Some of the written questions were open-ended and included an option for the participant to write in a response. I also asked oral questions during the sessions. Most of these oral questions reiterated the written questions and provided opportunities for participant feedback. Some of this feedback was oral, some involved the participants raising their hands in agreement, and some involved the participants getting up and moving around the room. For the Lost Sheep and the Tree and Fruit passages, the participants drew a picture of something they imagined in response to the passage. I was accompanied

47. Knight, *Small-Scale Research*, 51.
48. Krueger and Casey, *Focus Groups*, 42, 45.

in each session by an assistant who recorded the participants' non-written feedback on paper, while maintaining their anonymity.

Despite the larger number of participants, the RVG sample size was still too small for its results to be statistically valid. Since the overall study is qualitative, the empirical work does not need statistically defined results. Knight points out that it is a common practice in small-scale studies for researchers simply to tally their data,[49] and that was the main form of analysis I used for the RVG data. One of the aims of mixed method research is for the different methods to produce data that is "mutually illuminating."[50] This illumination may confirm, extend, or challenge the results produced by the main study. I collated the data from the RVGs specifically with the aim of cross-checking the interview findings. Table 6 summarizes the results.

TABLE 6

RVG Results Organized by the Code Under Investigation

Question	Number of respondents who agree*	Approximate percentage of respondents who agree
Plot-Driven Reading & Jesus as the Hero Taxes to Caesar		
Jesus and the religious leaders were in conflict.	52 out of 78	66%
Jesus was cleverer with words than the religious leaders.	68 out of 76	90%
The religious leaders used difficult questions to try to catch Jesus out.	63 out of 79	80%

---

49. Knight, *Small-Scale Research*, 176–77.
50. Bryman, *Social Research Methods*, 603.

Question	Number of respondents who agree*	Approximate percentage of respondents who agree
Character Empathy *Mary & Martha*		
I imagine how Martha feels.	66 out of 81	81%
I think Jesus is unfair to Martha.	Even distribution across Agree, Disagree, and Uncertain	
Which character is most like you?		Mary: 50% Martha: 33%
Respondents indicating that they did not relate to any of the characters in passage.	4 out of 82	5%
Reading for Personal Meaning *Mary & Martha and the Lost Sheep*		
Which character [in the Mary and Martha story] is most like you?	67 out of 82 related to a character	80%
In the story [of the Lost Sheep], I am most like:		Shepherd: 33% Lost Sheep: 33% 99 sheep: 33%
The story [of the Lost Sheep] makes me think about my own life.	45 out of 80	56%
The story [of the Lost Sheep] is about: how each person is special.**	36 out of 85	42%

Question	Number of respondents who agree*	Approximate percentage of respondents who agree
Teen Reading the Lost Sheep		
The lost sheep is like someone who is not popular at school.	32 out of 80	40%
The story [of the Lost Sheep] is about: how Jesus treats people who are not popular. **	12 out of 85	14%
If Jesus lived today he would tell this story differently.	44 out of 79	56%
Ethical Reading the Lost Sheep and Tree & Fruit		
The story [of the Lost Sheep] is about: saying sorry (or similar written in responses).***	72 out of 100	72%
The passage [of the Tree and Fruit] shows that: people can tell if you are good or bad by what you say (and/or do).****	65 out of 101	64%
Reading by Imagining Tree & Fruit		
When I hear this passage, I imagine . . .	159 out of 162 imagined in some form	98%
When I imagine this passage, I think of: Images from the real world	61 out of 110	55%
Images from other sources	45 out of 110	41%
My own images	4 out of 110	4%

Question	Number of respondents who agree*	Approximate percentage of respondents who agree
Reading by Puzzle-Solving *Tree & Fruit and the Lost Sheep*		
This passage [of the Tree and Fruit] has a hidden meaning.	63 out of 80	79%
Imagining this passage [of the Tree and Fruit] helps me to work out what it means.	54 out of 81	66%
The story [of the Lost Sheep] is about: people.	49 out of 56	87%

*These numbers represent those respondents who chose either the Agree or Strongly Agree option on the response sheet. Not all of the respondents were asked the same questions, hence the divergence in the "out of" numbers in this column.
**This option was one of six possible fixed responses.
***Although "saying sorry" was one of six fixed options, 15 participants wrote in alternative responses, 11 of which were ethical in intent. The numbers include both the fixed response and the written in responses.
****Although "people can tell" was one of four fixed options, 36 participants wrote in alternative responses, 31 of which were ethical in intent. The numbers include both the fixed response and the written in responses.

As Table 6 reveals, the findings from the RVGs generally supported the findings of the interviews and the IFGs in the eight codes under investigation. The numbers involved in the RVGs were too small to make any conclusive statements, but it is clear that their findings did not refute the interview findings. Only the codes tested through the Lost Sheep parable, "ethical reading" and "teen reading," received less than 50% of positive responses. This lower response rate aligns with the IFG data which subsumed these codes under the category, "how does that relate to me?" The lower response rate may also have been due to the choice of passage. The participants interpreted the parable in a variety of ways, diluting the numbers opting for the ethical and teen readings.

Interestingly, although the RVGs included both churched and non-churched children, the responses of the RVG participants tended to agree with those of the churched interviewees. A number of factors may have contributed to this result. It may be that the reading strategies that both types of participants brought to the passages were similar due to the influences of the curriculum and teaching methods of the target school. The common school experience may outweigh the divergence of the religious and non-religious communities represented in the school population. The result may thus suggest that child readers bring to the Bible particular types of strategies learned through their general reading experience. Although some religious traditions may alter these strategies relative to the Bible, this potential alteration was not evident in the RVG findings.

Using a mixed methods mode of research within the context of a qualitative study highlighted the limitations of quantitative research relative to qualitative research. The results of the RVGs were broad-brush relative to those of the interviews. The response sheets confined the participants to a limited set of responses which may or may not have accurately reflected the participants' engagement with the passages. Even the open-ended questions allowed for only brief written responses. Unlike in the interviews, the RVG participants' responses could not be probed for clarification or elaboration. The RVG participants' oral statements consisted of little more than a one or two sentence response to a question. It was impossible to replicate the dialogue opportunities provided by the interviews with groups of up to 30 RVG participants.

Similarly, the Gospel of Luke could only be minimally presented to the RVGs in the form of four passages. The brevity of the sessions allowed for minimal engagement with these passages, an engagement which entailed taking the passages out of their narrative context and treating them as isolated pericopes. Therefore some of the reading strategies evident in the interview data, such as using one part of the text to aid interpretation of a different part of the text, where wholly absent in the RVG data.

Summary

As the lengthy discussion in these two methodology chapters makes clear, the empirical research sought firstly to generate and then to analyze the children's readings of the Gospel of Luke. This present chapter has outlined how the empirical work was carried out, including: the selection and execution of the semi-structured interviews, the design and development of the interview script, and an overview of the transcription process. The method of analysis used in this study was grounded theory, which enabled the investigation to be heuristic and provided procedures for developing theories from the research data.

The grounded theory analysis led to codes which summarized and explained the data. These codes were classified into categories, and these categories were theorized. The resulting emerging theories were validated using two types of focus groups: IFGs with the original interviewees and RVGs with a broader cross-sample of the population of the target school. The top six code categories prioritized by the IFGs, as listed in column 2 of Table 4, represent the key theories that emerged from the empirical work. The code categories investigated through the RVGs, as listed in Table 5, are all represented in some form in the theories developed around the IFG codes.[51]

The IFG participants' top six code categories became the key subjects of the theoretical analysis. I combined two of these code categories, "how does Luke relate to me?" and "reading by puzzle-solving" into one theoretical category, "sense-orientated reading," since both code categories entailed the pursuit of meaning on the part of the reader. This amalgamation is explained more fully in chapter 10. The code category which the participants added, "reading Luke as a story," highlighted the need for a theoretical category concerned with the role that the text played in the readings. As a result, the five theoretical codes which I analyzed included: reading Luke as a story, reading by imagining, reading with empathy, seeking the sense of the text, and plot-driven reading. I look at these next.

---

51. For instance, the RVG codes "teen reading" and "ethical reading" are both subsumed under the theoretical category "How does that relate to me?" This grouping of code categories is discussed further in chapter 10 under "How Does That Relate to Me?"

Part Three
An Analysis of The Children's Readings of Luke

Chapter 7

A Framework for Analysis: Participatory Reading

Tarquin: Luke "is like a story that's along the road, and the separate bits along the way. Like you're walking down it and looking at them."

Rachel: I put myself "in the shoes of the people who were there. So it's not just that you're standing there, but you're actually really there."

Introduction to the Analysis

This part of the study, the analysis, explicates the theories that arose out of my empirical investigation. This analysis is divided into five chapters and each chapter explores one theoretical category identified in the findings, in the following order: reading Luke as a story, reading by imagining, reading with empathy, seeking the sense of the text, and plot-driven reading. Each of these categories represents a reading strategy. In the first category, the emphasis falls on how the discourse of the text directed the readers. In the other four categories, the emphasis falls more on the interpretive moves that the children made.

I would like to emphasize that my discussion of these reading strategies is consistently rooted in how the child participants conceived of and expressed their readings, rather than in the application of pre-existent categories to those readings. Although my labels for these five categories are etic, each label is based on ideas articulated by the children in the interviews. For instance, while none of the interviewees used the term "empathy" to describe their engagement with the characters in Luke, they repeatedly and frequently discussed the motives, emotions, and attitudes of Luke's characters, even when such discussion was not directly elicited by or even pertinent to a question on the interview script. The label "empathy" expresses this interview trend, which I explore more fully in chapter 9.

Each reading strategy represents a theoretical tree laden with data and concepts from the empirical findings. These five trees also combine to form one forest, that is, one overarching theoretical classification of all of the findings. I refer to this theoretical classification of the children's readings as participatory reading. Broadly speaking, the children's readings could be described as experiential, and this experience appeared to result from the readers' *participation* with the narrative world, a participation that took the form of the five reading strategies.[1]

The idea of participatory reading is so central to the findings of this research that it is necessary to discuss the overall framework first since it will shed light on the discussion of the five reading strategies that follows. Therefore this current chapter looks initially at participatory reading. It then proceeds to the first reading strategy, reading Luke as a story. This particular strategy highlights the role of the text in the children's interpretive maneuvers and therefore stands apart in certain respects from the other reading strategies.

Participatory Reading

When I began this study, my headline question was, "how do children read the Bible?" My conclusion from the empirical research is: by participating in text-reader transactions that produce inside experience of the text. I did not reach this conclusion rapidly. It was only during the analysis phase of the empirical work that I began to piece together the big picture of the children's readings—puzzle-solving in a way not incomparable to the child readers' approach to making sense of Luke, although a social researcher may prefer to call it inductive reasoning—and began to conceive of an overall theoretical framework for the children's reading strategies. My discovery around the same time of Lewis's epistemological discussion raised the question, "how did the child readers know what they knew about Luke?" His light beam analogy pointed the way to an epistemological framework for the theoretical categories emerging from the investigation. The child readers knew Luke, at least partially, through their experience of the narrative world.

---

1. It is interesting to note that Pennington encourages his readers "to enter into the narrative world of the Gospels experientially" and provides them with a method for doing so. He seems to assume that they will not read this way without guidance. The child readers, on the other hand, read experientially with no coaching. See Pennington, *Reading the Gospels Wisely*, 49, 169–210, but especially 202–3.

In other words, the way that the readers participated in the reading transaction was experiential. Reading was a way of experiencing Luke's narrative world and their readings were an expression of that experience. As Culler notes, the "value of literature has long been linked to the vicarious experience it gives readers, enabling them to know how it feels to be in particular situations and thus to acquire dispositions to act and feel in certain ways."[2] The empirical research rapidly revealed that the readers used interpretive strategies that were both cognitive and affective, that involved both their heads and their hearts. For these children, reading Luke was not merely an intellectual exercise but an act of wrestling with the text, sometimes embracing it, sometimes critiquing it, and sometimes rejecting it.

Comparing the results of the thirty-one interviews revealed two seemingly divergent trends: the readings were diverse so that no two readings were identical; and yet these readings shared striking similarities so that it was clear that they all functioned as expressions of a common document. These trends reflected the two factors that were at work producing these readings: the individuality of the readers and the constancy of the text. This diversity-in-similarity effect may be seen as evidence of the dialogue that took place between the text and the readers. This dialogue was a communicative transaction that seemed to be guided by the text but was contingent upon the readers' participation.

Chatman notes that a narrative expects dialogue and that readers respond with an "interpretation" since "they cannot avoid participating in the transaction."[3] The reader responds to a narrative world with a reading of that world. My empirical findings suggest that the children's readings were conceptualizations of Luke's narrative world within the framework of the readers' understanding. Even those readers who reacted against some aspect of Luke still took the text as their starting point. A useful description of the text's contribution to this dialogue comes from Rosenblatt who indicates that because a text "is organized and self-contained, it concentrates the reader's attention and regulates what will enter into his consciousness."[4] The text directs the focus of the dialogue.

Rosenblatt, however, limits the text to a set of linguistic symbols, construing it as an object which the reader processes. Accordingly she defines the literary work, not as the text, but as the construct resulting from the text-reader transaction.[5] In contrast, I refer to this construct as a *reading*

2. Culler, *Literary Theory*, 112.
3. Chatman, *Story and Discourse*, 28.
4. Rosenblatt, *Literature as Exploration*, 33.
5. Rosenblatt, *The Reader, The Text, The Poem*, 12.

since it is the product of the transaction. I view the Gospel of Luke as the literary work for it functioned as one of the partners in the dialogue and served as the seed from which all of the readings germinated. The discourse of Luke directed the act of reading and Luke's contents were the focus of that act, while the readers interpreted Luke using particular reading strategies.

Lewis draws a helpful contrast between a child's reading of a story and a critic's reading, a contrast which highlights the significance of participatory reading. The critic weaves theory around the story, producing literary abstractions a step removed from the text. The child, on the other hand, brings the story to life by envisaging its contents and vicariously experiencing the events and vicissitudes of its narrative world.[6] This was evident in a statement made by one of the child readers in an IFG: James A. declared that Luke was "not abstract or philosophical" but "mainly physical" and comprised of "actual things." Lewis argues that all readers, even critics, must seek to bring a narrative to life in order to read it effectively. Mature reading does not mean moving beyond interacting with the contents of a narrative but rather building upon that interaction.[7] This being the case, the children's participatory reading strategies may have implications for interpretation in general.

An Example of Participatory Reading

In order to illustrate how the child readers participated in a reading dialogue with Luke, I analyze here John's reading of the Luke 8:16–17 Lamp Under a Bowl saying. This reading demonstrates how both the text and the reader contribute to the reading transaction. It also exemplifies a number of the reading strategies and thus sets up the topics of discussion found in this and the following chapters.

To begin with, the text appeared to guide John's act of reading. Indeed, John viewed himself as directed by the text and described how that process worked: "When I was reading it, [the text stated], 'You don't get a lamp,' and so I imagined a lamp. 'You don't get a bowl,' and I imagined the bowl, putting it over the lamp and then suddenly under the bed." John focused on the concrete elements brought into view by the text and these served as the building blocks of his reading. The saying includes a temporal sequence and John's visualization of its contents followed that order, "I imagined it hopping between these three scenarios: firstly a lamp, then a bowl, and then under the bed."

6. Lewis, "Hamlet," 104–5.
7. Ibid., 105.

As these statements indicate, John used his imagination to follow the textual directives. His imagination brought the saying's contents into focus and filled in the saying's broad brush outlines. Iser asserts that gaps in a narrative provide space for a reader's imagination to work[8] and John's reading substantiates this assertion. The saying's lack of descriptive detail functioned as a gap for John and he added in color, location, and size: "I imagined an old bed probably a bit like my bed, but in the middle of a room, in a grey room, a clay bowl, and a small candle like that big" {demonstrates small size}. While John's gap-filling fleshed out the scene, it also remained within the bounds of the text. The saying is a metaphor and the GNB refers to the agent of its action generically as "people." Accordingly John did not treat the saying as a story and he did not fill in gaps pertaining to either characters or plot: "I can't imagine anyone actually putting [the lamp] under the bed." The focus of the saying determined the focus of John's reading.

Yet John's reading went well beyond mere observation of the concrete elements in the text. The reading was also shaped by John's affective response to the saying, an affect rooted in humor. In the interview, John initiated discussion of this saying because of his own experience of reading it:

> It's so obvious it's almost like a joke. Like where it says, "People don't light a lamp and put it under a bowl"—well obviously. So I imagine everyone going, "Ha!" {laughs}. Then going from that to everyone listening . . . It takes something which is quite funny and turns it into a clever message.

This reader likened the saying to a literary form with which he was familiar: a joke. His enjoyment of the saying appeared to produce this comparison. The saying positioned John alongside the implied listener in the story world, the narratee; accordingly, John's reading took the form of a direct personal response. The response of the listener is not alluded to in the saying but John attributed to this listener his own experience of the saying's humor, which he assumed was both intended and normative.

Commentators on this passage note, like John, the unlikelihood of the various locations of the lamp in verse 16: both Green and Nolland refer to these locations as "bizarre,"[9] while Marshall calls them "patently foolish."[10] Yet none of these critics consider, as John did, the impact of these odd locations upon the listener. Instead the critics make serious points about what the light of the lamp might represent: the missionary endeavors of

---

8. Iser, *The Implied Reader*, 37–40.
9. Green, *Luke*, 329; Nolland, *Luke 1—9:20*, 391.
10. Marshall, *Gospel of Luke*, 329.

the church,[11] the revelation of human conduct,[12] the need for the disciples to make Jesus' message plain to others,[13] or Jesus' intention to reveal God through his teaching.[14] The experiential effect of the saying is overlooked in the pursuit of theological significance.

Like these scholars, John sought to make sense of the saying, but his sense-seeking included his experience of the saying. He classified the saying as a humorous device designed to gain the listener's attention in order to deliver its point: "It attracts the attention with the joke, and then tells you serious stuff." The reader assumed that, like him, the humor would lead the listener to seek the meaning of the saying. John summarized the saying's point as, "don't hide things, because if you do, then God will always know." The critics' readings are theologically worthy but John's reading aligns with that of the implied reader and has theological implications which pertain directly to the life of the listener. John's reading reflects the persuasive intent of the text: the saying exists not just to make an abstract theological point but to be transformative.

As Marguerat and Bourquin state, "to arrive at its destination the text needs the participation of the reader."[15] John's reading of Luke 8:16–17 was built out of a complex transaction between Luke and the reader. John, for his part, visualized the contents of the text, experienced its humor, and sought to puzzle out the sense of the saying. The reader's participation may be described as holistic, since it encompasses imaginative, emotive, cognitive, and personal elements. This participation took the form of direct engagement with the text. The text, for its part, directed the act of communication: the contents, order, perspective, and literary form guided the production of the reading. The reading was the product of both dialogue partners: as the reader looked *along* the path of the saying, the text provided the view and direction, while the reader brought that view to life.

Drawing a Few Boundaries

Prior to launching into an analysis of the children's five reading strategies, I need to make a few points that clarify the boundaries of my discussion. It is important to stress that the aim of this discussion is neither to measure the children's readings against some pre-established critical range, nor to

11. Nolland, *Luke 1—9:20*, 391; Tannehill, *Luke*, 142.
12. Green, *Luke*, 329.
13. Marshall, *Gospel of Luke*, 328.
14. Craddock, *Luke*, 113.
15. Marguerat and Bourquin, *How to Read*, 121.

determine what an appropriate range might be relative to this group of child readers. Rather the aim is to examine the readings to see what they reveal about the reading strategies the children used with Luke. I do at times compare the children's readings to those of critics but with the purpose of highlighting the distinctive aspects of the children's readings. Sometimes these comparisons suggest what participatory reading might add to the scholarly discussion.

This study did not attempt to assess what took place during the actual act of reading. Such an investigation would be difficult indeed. Rather the focus is upon the outcome of this act: the readings it produced. All of the discussion about the children's reading strategies derive from the readings. It is also worth noting that my discussion seeks neither to adjudicate between different reading theories nor to claim that a particular approach is the "right" one. Rather I seek to conduct a theoretical analysis that is appropriate to the empirical findings. I examine the readings in order to evaluate their salient features, in pursuit of those features of the text-reader dialogue that may be considered characteristic of this particular group of readers.

To read the Gospel of Luke, the readers immersed themselves in its narrative world. As the researcher, my task, on the other hand, is to analyze this dialogue from the outside. I have to take a looking *at* position in order to assess the readers' looking *along* positions. Thus ironically, my discussion of participatory reading derives from a non-participatory position. If I had attempted to participate with the children in their reading of Luke, my participation would invariably have altered their engagement with the text and the resultant readings would have reflected not so much the transactions of child readers as the transactions resulting from the co-working of a child and adult.

Finally, the readings I analyze are representative rather than comprehensive. The raw data from the interviews and the focus groups were vast and the full details could not be presented in a few brief chapters. The readings under discussion have been selected because they provide salient examples of the findings. This selection aims to cover as many angles of the findings as possible while focusing on *the central characteristics of the readings and the processes that seemed to produce them*. My choice of readings is inevitably subjective but this is unavoidable. In order to mitigate the effect of this personal bias, I include a range of readings in each section, to enable my reader—who is no doubt looking *at* this text—to conduct her or his own evaluation alongside of my own.

Reading Luke as a Story

The remainder of this chapter looks at one of the reading strategies arising from the empirical findings: reading Luke as a story. In the second IFG session, I asked the participants, "has reading Luke affected your interaction with the Bible in any way?" To which Hannah M. responded, "I was confused before [I read the Gospel]. Now I realize that Luke's more like a story." The other participants assented to this statement. Reading Luke appeared to lead these child readers to view the Gospel as a narrative. As discussed in chapter 3, Meek argues that a narrative is the best guide for teaching children how to read a narrative.[16] The findings suggest that although the readers brought to their reading transaction with Luke various expectations gleaned from their church, school, and home contexts, their encounters with the whole Gospel made them aware of its narrative shape. They read Luke not only *for* its story, but also *as* a story.

The children reading Luke *for* its story is the topic of the final chapter of this analysis. I focus here upon how the children read Luke *as* a story and thus engaged with its discourse. Tannehill helpfully describes this discourse as the "literary means" that Luke uses to guide its readers.[17] Luke's discourse seeks to direct its reader's focus onto the story contents but is itself often implicit. Nonetheless the readers were at times aware of the text's direction, sometimes following it and at other times resisting it. In the remainder of this chapter, I delineate some of the key discourse devices that guided the text-reader dialogue and argue that the text thereby directed but was not determinative of the children's readings.

The discourse devices to which the readers responded were myriad and I cannot hope to address them all, but have selected the most prominent for exploration. My main selection criteria were the frequency with which these devices appeared in the readings and their representation of discrete facets of the text. The discourse devices I discuss are literary genre, perspective, voice, and order.

"It Does Parables and What's Happening"

The type of discourse used by a text is largely determined by its literary genre. As established in chapter 2, Luke is a narrative but also includes a variety of embedded literary forms such as parables, metaphoric sayings, and apocalyptic warnings. These forms make different demands on the

---

16. Meek, *How Texts Teach*, 19–20.
17. Tannehill, *Luke*, 31.

reader. The children's readings generally distinguished between the forms. Lucy described Luke's structure by pointing out its alteration of two literary forms: "It does parables, and what's actually happening, and then parables." This reading uses the term "parables" to refer to all of Jesus' teaching. Lucy found the inclusion of the different forms appealing: "I thought it was good how it mixed everything together." Most of the readers adapted their interpretations of Luke to the different demands of these forms, showing at least implicit awareness of literary genre.

For literary forms such as metaphors, similes, and apocalyptic warnings, Luke's imagery often guided the readings. Grace explained how she read the first part of the Luke 6:43–45 Tree and Fruit saying: "When it says, 'bad tree,' I imagined a crinkled bush or tree. One that you might get in all these fantasy stories, that it's winter and no snow, but it's all black and horrible." The GNB actually uses the phrase "poor tree," but Grace's reading incorporated the saying's associated "bad fruit" into her rendering of the tree. The text's terminology evoked for her a familiar literary image that could symbolize moral decrepitude or evil. The reader's emotive description of the scene as "horrible" expressed her aversion to the image, a response which could be deemed appropriate to the import of the saying.

Green, in his discussion of these verses, calls the fruit image a metaphor for the human conduct that exposes the heart. He supposes that Jesus' audience would have agreed with this use of the fruit and tree imagery, intellectually setting them up for the remainder of the passage.[18] This scholar's reading limits the metaphor's impact to cognitive assent on the part of the hearer or reader, whereas in Grace's reading the metaphor prompted the reader to disassociate from the poor tree and all it represented. The saying's imagery did not just inform the reader; it swayed her.

For the parables, the readings were guided by the characters and plot. Abby particularly liked the Luke 15:8–10 parable of the Lost Coin and initially described it by retelling its main actions, following the plot sequence. The searching woman, the focal character of the parable, was at the center of her reading. The text describes the woman's celebration at discovering her coin including her declaration of "I am so happy I found the coin I lost." Abby responded empathetically and elaborated on this happiness: "She's so grateful when she finds this one small thing because it means so much to her, even though she has others. It's like everything is worth something to her." Abby's reading attributed the woman's happiness to gratitude and she even surmised that this gratitude typified the woman's life.

---

18. Green, *Luke*, 279–80.

After exploring a parable's plot and characters, the readings tended to interpret the parables metaphorically, usually through some form of analogy. The Lost Coin parable closes with a summarizing simile which begins: "In the same way . . ." This phrase signals an analogous reading and Abby extrapolated from this to the other Lukan parables, declaring "all of these parables are all about people really." Following the connection made in the simile, her reading associated the lost coin with the similitude's "sinner who repents" and assumed that the purpose of the parable was to show "how grateful the angels are" for repentant sinners. Abby declared that she found the woman's gratitude personally inspiring, and her reading attributed to both the woman and the angels the gratitude which she experienced through her empathy with the woman. Although the parable's protagonist may be deemed to represent God, Abby's reading marginalized the parable's theological implications in favor of personal values.

The micro-narratives of events in Jesus' life, what Lucy referred to as "what's actually happening," evoked similar interpretive maneuvers to those of the parables with one clear difference. The children's readings of the micro-narratives were inextricably linked to their reading of Luke's macro-narrative. The macro-narrative of Jesus' life often guided the readers' interpretation of the micro-narratives. For instance, in the Luke 5:17–26 story of the Healing of the Paralyzed Man, the story's plot is initially focalized through the paralyzed man's friends and follows their successful efforts to get the paralyzed man to Jesus. Many of the readings of this story aligned with this focalization and focused on the actions of the friends. In the macro-narrative, Jesus' identity as a healer is already established and, for Jeremy, Jesus' status provided motivation for the friends' conduct: the story "made me think of the lengths that some people were prepared to go to just to see if there was even a hope that Jesus could heal."

This interpretive influence was not one-way: the micro-narratives also shaped the readers' understanding of the macro-narrative. Prior to the Luke 5 story of the Healing of the Paralyzed Man, Jesus has already been established as the protagonist of the macro-narrative, positioning the readers to side with him and against those who antagonize him. This Luke 5 story depicts the first clash between the religious leaders and Jesus, and its contents help to distance the readers from the religious leaders. The child readers, having initially aligned with the paralyzed man's friends, seemed to view any obstacle to the friends' quest as unwelcome, including the questioning of the religious leaders. Zak not only refused to take the viewpoint of the religious leaders but also emphasized his distance from them: "I imagined myself as one of the crowd looking back at the Pharisees and watching them." This micro-narrative sets up the viewpoint of the religious leaders in the macro-narrative as an obstacle to surmount[19] not a perspective to embrace.

"Seeing from All Different Angles"

Looking *along* a text means viewing the narrative world from a particular perspective, usually a perspective that is embedded in the text. Gary Yamasaki compares textual point of view to the use of camera angles in a film since both control what the readers and audience "see."[20] Luke's embedded perspectives directed the readers' focus and thereby guided what they participated with in the narrative world.

The readings showed awareness of the different perspectives in Luke. Echoing Yamasaki, Zak described his experience of the text's changes in perspective using film terminology: "If it was made into a movie, it would be like me on top of the hill and then when there's a big pause in a sentence, jump over to actually in the action, maybe into a person." Zak's hill top perspective was that of the narratee who sees the narrative through a wide angle lens, while Zak's entrance into the plot or a "person" expressed his alignment with a character's point of view. His phrase, "a big pause," cues the change in perspective.

As Zak's reading indicates, the readings often aligned with the perspectives in the text, and swapped between them based on textual cues. The most commonly assumed perspectives were those of the narratee, the crowd, and the characters. I look at each of these in turn.

The Narratee as a "Camera Man"

The most dominant perspective in Luke is the one directed by the narrator, the perspective which orientates the whole narrative world. This perspective may be described as that of the narratee: the one who sees what the narrator shows. As Marguerat and Bourquin state, the "position of the narratee is occupied by the receiver of the story, which is symmetrical to the narrator."[21] The readings frequently assumed this perspective and even appeared to take it for granted. Jeremy articulated the viewpoint as "just one that's there." When they aligned with the narratee, the readings tended to follow the

---

19. Tannehill makes a similar point in his discussion of this story as a quest narrative. See Tannehill, *Luke*, 105.
20. Yamasaki, "Point of View in a Gospel Story," 91.
21. Marguerat and Bourquin, *How to Read*, 14.

grain of the text. James A. spoke for many of the readers when he asserted: "I just watch [the characters] doing what they're doing." Where the narrator led, the readers followed. Stephanie referred to this as the pensieve effect, explaining the perspective by way of an inter-textual reference to J. K. Rowling's narrative world: it's like "when Harry goes into the pensieve and you can follow everyone around but you can't actually speak to them."[22]

This viewpoint positioned the readers outside of the story frame. Consequently a key action on the part of the readers was observing the story. Numerous readings compared their alignment with this perspective to the role of a camera operator, the one who "sees." Ebby explained: "You know how in those concerts that have a camera man all over the place and you can never see him? It's like that. Because I could see it from all different angles but I could never really see where I was." The reader followed the events of the story much like a camera operator follows the events of a concert or a film. This perspective separated Ebby from the story, just as the camera operator records the action of a film yet is not visible in the final product.

As the camera operators, the readers entered into a tacit partnership with Luke. They observed what the narrator revealed while concomitantly animating the narrative world through their imaginations. Boris explained: "I try to visualize each character and think of it as a film, like I'm watching it but reading it at the same time." His reading gave Luke's contents shape and substance in the form of mental images. Percy felt that this perspective caused him to assume "a bystander's point of view. And not even a very interactive bystander at that. It's just standing there watching." Yet this perspective did not reduce the readers to inertia. Lucy pointed out that the experience of reading Luke drew her further into its narrative world than the experience of watching a film. When watching a film she was passive, but when she read, she actively observed.[23] Even Percy, who viewed himself

---

22. For the effect of the pensieve, see Rowling, *Harry Potter and the Goblet of Fire*, 505–25.

23. This description of the readers' active engagement with the Gospel might imply that the children's reading strategies were comparable to the meditative reading method of St. Ignatius of Loyola. This was not the case. St. Ignatius' approach to the Gospels is based on the imagination and seeks to apply the five senses to Gospel excerpts as a means of meditation. Unlike the child readers, who observed the narrative world from the perspective of the narratee and in relation to the whole macro-narrative, the Ignatian exercitant imagines the textual world through the guidance of a spiritual director and based on excerpts, or mysteries, each of which consists of a few sentences from a Gospel embedded in a brief summary of the story from which it is drawn. The exercitant sees the Gospel world through the medium of St. Ignatius. The excerpts follow the basic chronology of Jesus' life but draw from the fourfold Gospel and omit vast portions of the Gospels. They do not sustain, or even attempt to produce, any form of narrative experience. The Ignatian exercitant engages with the excerpts through the imagination

as inactive, fleshed out the setting of the Luke 9:10–17 story of the Feeding of the 5000: "I pictured it as though it's a small hill. There's a little dip and tree and I was standing on the hill, seeing it from different areas in the place where it's happening." His reading added details which brought the story to life.

Luke's embedded teaching had a different effect. For these passages, the narratee's perspective often heightened the readers' participation. The teaching sections are narrated by Jesus and not the third person narrator. In his literary-critical study of Luke, David Lee points out that the Gospel's teaching sections tend to omit the temporal and spatial markers of narrative and as a result these sections produce "the narrative effect of Jesus teaching *the narratee*."[24] This teaching uses second person pronouns, giving the impression of direct personal address by Jesus. It also lacks characters whom the readers may observe from an external position. When the readers adopted the perspective of the narratee for these passages, they frequently responded directly to the text as themselves.

The resulting readings were consistently personal. Allie appeared to experience conviction through Jesus' Speck in the Eye saying in Luke 6:41–42: "It makes you feel quite bad about yourself." She expressed contrition over her fights with her siblings and adopted the saying's imagery to describe herself: "I'm good at dirt as well." The reader cited this saying as one of her favorites in the Gospel, perhaps because it evoked a self-evaluative response. Allie's reading counters Tannehill's assertion that this saying's accusatory language "might primarily produce anger and defensiveness if applied to an individual," while those who overhear it "spoken to no one in particular" may be more receptive to its implications.[25] Allie's reading neither derived from an indirect approach nor was it defensive. Tannehill seems to assume that the reader will not follow the guidance of the text and align with the narratee's perspective. The real reader, Allie, proved more receptive to the directives of the text than the hypothetical readers posited by this scholar.

---

using what Ignatius refers to as an "application of the senses," while for the child readers, use of their imagination was one of a several reading strategies. Also the goals of the two forms of reading are different. The children engaged in order both to understand and to find out what happened in the narrative, but the exercitant meditates on the mysteries specifically for spiritual benefit, so that the meditation is directed towards personal ends. See St. Ignatius of Loyola, *The Spiritual Exercises of St Ignatius*, esp. 72, for an example of the meditation method and pp. 109–26 for the mysteries.

24. Lee, *Luke's Stories of Jesus*, 229; italics in the original.
25. Tannehill, *Luke*, 122.

In the Crowd

Luke includes one group character whose role echoes that of the narratee: the crowd. The key role of the crowd in the narrative world, like the role of the narratee in the discourse, is to observe: both see Jesus. But as a group character, the crowd has direct access to the protagonist because it exists in the story world. For some of the micro-narratives, the readings merged the narratee's perspective with that of the crowd. This merged perspective positioned the readers within the narrative world, enhancing their participation. James S. joined the crowd in his reading of the Luke 8:42b–48 story of the Bleeding Woman: I was "watching the woman touch the cloak." His choice of position was deliberate for it "gave a better view of things. People in the crowd come to see Jesus and what he does. So if you're in the crowd, you see what he is doing, and what other people are doing as well." This reader participated in the micro-narrative much like the crowd members surrounding Jesus participated in his ministry: present but at a distance.

This perspective frequently produced empathy with the crowd. Rachel took the perspective of a crowd member for the Luke 9:10–17 story of the Feeding of the 5000 while maintaining her own identity. Being a crowd member allowed her to put herself "in the shoes of the people who were there. So it's not just that you're standing there, but you're actually really there." From this position, she imagined herself being fed the miraculous food, she empathized with the crowd's surprise, and she capitulated to the inexplicability of the miracle. The result was an experience of the story that paralleled the impact of the miracle upon the characters whose role she had assumed.

Like Rachel, many of the readers who discussed this story adopted the crowd's perspective. The commentators on Luke, on the other hand, repeatedly discuss this story in relation to its impact on the disciples primarily because the disciples function as the story's focal characters, but also due to the story's location between the co-texts of the sending of the twelve and Peter's confession.[26] Johnson, for instance, describes the provision of food as a "lesson" for the twelve disciples which, among other things, reinforces what they have already "learned on their own journey."[27] This scholarly focus reflects a key dynamic within the narrative world: the disciples' developing understanding of Jesus' identity and participation in his ministry. Yet this focus overlooks the potential impact of the micro-narrative upon readers who assume the more detached perspective of the crowd. Rachel's

---

26. See: Ibid., 154–55; Johnson, *Luke*, 149; Craddock, *Luke*, 125.
27. Johnson, *Luke*, 149.

alignment with this perspective rendered her a witness to the story, much like the crowd.

Into a Character

As Lee points out, Luke's narrator often steps out of the way to allow stories in the Gospel to be seen from the perspective of a character.[28] The readers usually followed this change in perspective and adopted the viewpoint of that character. Many of the readers, for instance, viewed the Luke 15:8–10 parable of the Lost Coin from the perspective of the searching woman, while others viewed the Luke 10:38–42 story of Mary and Martha from the perspective of Martha. Aligning with a character's viewpoint generally led the readers to interpret the story in line with that character's situation.

Grace's detailed and insightful reading of the Luke 19:1–10 story of Zacchaeus assumed the perspective of the central character, Zacchaeus. This alignment positioned her against the crowd who obstruct Zacchaeus on several levels. Grace imagined the difficulty Zacchaeus experienced in getting around the crowd: "He goes to the great length that he actually climbs a tree to see Jesus." She probed why Jesus singled Zacchaeus out: "Jesus thinks that Zacchaeus is one of the most important people in the crowd because he is going to repent of his ways." The role of the crowd, in contrast, is to complain about Zacchaeus and they remain inert: "All these people, they're just standing there looking." Meanwhile the central character is changed through his encounter with Jesus: Zacchaeus "actually does something to show that he's really sorry." Aligning with this character's perspective led Grace to ponder the story's theology of repentance.

Tannehill likewise highlights the story's juxtaposition of Zacchaeus and the crowd. According to this commentator, the crowd's grumbling creates a scenario in which "the narrative tries to persuade" its readership that Zacchaeus "rightly belongs to the children of Abraham . . . and to the outcasts whom Jesus came to save." That is, the crowd's view of Zacchaeus potentially represents that of the reader.[29] Tannehill does not discuss how the story may be experienced by those who take the perspective of the central character. What Tannehill does not note, but Grace did, is that the crowd's grumbling signals opposition to Jesus' ministry, a pattern that is already well-established and not encouraged in the narrative world. Both the crowds and Zacchaeus see Jesus, but for Grace the key difference was their attitude towards what was seen.

28. Lee, *Luke's Stories of Jesus*, 228.
29. Tannehill, *Luke*, 275–78.

"Being Told the Story"

I have been discussing the perspectives in Luke. What the readers who align with these perspectives "see" is dependent upon what they are shown. This showing is done by the narrative voice, a discourse device that specifically directs readers.[30] The most salient voices in Luke are those of the narrator and of Jesus. The interplay of these two voices has been the subject of some debate, with Dawsey arguing that the narrator and Jesus deliver divergent messages[31] while Tannehill criticizes Dawsey on literary grounds. Tannehill points out that the Lukan narrator primarily uses the technique of showing rather than telling and thereby foregrounds rather than contradicts, as Dawsey suggests, the speech of the protagonist.[32]

It was clear from the empirical findings that the readers distinguished between these two voices. Indeed some of the readers used complex reading strategies in order to account for their differences. Stephanie described how she used a visual strategy to differentiate the macro-narrative for which the narrator provides the voice and in which Jesus is the protagonist, from parables for which Jesus provides the voice: "Whenever Jesus tells a parable, I imagine him sitting on a rock telling it to everyone. But you also imagine the place that Jesus is telling it about." Visualizing two different scenes helped this reader to distinguish between the voices as well as to work out their relationship. This reading treated the two voices as complementary, an approach aligning with Tannehill's position rather than Dawsey's.

Stephanie's reading of the Luke 20:9–18 parable of the Tenants in the Vineyard provides an example: "I imagined it being a flashback with the tenants and the owner of the vineyard in this big house and a vineyard in the front garden. Then I imagined Jesus, in the future but in the same place, talking." Notice how the storyteller, Jesus, is temporally separated from yet spatially located in the same setting as his story. The parable functions as a "flashback": the embedded story is relegated to the past, while Jesus and his narrative world as described by the narrator are in the present and primary.

The voice of the narrator tells the overall story and enables the readers to access the narrative world. From Luke 1:5 onwards, the narrative is told in the third person so that the narrator is effaced. But this omniscient narrator first provides grounds for his reliability in the Prologue, Luke 1:1–4. Green deems the opening to the Gospel significant for it "ushers readers

---

30. "Voice" is a term coined by Gérard Genette. See Genette, *Narrative Discourse*, 212–15.

31. Dawsey, *The Lukan Voice*, 73–102.

32. Tannehill, *The Narrative Unity of Luke-Acts*, 1:7.

from the world outside the text into the world of the text."³³ In the Prologue, the narrator speaks in first person, personalizing the narrator's voice and creating a collusion between the reader and the narrator over the "full truth" (Luke 1:4) of the narrated events. The child readers consistently yielded to this voice. According to Jake: "It's like you're sitting back and being told the story even though you're reading it." The narrator's voice draws constant attention to the life and sayings of Jesus while also guiding the reader's conceptualization of Jesus' world.

The narrator uses an episode-based and event-orientated form of discourse. This voice *shows* Jesus and divulges the plot. The voice of Jesus, in contrast, often speaks in second person which has the effect of directly addressing the reader. The narrator's presentation of Jesus as the agent-hero encourages the reader to rely on Jesus' voice. Jesus' form of discourse is "often aphoristic, metaphorical, and hyperbolic, appealing to the imagination," with the result that his "words gain transformative power but renounce precise control."³⁴ Jesus' figurative discourse creates an openness in Luke that provides ample space for divergent readings.³⁵

A comparison of some of the children's readings of the Luke 8:4–8 parable of the Sower and the Seeds reveals the effect of this openness. The need to read this parable figuratively seemed to be the primary cue which the readers took from its interpretation in Luke 8:11–15. Sophie M.'s reading of the parable was socio-cultural and concerned with the success of different social classes. Percy interpreted the weeds as peer pressure, leading to a teen reading. Boris' reading was ethical and focused on the fruit of the good soil which for him represented the heritage that results from worthy conduct. James A.'s reading was theological: he thought that the good soil represented those who "learn more about God." Ebby produced a personal reading, describing the parable as giving him "a revelation of what I was doing wrong." Jack, in contrast, resisted the figurative discourse: "I'm not a seed." He went on to question the use of figurative discourse in general: "Why are you seeds? Why are you sheep?"

A similar diversity may be found by comparing the commentators' readings of this parable.³⁶ The sheer variety of such readings exemplifies how a discourse strategy such as voice may be directive but not determinative. The young readers' personal concerns appeared to influence how

33. Green, *Luke*, 33.

34. Tannehill, "Freedom and Responsibility," 267–68.

35. See my discussion of Luke as an open text in chapter 2 under "Luke as Narrative."

36. Cf. Green, *Luke*, 327–28; Tannehill, *Luke*, 142; Nolland, *Luke 1—9:20*, 387–88; Johnson, *Luke*, 134–35.

they interpreted the figurative language of the parable. These concerns were woven into their readings with the result that the readings often pertained to the readers' contexts. To be heard, the voice of the text must address its reader and the reader invariably filters that voice through her or his context. A text may thus address the reader *in situ*.

One other voice in the Gospel is worth noting: the voice of Jesus' opponents, particularly the religious leaders, Satan, and the political authorities. These characters, as a group, provide a voice of ambivalence and dissent in the narrative and the readers consistently reacted against this voice. Ebby described the religious leaders as verbally picking on Jesus while he admired Jesus because "he was right on top of everything that they said." Although such characters potentially presented an alternative account within the narrative world, as far as the readers were concerned their voice was there to be proved wrong.

"A Story that's Along the Road"

Luke's narrative sequence determines the order in which its readers process its contents, assuming they read the narrative from beginning to end as the readers in this study did. Chatman views order as one of the principal features of discourse and describes narrative as "a sequential composite."[37] Luke's order appeared to guide Tarquin's reading experience: "I actually read it in my mind—just make up a picture in your mind and go along. It's like a story that's along the road, and the separate bits along the way. Like you're walking down it and looking at them." This reading's "separate bits" refers to Luke's episodes. Tarquin equated reading Luke to a journey which follows the narrative order and envisages the different episodes as they come into view. Tarquin's approach to the narrative trajectory was not passive, but it was receptive: he took the stroll but followed the path that the text provided.

In a narrative world, the order is part of the structure of the overall plot. Sophie A. thought that reading the whole Gospel "gets the message across much more strongly" than reading individual episodes. The plot makes sense of the ordering of the macro-narrative by connecting its events and supplying them with significance. Through the plot, the events of a narrative "tend to be related or mutually entailing."[38] Zak viewed the order of the macro-narrative as chronological and thought that the plot filled in the main "gaps of what happened." Boris described the structure of Luke as "a photo album with pictures in stories." He equated the "small stories" in Luke

---

37. Chatman, *Story and Discourse*, 28, 21.
38. Ibid., 21.

to "snapshots" that were "a bit jumbled up, but still in an order." Despite Luke's episodic structure, this reader expected all of the parts of Luke to cohere and he disliked any small sections that he felt "didn't really help" to tell the overall story.

Narrative order guided the readers' interpretation of not only the macro-narrative, but also the micro-narratives and parables. Darr points out that as a reader progresses through a story, she or he "begins to formulate expectations and opinions which then become the basis upon which subsequent data is processed." The reader also "reassesses previously-formed expectations and opinions in the light of new information and insights."[39] The reader looks forward and backwards in a story, accumulating data in pursuit of a coherent interpretation of that story.

Some of the effects of this cumulative processing of story data may be seen in Sophie M.'s reading of the Luke 15:4–7 parable of the Lost Sheep. This parable initially made her think about the sheep and shepherds "cause that was the words on the page." Her mental progression through the passage followed the sequence of the story:

> First of all, I had the idea of a sheep going away and [the shepherd] goes searching and looks for it, and comes back with it—a slightly comical image of the sheep on his shoulders. Then there was the idea of everybody in heaven and all these good people easily just walking through the gates. Then one sinner, and God and Jesus stand up and they seem so happy to see him because he's come that bit further and he's changed.

It is worth noting that Sophie M. supplied "God and Jesus" as characters; neither is named in the parable. Yet as Green points out, the parable provides insight "into God's own disposition vis-à-vis sinners"[40] and Sophie M.'s supplied characters serve as veritable embodiments of this disposition. The reading treated the lost sheep and the sinner in parallel, and likewise the shepherd and God, referring back to the parabolic part of the passage to interpret the passage's final statement about the sinner.

This reading configured the entirety of the passage within the bounds of the story world. The reader's divine characters enacted the statement "there will be more joy in heaven," turning what may otherwise be viewed as an abstract theological assertion at the end of the parable into a continuation of its story. This configuration is *contra* Nolland who asserts that "the place of repentance here takes us right outside the framework of the parable." While Nolland separates out the actions of the shepherd and the sheep

39. Darr, *Character Building*, 30.
40. Green, *Luke*, 569.

from the repentance of the sinner,[41] Sophie M.'s reading assumed narrative progression and used the beginning of the parable to interpret the end of the passage.

Sophie M.'s reading also moved outside of the story frame but only after the passage concluded. Sophie M. then wondered, "is it ever too late to change?" and she considered the possibilities of change for the people she knew. These ponderings were the culmination of her processing of the passage in its narrative order. Sophie M.'s interpretation began with the world of the text and her ponderings about the world of the reader grew out of her interpretation of the narrative world. Her thoughtful, systematic reading rippled outward from the parable of the sheep and shepherd, then to the theological implications for the sinner, before finally spilling out into the reader's world. The order of the passage directed the reader and led her, finally, to a position of personal reflection.

Summary

I began this chapter with an introduction to participatory reading as the overall explanatory framework for the children's interpretive strategies. This framework conceptualizes the children's reading strategies as expressions of how the readers sought to know Luke: the reading strategies have an epistemological orientation. In the second part of this chapter, I have been concerned with how the children read Luke as a story and I have demonstrated how the text's discourse seemed to direct the readers without being determinative of their readings. Luke's literary genres guided how the readers approached the text. The perspectives in Luke enabled the readers to "see" the text's contents, sometimes from the position of an observer and at other times through alignment with a character. This seeing was not passive but it was responsive to the narrative voices that directed the seeing. The readers distinguished between the two key narrative voices, that of the narrator and that of Jesus, usually relying upon the narrator's directions while interpreting Jesus' figurative teaching more freely. The findings suggest that the narrative order guided how the readers processed the text's contents.

Reading Luke as a story is a reading strategy that approaches the narrative *as* a narrative and is contingent on the narrative's discourse. This chapter has already touched upon the other key reading strategies that the readers used in their dialogue with Luke. I look next at reading by imagining.

---

41. Nolland, *Luke 9:21—18:34*, 772–73.

Chapter 8

Reading by Imagining

Fishy: "It helps to understand the thing—imagining it."

Elaine: "Once I've pictured something in a book, if I come back years later and revisit that book, I'll get the same image."

Introduction

One of the theoretical questions guiding my empirical work was, "what role does the reader's imagination play in the readings?"[1] At the beginning of the interview phase, I explored this role using a single interview question which was located near the end of the interview script. The purpose of that question was primarily to probe the impact of children's bibles, Sunday School materials, and visual media on the participants' readings of Luke. However, the initial interviews made clear that the readers' imaginations played a much larger role in their interpretive strategies than merely eliciting memories derived from external sources. Consequently, I soon expanded the imagination question to two questions and moved these to a location earlier in the interview script, making the imagination a potential topic of reference for later conversation in each interview. I thereby generated a large supply of data about the readers' imaginative reading strategies.

This data revealed that imagining was a common component of the text-reader dialogue. The IFGs placed "reading by imagining" at the top of their list of reading strategies.[2] The readers appeared to interact with the narrative by giving its contents a concrete form in their minds. Iser helpfully explains that imagining occurs when a text initiates "a sequence of mental images which lead to the text translating itself into the reader's conscious-

---

1. See Table 1 in chapter 6.
2. See the list in Table 4 of chapter 6.

ness." The forms that these images take are shaped by the reader's "stock of experience, which acts as a referential background against which the unfamiliar can be conceived and processed."[3] The child readers' imagining often took the form of visualization, as Iser suggests, although sometimes it was more idea-based.

This imagining enabled the readers to follow the text, to "see" what was happening. What is more, it also served as a tool for interpretation so that the readers claimed to use their imaginations to engage in the metaphoric form of "seeing," that is, understanding. As James S. explained, imagining "helps me with my own opinion. If I visualize it myself, that gives me my own opinion on the thing, how I would see it."

This chapter considers both *how* the readers used their imaginations to engage with Luke's narrative world as well as *why* they did so. Its discussion draws on the fields of psychology and philosophy. This is because the theoretical side of the research straddles children's literature theory and biblical studies, and the former draws mainly on psychology while the latter draws mainly on philosophy in their discussions of the imagination. The use of the term "imagination" in this study, however, is rooted in the child participants' use of the term and I begin by clarifying that use. I then explore some of the key findings which suggest that the readers' used their imaginations as a tool for participating in a dialogue with Luke. Next I consider how the readers' memories contributed to their imaginative participation. Finally, I argue that the main function of the imagination in the readings was interpretive: the readers imagined in order to make sense of the text.

A Working Definition of "Imagination"

The imagination as a topic of discussion has a long history within Western thought, dating back at least to the time of Aristotle's *Poetics* in the fourth century BC. The term itself was introduced into the English language in the thirteenth century.[4] As may be expected with such a history, uses of the term have varied considerably, ranging from basic definitions such as "mental imaging" to the Enlightenment philosophers' conception of the imagination as a perceptual tool.[5] Because my concern is with the role of the imagination in reading, my discussion is limited to ideas that pertain to this role. Even within these more limited parameters, "imagination" still

---

3. Iser, *The Act of Reading*, 38.
4. Searle, *The Eyes of Your Heart*, 40.
5. For a thorough discussion see Warnock, *Imagination*, 13–71. She discusses, among others: Hume, *A Treatise of Human Nature*; and Kant, *Critique of Judgement*.

proves a slippery term and some scholars avoid this problem by not defining it at all before plunging into an examination of its function.[6] Since my focus is on the child readers' use of the imagination, my working definition, while drawing upon the scholarly views, is rooted in the readers' employment of the term.

Many definitions of "imagination" have at their heart the term's root concept: the capacity to create images in the mind.[7] Tolkien adds precision to this definition, making a philological argument for confining the term to the cognitive ability to form "mental images of things not actually present,"[8] whether spatially or temporally. As far as the readers were concerned, their imagination was primarily an imaging tool. When they discussed imagining the text, they typically referred to mental representations albeit in a variety of forms. But the readers' implementation of the imagination did not end there. The imagination was not, for them, merely a means of observation but also a means of engaging with the text. Garrett Green helpfully classifies the imagination as a faculty and clarifies that a "faculty is an ability, a skill, a way of behaving that allows one to do something. What it is that one does with imagination . . . is the crucial issue."[9] What the readers did with their imaginations can be described under two headings: experiencing the narrative world and making sense of the text. I look briefly at the scholarly discussion of each of these uses.

The Imaginative Experience

Beginning with the experiential side of imagination, scholars from a variety of fields hold that the imagination is a cognitive act that enables a vicarious experience of the thing or situation imagined.[10] Green specifies that the imagination "makes present through images what is inaccessible to direct experience."[11] By supplying representations of absent things, the

---

6. For example: Hart, "Imagination and Responsible Reading"; De Hulster, "Imagination." De Hulster claims the advantages of "imagination" as a term over "intuition" without clarifying his use of the former term.

7. See Warnock, *Imagination*, 40; Searle, *The Eyes of Your Heart*, 39; McIntyre, *Faith Theology and Imagination*, 25.

8. Tolkien, "On Fairy-Stories," 68. Tolkien's delimitation of "imagination" is a purposeful step in his argument for defining "fantasy" as a related but separate concept; see "On Fairy Stories," 69.

9. Green, *Imagining God*, 40.

10. For example, Harris, *The Work of the Imagination*, 49; McIntyre, *Faith Theology and Imagination*, 74–79.

11. Green, *Imagining God*, 62.

imagination may lift the imaginer out of the bounds of her or his spatio-temporal context and enable an indirect experience that is not confined to that context. Imagination is a form of thinking that allows projections into the future, past, or other places. Vanhoozer, in his discussion of Lewis's looking *at* versus looking *along* analogy, advocates the imagination as a key means of achieving a looking *along* position relative to a text. This is because the "imagination is our port of entry into other worlds."[12] In short, the imagination may enable a vicarious experience of a narrative world.

Although the imagination is a form of thought process, the experience it produces is not limited to the cognitive. As discussed in chapter 3, Oatley's findings suggest that the imagination may be the means by which the linguistic form of a story is transformed into "an inner mental enactment" that takes the story into the realm of intuition and association.[13] The imaginative processing of a story may engage a reader's emotions.[14] Since the imagination is associative, it draws on the reader's previous experience to generate images. An imaginative experience, then, may encompass cognitive, emotive, and personal responses.

This imaginative experience is an experience *of* the narrative. Mikkelsen, based on her work with child readers, labels the reader's use of the imagination as "aesthetic literacy" and defines this as: "Living through a work with full absorption and strong engagement in forming mental images about characters, settings, and events."[15] When the imaginative experience builds on a reader's memory and previous experience, the imagination becomes personally involving. The reader's use of personally-generated images to engage with a narrative world produces an experience which, while not "real" in the material sense, may have an emotive or cognitive impact upon the reader which authenticates it within the context of the reader's own life.

Imaginative Thinking

As a type of thought process, the imagination enables thinking about something, whether an idea, situation, problem, or narrative world. George MacDonald maintains that the imagination is the faculty "which gives form to

---

12. Vanhoozer, *First Theology*, 37.

13. Oatley, *Such Stuff as Dreams*, 77; see also my discussion in chapter 3 under "Children Reading Narrative."

14. Ibid., 115, 119; see also my discussion in chapter 3 under "Children Reading Narrative."

15. Mikkelsen, *Powerful Magic*, 4; original italics removed.

thought."[16] In the case of reading, these thoughts may be about the contents of, as well as the ideas elicited by, the text. Building on MacDonald and Sartre, McIntyre adds that the imagination is "the mediating consciousness by which . . . the non-perceived is thought and talked about."[17] The products of the imagination serve as the means by which an absent reality is contemplated. When reading, the reader's imagination gives form to the contents of the text so that those contents may be pondered by the reader.

The findings of my study suggest that the readers' imaginations were one of their key tools for thinking about the Lukan world. Johnson affirms this in his discussion of the imagination and theology: if the Bible "is ever again to be a living source for theology, those who practice theology must become less preoccupied with the world that produced Scripture and learn again to live in the world Scripture produces. This will be a matter of imagination."[18] As discussed in chapter 2, the logic of Luke's narrative world is theological. If imaginative thinking contributes to an understanding of this world, then the imagination may play a role in theological thinking.

Defining Imagination

Putting together these ideas, in this study I define "imagination" as:

> the thinking process that enables readers to form mental impressions of the world of the text which facilitate engagement with that world, by helping the reader both to experience that world and to make sense of it.

The imagination is one of the tools a reader may use to engage with a narrative world. The imagination may, of course, have other roles beyond the world of narrative, but they are not the concern of this study.

Imagination and Fantasy

Before concluding this section, it may be useful to distinguish between the imagination and fantasy since these terms are used at times almost interchangeably, particularly in popular discourse. Although I do not seek to challenge the popular use of the terms, I do need to establish clear boundaries for the sake of my discussion. I have indicated that the imagination is a

---

16. MacDonald even locates the imagination in the *imago dei*. See MacDonald, "The Imagination," 9–12.

17. McIntyre, *Faith Theology and Imagination*, 120.

18. Johnson, "Imagining the World Scripture Imagines," 165.

faculty of thought. It is the act of the mind that enables the imaginer to "see" what is not physically present, whether a narrative world, a future not yet realized, or a historic place such as ancient Nazareth. It does not follow that all things imagined are imaginary, although some may well be.

Fantasy is narrower than the imagination and may be considered a sub-category of it, for fantasy is a product of the imagination. I am not referring here to fantasy as a genre of literature,[19] but rather to fantasy as the use of the imagination to create an alternative set of circumstances that are disconnected from or significantly alter the workings of the primary world. Although the imagination may deal with both the fantastic and the mimetic, fantasy deals solely with the fantastic. Fantasy exists at times for the sake of the realistic but its purposes should not be confused with its contents. Fantasizing and imagining are not the same things.[20] Imagining explores possibilities while fantasizing creates impossibilities; although these impossibilities may shed light upon the possibilities, they remain impossibilities.

My distinction so far has been pertinent to distinguishing between the roles of fantasy and the imagination in generating narrative worlds, but this distinction takes another form in this study. Within the context of reading, the imagination may be used to think about narrative worlds of all varieties, whether mimetic, fantastic, or any combination of the two. I may, and indeed often do, use my imagination to access a fantasy world; I have to, for that is the only way that I will ever get there. But I also use my imagination to access aspects of the primary world that are signified in a text. To imagine a narrative world is to give that world a mental form. To fantasize about a narrative world is to extrapolate from it, moving outside the bounds of the text-reader dialogue. My focus is on the former: the readers' use of their imaginations to make sense of the narrative world.

To Read is to Imagine

Most of the readers in this study described imagining as a normal part of their reading experience. Chatman gives a reason for this: "Narrative evokes a world, and since it is no more than an evocation, we are left free to enrich it with whatever real or fictive experience we acquire."[21] Fishy explained how this imagining worked for his reading of Luke: "You imagine your own version of it . . . You just fill in the main things." The language of "filling in"

---

19. Cf. Carpenter and Prichard, "Fantasy," 181–82.
20. There is a reason why John Lennon sang "Imagine" rather than "Fantasize."
21. Chatman, *Story and Discourse*, 120.

suggests Iser's theory of how a reader responds to narrative gaps.[22] However, based on my study's findings, a more useful analogy may be anatomical. The text provided the skeletal framework which the readers fleshed out imaginatively. While "gap-filling" implies addition, "fleshing out" implies the enlivening of something that is already present. The readings did not so much add extra elements into the narrative as give life to the elements that were already present.

This fleshing out process was tantamount to the readers bringing the narrative world to life. It involved thinking of Luke in concrete terms and is part of the literal reading strategy which I discussed earlier in this study.[23] Literal reading, in this sense, means approaching a narrative world as a narrative world and experiencing it through its narrative elements. In this section, I consider how the readers used their imaginations to experience Luke's narrative world. I begin by delineating the key features of the readings that illuminate imagining as a reading strategy and then I consider how the children's readings gave form to the contents of Luke.

"It's Like I'm Watching It"

The readers' imaginative reading strategy appeared to generate a sensory experience of the narrative world. Although this sensory experience did not reduce to the visual, visualization did seem to dominate the process. Robyn said of her reading in general: "It's like I'm watching it, like it's on a t.v. screen. It just happens. It's like I can't help it. When I read a book, I can't really help seeing things." Of the thirty-one readers interviewed only one, Abby, claimed not to visualize the text. Abby, who is a voracious but goal-orientated reader, stated that she did not visualize any of the stories she read because visualizing slowed her down.

A number of readings included auditory forms of imagining. Michael imagined the demons in Luke in some detail, and his imagining included the noise that they made during an exorcism: "Ruuuurrrhhh!" Boris described hearing the complaints of the crowd in the Luke 9:10–17 story of the Feeding of the 5000. He also talked about the noisy "hustle and bustle" of other crowd scenes. Boris said of his imagining, "sometimes it was visual, but a lot of the times it was just like the sound you would hear if you were there." These sounds contributed to his understanding of the narrative.

The readers' use of the imagination could be considered an appropriate response to Luke's discourse which often communicates through imagery.

22. Iser, *The Implied Reader*, 38–39.
23. See my discussion in chapter 4 under "Reading Literally."

As Parsons states, Luke describes events in "vivid and corporeal language," writing "for the eye as much as the ear."[24] Lisa referred to Luke's images as mental stimuli: "If an image is created [by Luke] when I read, I'll think of an image in my head." Luke's images appeared to elicit an imaginative experience for most of the readers.

Imagining the elements of a passage was occasionally a reader's primary form of imaginative engagement with that passage. For the Luke 6:43–45 Tree and Fruit saying, Stephanie visualized the trees in the first part of the saying and for the second part of the saying, she envisaged, "a person standing and then something's coming out of his chest, like the heart and crown." Her engagement with the saying stopped at that point. She neither connected the two halves of the saying nor reflected on the saying's import. Such imagining was an end in itself. As one RVG participant explained, the "imagination makes stories more fun."

But in most of the readings, imagining led to some form of reflection. For Jesus' Speck in the Eye saying in Luke 6:41–42, Lisa visualized the speck and log images, and declared: "I liked that cause it was easier to think about, and the image stuck with me a bit more than it would have done if it had just said, 'Don't be horrible to people.'" In this reading, imagining enhanced both reflection and retention. By visualizing the saying's images, Lisa came to an understanding of the saying which she then articulated as an abstract command. Her visualizations also functioned as a hook into her memory which may in turn augment her retention of the import of the saying.

The readers' imaginings were selective and rarely reproduced the entirety of a passage. Jeremy specifically visualized the actions in the Luke 5:17–26 story of the Healing of the Paralyzed Man: "I imagined snippets of it, like him being lowered down and Jesus healing him. Then people crowding round to see what was going on." Other readers described their visualizations as "vague" and "not detailed." Green's distinction between the function of an image versus the function of a picture is helpful for understanding the role of this selectivity. Green states: "A picture reproduces; an image exemplifies. An image is a picture in which nonessential features have been suppressed and essential ones highlighted. A picture . . . represents features indiscriminately; an image . . . represents selectively."[25] The readers, comparably, used their imaginations to form the images of a story which enabled them to understand that story, not to represent the story comprehensively.

---

24. Parsons, *Luke*, 27.
25. Green, *Imagining God*, 93.

The Contents Triad: Setting, Characters, and Action

As I have already suggested, the contents of Luke were key stimuli for the readers' imaginations. Tannehill makes the useful point that in Luke "what is said" leads the reader "to construct an imaginative scene, and this imaginative scene is able to provoke imaginative thought on a particular issue or situation highlighted in the scene."[26] The text comes first and the imaginative thought grows out of interaction with the text. In the case of my study, the contents of Luke guided the readers' imagination: the imagination was not used for fanciful flights away from the text but rather to bring its contents into focus. The readers treated these contents as literal in the literary sense, or, as Martin refers to it, the "narrative sense":[27] the concrete contents of Luke were the foci of their engagement with the narrative. The findings indicate that the contents that were the main foci of the readers' imaginings were its settings, characters, and actions. I discuss each of these components in turn.

Setting: "There was a Street"

The readers' imaginative thinking often fleshed out Luke's settings, giving the narrative world spatial dimensions. A number of the readings adopted settings virtually wholesale from the primary world. Stephanie visualized a number of Luke's stories in her church, a setting which she associated with the Gospel. Lucy described how she usually set all of the stories she read in houses with which she was familiar. Personal experience was often paramount as a source for the imagined settings. The Luke 5:1–11 story of the Disciples Fishing is accompanied by a line drawing in the GNB, yet Fishy rejected this picture and fleshed out the setting with details from his own experience: "You imagine your own lake, your own boat, and your own people. They usually end up being related to something you've seen before." His reading treated the line drawing as suggestive rather than determinative.

Other readings stuck closely to the descriptions of the settings in Luke but added precision to those descriptions. This precision often had interpretive significance. In the Luke 18:35–43 story of the Healing of the Blind Beggar, the scene is set in the GNB by the statement: "As Jesus was coming near Jericho, there was a blind man sitting by the road, begging." Jake's imaginative reading revealed his understanding of the beggar's plight: "There was a

---

26. Tannehill, "Freedom and Responsibility," 267.

27. Martin, *Pedagogy of the Bible*, 53. See also my discussion in chapter 4 under "Reading Literally."

beggar sitting facing a wall in a crowded street." This reading placed the man in a humble and potentially humiliating position, facing a wall, a posture that may also symbolize the impenetrability of his blindness. A number of scholars highlight the shame and poverty of this beggar,[28] a status which finds effective visual expression in the hopelessness of sitting stationary before a wall in the midst of a faceless crowd on a busy thoroughfare.

In many of the readings, the imagined settings blended the text's specifications with details from the reader's experience. This may be seen in Jenny's description of the setting of the Luke 8:49–56 story of the Healing of Jairus' Daughter: "There was a street, then you went into this house, and then there was a bed made of hay with a brown blanket on it." Neither the bed nor the blanket is present in the passage. Yet Jenny's visualization was text-directed for Jesus declares in verse 52 that the girl was sleeping, an activity that a twenty-first-century British teenager would normally associate with a bed. Jenny envisaged the bed as made of hay rather than a mattress, perhaps deriving these details from her previous encounters with visual depictions of the Luke 2 manger scene.

Jenny's imagined setting was interpretive, gradually narrowing the focus of the scene from a street, to a house, to a bed, and thus to the bed's occupant. The young girl was the central character in her reading, an interpretation which aligns with Johnson's description of the girl as one of the two "daughters" at the center of the overall passage (Luke 8:40–56). This is *contra* Tannehill who treats Jairus, rather than his daughter, as a key character.[29]

The readings tended to maintain the background status of Luke's settings and neither developed the settings fully, nor treated them as a central focus. Fishy emphasized that he imagined only the necessary details of the settings: "You think of, say, on the street, but you don't actually think of what the houses look like." Nonetheless he thought that establishing the setting was essential: "Those things you don't actually need, you put in the background—you don't take much notice. But they have to be there." Although Fishy's reading did not express a reason for needing a setting, Jake explained that establishing the setting helped him to contextualize the story, which in turn enabled him both to make sense of and to remember what he read.

---

28. Johnson, *Luke*, 283, 287; Green, *Luke*, 662–63.
29. Johnson, *Luke*, 142–43; Tannehill, *Luke*, 148–51.

Characters: "Jesus was Played by this Guy"

One of the readers' key means of engaging with Luke was through its characters. I will discuss character empathy in the next chapter, and focus here only upon how the readers formed ideas and images of the characters. As with the settings, a number of the readings utilized external sources. Vanessa indicated that she peopled Luke with characters from other books that she thought were similar in some way to the characters in Luke. B.C., in comparison, treated the narrative as a type of script and placed himself in the role of a casting director: "I read it like a play. I imagined that Jesus was being played by this guy." B.C.'s reading constructed the characters in Luke out of external sources. For Jesus, B.C. combined four familiar characters: "I put Santa Claus and a preacher together, with some other stuff to make Jesus. There was a bit of a story writer, like Antony Horowitz. And a hero because he dies to save everyone else." Notice that each external source expresses a facet of Jesus' mission: he brings good to those he meets, teaches persuasively, tells stories, and dies self-sacrificially.

More commonly, the readings constructed characters based on the characters' actions and attitudes in the narrative. Allie's creative reading of the Luke 9:37–43 story of the Healing of the Demon-Possessed Boy provides an example. In the GNB, the boy's father describes the effect of the boy's possession: "A spirit attacks him with a sudden shout and throws him into a fit, so that he foams at the mouth." When Jesus descends the Mount of Transfiguration, he says to the father: "Bring your son here." The narrator then states: "As the boy was coming, the demon knocked him to the ground and threw him into a fit."

Note the development of these characters in Allie's reading, which began:

> Jesus is on a hill and then the dude comes up and he's dragging the boy. The boy's quite wild and savage, a bit like a dog, and he's foaming at the mouth. His eyes are rolling and then he goes stiff. He's having a fit. Then Jesus tries and saves him.

The reading's descriptions of Jesus, the boy, and the father began with the text and developed from there. The story does not state how the father responded to Jesus' command, but according to the reading he dragged his son to Jesus. The reading endowed the boy with characteristics that could be attributed to demon possession: he behaved like a savage dog, his eyes rolled in his head, and he went stiff. All of these characterizations conform to the rudiments of the text so that Allie's reading fleshed out the story. Joel Green believes that the boy's "list of symptoms elicits pathos from the reader."[30] Allie's reading certainly displayed her awareness of the plight of the boy, but it also added a layer of affliction that expressed the horror of demonic possession.

Allie's reading went on to develop the exorcism. The narrator does not describe the exorcism, but merely asserts its occurrence: "Jesus gave a command to the evil spirit, healed the boy, and gave him back to his father." At this point Allie's reading focused on the demon, describing it as a little monster without a body but taking the form of a spirit. This monster-spirit "comes out [the boy's] ear. A big hole appears in the ground, and the spirit gets sucked down into the ground." The story thus became a full scene that specified how the demon left the boy and where it went afterwards. The reader's horror of the demon appeared to lead her to give the demon more attention than is sanctioned by the text. Her reading ensured that not only the boy, but also the demon had closure, in the latter case imprisonment underground where he could do no further harm.

"Catching All the Action"

When the readers recounted parts of the narrative in the interviews, they invariably did so by highlighting the action. For them the narrative was not static. Fowler points out that third-person biblical narration, because it effaces the narrator, leads readers to "get caught up in the story" so that they "visualize the action taking place now, before [their] eyes, in a direct, unmediated way."[31] Echoing Fowler's point, the readings often treated action as the heart of Luke's stories. Zak asserted that he imagined in order to "catch all the action." The readers' imaginings rendered the narrative as a series of related actions, not unlike a film sequence or comic strip. Robyn described her focus on the action using film discourse: "I imagine, like, I just see the people doing it when I read. It's like a little video in my head."

Action was so fundamental to the readers' understanding of the narrative that their readings sometimes rendered passages in terms of action, regardless of how the passages are presented in the story world. This can be seen in Tarquin's reading of the Luke 22:7–13 story of Jesus' Disciples Preparing for the Passover, a story he claimed he had never seen visually depicted:

> So I imagined [Jesus] outside the city walls, and him with his disciples, and him telling them. You imagine them going into

---

30. Green, *Luke*, 387.
31. Fowler, *Let the Reader Understand*, 65.

the city and you can see them walking down the street. You see someone with the water and then they follow him into the house, upstairs, and get the meal ready.

Notice that Tarquin's account is a series of connected actions, reducing the story to plot. He imagined both the setting and action. But what is remarkable here is that, while the Lukan account consists primarily of dialogue, what Tarquin imagined were the actions that took place as a result of this dialogue.

In Tarquin's reading, the enactment of Jesus' instructions became the events of the story. The GNB merely summarizes the disciples' actions as: "They went off and found everything just as Jesus had told them, and they prepared the Passover meal" (Luke 22:13). By transforming Jesus' instructions into action, Tarquin could "see" what was happening in the episode. As a result, he appeared to experience the story as a series of events. This re-configuration of the passage suggests that child readers may use plot as a framework for interpreting a narrative: what happens guides their interpretation of a story.

Remembering Luke

In the previous section, I examined how the readers imagined the spatially absent contents of Luke. Here I take up the topic of temporal absence and discuss the contribution of the readers' memories to their readings. Garrett Green helpfully clarifies the connection between memory and imagination: "There are two chief modes of physical nonpresence, temporal and spatial . . . The clearest case of *temporal* absence is past reality . . . and it has long been recognized . . . that memory requires an act of imagination."[32] If the imagination makes present that which is absent and if memories are retainers of experiences that are temporally absent, then the imagination may recall and make use of memories.

The findings of this study indicate that the readers' memories served as fuel for their imagination. Their readings were not solely the product of their encounter with Luke as generated by the empirical research, since none of the participants approached Luke as virgin readers. Most of the interviewees attend church regularly and even the few who do not have been exposed to the Bible through occasional church services, school, visual media, and the text's ubiquitous, albeit caricatured, presence in Western culture. An

---

32. Green, *Imagining God*, 64; italics in the original.

important consequence of this previous exposure was that a version of the narrative world already existed in the readers' memories.

I discuss here two aspects of the connection between imagination and memory that were evident in the findings. First I consider the contribution of the readers' memories to their readings of Luke. Then I investigate how the readers negotiated the differences between their memories and the text.

"I Remember That"

The readers' previous encounters with Luke's narrative world, no matter how incomplete or caricatured, functioned as the starting point from which they built their developing understanding of that world. Elaine, a churched-child who had considerable exposure to the Bible from early childhood, called her experience of reading Luke a "remembering." When asked if she saw the story happening in her imagination as she was reading, she replied: "It was more like a memory." She described her visualization of the landscape of Luke as "collage-style," put together from images generated through her exposure to all four Gospels, children's bibles, visual media, and church teaching. Images from these sources no doubt lodged in her mind at an early age so that she experienced them as memories.

This finding aligns with Meek's point that children's readings of a text may develop gradually, building upon their exposure to an inter-text of oral and written media.[33] The images already established in the readers' memories appeared to take priority, so that subsequent encounters with the biblical narrative served as a development of those images. Elaine said of reading Luke: "It's not as if I had to make up the whole thing. I did picture it happening, but I had already pictured it happening. So it was more like, 'Oh yes. This is what is happening. I remember that.'" Although her dialogue with Luke at times fleshed out, altered, or even dismantled her previous view of the narrative world, it did so with reference to her established memories.

For Elaine, this "remembering" was a common reading experience: "Once I've pictured something in a book, if I come back years later and revisit that book, I'll get the same image." Imagining a narrative world may have more than a temporary impact if the images lodge in the reader's memory and become part of her or his on-going experience of that narrative. What is more, as memories, these images have the potential to permeate beyond the confines of experience of the narrative world and to become part of the reader's more general thought process.

---

33. Meek, *How Texts Teach*, 22; see my discussion in chapter 3 under "Children Reading Narrative."

Reading Luke appeared at times to refine the readers' memories. Since none of the participants had read the entirety of Luke prior to the interview, they repeatedly discovered that the memories they connected with Luke were under-developed relative to the narrative world. Elaine found that the Gospel was "more precise than what I had in my head." Her experience of Luke was of reading something familiar but at the same time needing to fill in the details. Fishy found that his memories augmented his ability to make sense of the narrative while also needing to be developed: "I think it helps if you've heard [the Lukan stories] before, because then you understand them better. Cause the first time you hear it, you get the big things. Then when you hear it more, you notice more of the little things." Reading Luke stimulated both of these readers to develop their mental images of Luke, leading to a clearer view of the narrative world. Their memories were tantamount to a big but somewhat vague canvas upon which the readers located their growing understanding of the text.

On the other hand, a number of the readers indicated that they skimmed over the familiar parts of Luke. Rather than developing their extant memories, these readers appeared to use their reading to extend their view of Luke's world into new areas. Jeremy compared his engagement with familiar versus unfamiliar parables: "You don't need to really put yourself in some of the parables that you might have already heard. Whereas there are others where you've got to try and think." For such readers, it was the unfamiliar parts of Luke that stimulated their imaginative experience, building new memories to store alongside of the old. Negative memories occasionally prejudiced readers against a familiar story. Kit declared that his church's repeated teaching on the Luke 2:40–52 story of the Boy Jesus in the Temple "made me really not like it."

Sometimes the readers' memories served as a guide for generating new images. Jake described how he imagined the unfamiliar parts of Luke using his memories: "I remember scenes of Jesus healing and I used that as a template to how I imagined [an unfamiliar healing] scene." This finding substantiates that of Fry, who found that child readers draw upon remembered images to aid their visualization of a story.[34] Jake appeared to expect the unfamiliar stories to cohere with his extant view of the narrative world, prompting him to use images from familiar stories to construct images for unfamiliar stories. The result was further reinforcement of his view of the narrative world and potentially the impeding of the development of this view. The figure Jake saw in the carpet, while becoming clearer, maintained its already-established shape.

---

34. Fry, *Children Talk about Books*, 66.

"It Changed My Understanding"

Invariably, some of the contents of Luke ran counter to the readers' memories. The readers negotiated these differences in a variety of ways: some succumbed to cognitive dissonance; some retained their already established view of the narrative world; but many responded with further reflection upon the narrative. I look at each of these in turn.

Internal conflict resulted when the readers could not reconcile the contents of Luke with their extant view of its world. Elaine struggled with the Luke 12:49–53 saying that Jesus Will Cause Division for it seemed to counter her established view of Jesus as a peacemaker: "If Jesus has come to divide, isn't that a bad thing? I was a bit bewildered." The resulting confusion prevented Elaine from reflecting further on this saying, although she did conclude that "all those theologian people seem to be thinking that Jesus is a good person so it must mean something good, otherwise they would have been a bit worried too." Unable to resolve the conflict, this young reader looked to those whom she deemed more competent than herself at reading the text for a model of response. Note that her aim was not to ask for their assistance, but rather to gain assurance that it was possible to resolve the dissonance.

Previous exposure to depictions of the narrative world sometimes proved more powerful than engagement with the text. Percy had seen the *Miracle Maker* film which depicts Jesus carrying his own cross. The GNB, in contrast, includes a picture of the cross being carried by Simon of Cyrene, corroborating the text at Luke 23:26. When he looked at the GNB picture, Percy found that his "mental image changed into that full cross carried by Simon. But looking back on [my reading], I actually imagined Jesus with the cross bar, carrying it." Despite the influence of the GNB picture and text, Percy's image of this scene remained rooted in his established memory of Jesus carrying the cross. His reading reconciled the collision between text and memory in favor of the memory.

On the other hand, when a reader re-evaluated an established memory of the narrative world, this was often directly connected to a new understanding of that world. Trevor also experienced a conflict between memory and narrative over Jesus' walk to Golgotha. He too had seen the *Miracle Maker* film, but the difference between the text and his memory led Trevor to rethink his understanding of Jesus' death:

> It completely changed my understanding of the walk up to the cross. I'd always thought Jesus carried it up on his back. But actually it was this other guy who did it for him. It just really, really

shook me. I found it hard to imagine how Jesus would have reacted to it, having someone else carrying his cross up for him.

Altering his image of the story had an emotional impact on Trevor because of its implications for his beliefs about Jesus. Earlier in the interview, Trevor described the view of Jesus that he brought to the text: Jesus was a perfect person who provided an untarnished model to which a teenage boy could not attain. This reader was surprised to discover that Luke's portrayal of Jesus, including this scene with the cross, did not support his previous view. Trevor thought that a perfect, self-sufficient Jesus should be able to manage his own cross. A Jesus who needs someone else to carry his cross is a Jesus in need of others, a Jesus who displays real humanity. The alteration in Trevor's image of Jesus had a theological impact upon his already developing Christology.

The Imagination as the Organ of Meaning

Imaginative reading had implications for how the readers understood Luke. This was made clear to me during one of the early interviews, when Fishy and I were discussing how he imagined Luke. Following a brief pause in our conversation he asserted, unsolicited, "It does help." "What helps?" I responded, a little lost. He answered: "It helps to understand the thing—imagining it." I had been seeking to understand *how* he imagined, but Fishy had changed topics to *why* he imagined. This made me sit up. Here was an area I had not, at that point, even begun to explore.

If, as Fishy so cogently explained, one of the imagination's roles in the text-reader dialogue is to enable the reader to understand the world of the text, then we have ventured into the field of interpretation and meaning. A number of other readers made similar assertions and I followed up the idea in the subsequent interviews and the focus groups. In the second RVG, a girl stated that "imagining helps you to understand the story." Three-quarters of this group raised their hands to say they agreed with her statement. On the RVG response sheet, one of the written responses to the Luke 6:43–45 Tree and Fruit saying was: "Imagining this passage helps me to work out what it means." Two-thirds of the total RVG participants either agreed or strongly agreed with this statement.[35] Based on these findings, a key function of the imagination in reading seemed to be enabling the readers to make sense of the text.

---

35. For the remaining third, it was unclear from the response sheets whether the participants imagined but were unable to work out a meaning for the saying, or whether they did not imagine at all.

The importance of imaginative thinking for working out meaning may be clearer if it is considered from a different angle. Numerous theorists posit the imagination as the source of creative writing[36] and Lewis specifies that the "imagination is the organ of meaning. Imagination, producing new metaphors and revivifying old, is not the cause of truth, but its condition."[37] Lewis's concern is with the construction of metaphors as a way of enabling thinking; he argues that metaphors are the means by which we understand concepts.[38] If, as Lewis argues, conveyances of meaning such as metaphors are created through the imagination, then the imagination may also play a role in interpreting these conveyances. In short, not only communicating meaning (which is the focus of Lewis's discussion) but also determining it (which is the focus of mine), requires the imagination.

Imagining allowed the readers to move beyond the limits of semantics in their pursuit of meaning, since the imagination's method of reasoning is associative and sensory. Hannah C. explained how this worked for her: "I read it. Then after a while I imagine it. Instead of looking at the words I imagine it in my head and it's a bit clearer to me when I do that." This reader's imagination brought Luke's contents into focus and pondered those contents by mentally translating the words into images and ideas. Notice that what Hannah C. was striving to do was to understand Luke, not to create an imaginary scenario separate from it.

The readings suggested that the readers used their imagination to make sense of Luke in two slightly different ways, depending upon the literary genre. For Luke's metaphoric teaching, the readers used the images in the text to work out the sense of the text. For the parables and the micronarratives, meaning derived from imagining the actions and development of the characters. I look at each of these in turn.

"Jesus Put These in So It Made More Sense"

The readers appeared so closely to associate imagining with meaning that, for their readings of the metaphoric teaching in Luke, some of them assumed that the purpose of the images was to enhance the accessibility of the text. In order to explain the imagery used in the Luke 6:43-45 Tree and Fruit saying, Zak stated that:

36. This is particularly a theme of the Romantics; see especially Coleridge, *Biographia Literaria*. See also: Searle, *The Eyes of Your Heart*, 106; Gerrig, *Experiencing Narrative Worlds*, 122-24.

37. Lewis, "Bluspels and Flalansferes," 265.

38. Ibid., 262.

Jesus put these [images] in so it made more sense. Cause if he just said, "You're a bad person. You do bad things. You'll get bad things back if you do"—it would be hard to imagine. But I think he makes it into something that people can easily imagine.

This reading virtually equates imagining with the process of interpreting the text. Zak appeared to prefer to think about the abstract through the concrete, reflecting the findings of Piaget that children use tangible objects to think about the world.[39]

This process of interpretation usually began with the contemplation of the images in Luke and a single metaphoric image often generated multiple readings. In her work on the imagination, Alison Searle helpfully explains the source of this diversity by observing that metaphors are multivalent; metaphors are not simply a figurative alternative to a literal statement.[40] Metaphors open up meaning rather than pinning it down, with the result that the interpretation of a metaphoric image may go in a variety of directions.

Returning to Luke 6:43–45 as an example, the image of the heart in that saying shaped the readers' interpretation of the second half of the saying. A number of the readings concentrated on the heart in action: one reader imagined "a heart and hearing what's coming out—all the bad thoughts and good thoughts are coming out and being spoken." Other readings highlighted the hidden location of the heart: "It doesn't matter what's on the outside [i.e. your physical appearance]. It's what your heart is full of and what's actually underneath that matters." One reader pretended to hold a real human heart, complete with the requisite squeamishness, while observing, "it all depends what your heart is made of. What your heart is made of is what your words are made of." The emphasis of each of these readings is different, yet these differences reflect the richness of the metaphor. The heart's activity, its location, and its substance are all potential interpretive foci, each providing a window onto the sense of the text.

An issue here is the potential for each reader simply to project her or his own idea of "heart" onto the text. This would be the case if the text did not have input into the interpretive process. In his discussion of imaginative readings of the Bible, Stephen Chapman helpfully distinguishes between the use of the imagination as "a launching pad for any kind of interpretive 'what-if'" which leads the reader away from the text, and the use of the imagination to provide attentiveness to the text, thus orientating the reader

---

39. See my discussion of Piaget in chapter 3 under "Childhood Development."
40. Searle, *The Eyes of Your Heart*, 169.

towards the text.[41] Chapman holds that attentive imaginative reading uses the text as "a crucial criterion for a determination of its content."[42] He does not explicate how such an interpretive method might proceed; however, his suggestion that text-orientated imagining may lead the reader towards the text aptly describes the orientation of many of the children's readings. Both the readers and the text were parties in the process, as the readers sought to understand the text through the images it conveyed.

"I Picture What's Happening"

While imaginative thinking about Luke's metaphoric teaching tended to focus on static images, for Luke's micro-narratives and parables, this thinking tended to focus upon the characters and action. Zak described how he imagined the plot-driven parts of the narrative: "Usually when I read, I read the description of what's happening and then I picture that. After that, I realize what're the actions that are going on." This reading's "realization" refers to the reader's understanding of the development of the plot. The reader envisaged the actions in Luke in order to work out the meaning of the narrative events.

Because the imagination as a reading strategy focuses upon the concrete contents of the text, the readers' interpretations were often an articulation of the significance of those contents. Elaine's reading of the opening section of the Luke 5:17–26 story of the Paralyzed Man provides an example. This reader imagined the initial actions in the story: the man's friends "are so desperate to get to Jesus that they cut a big hole in someone's ceiling." The reader found these actions "funny" and declared, "I wanted to laugh." She thought that the friends' actions revealed their determination to get to Jesus, but she also pointed out the outrageousness of cutting a hole in the roof of a house in order to enter that house.

This story was one of the most popular in the Gospel: numerous readers initiated conversation about it in the interviews. The paralyzed man's friends initiate the sequence of events in verse 18. In the GNB, the verse begins: "Some men came carrying . . ." This statement evoked the effect of the Greek which begins the verse with: "and behold men . . ." Over and over the readings began with the friends as the readers "beheld" the friends' actions in their imaginations. Both the wrecking of the roof and the unexpected appearance of the paralyzed man from above Jesus' head attracted the readers to this story, positioning them to interpret these contents. Elaine

41. Chapman, "Imaginative Readings," 412–13.
42. Ibid., 425.

specifically asserted that she "liked" the story due to the determination of the friends which, according to verse 20, functions as a display of their faith. Thus in her reading, faith became associated with determination and even outrageous action.

Unlike Elaine's reading, the actions of the friends receive minimal attention from the commentators. Numerous scholars discuss the role of faith in the story, taking their cue from the text, but some, such as Johnson and Nolland, manage to do so without mentioning the friends.[43] A few commentators even ignore the friends' actions, in verse 19, in favor of trying to explain the nature of the "tiles" of the roof.[44] Other scholars acknowledge the role of the friends, but limit their discussion to a brief synopsis: Craddock calls the friends' actions "very dramatic and most unusual"[45] and Marshall believes that their behavior displays "perseverance and ingenuity."[46] Only Tannehill ponders the friends' conduct. He calls their action "bold" and indicates that it demonstrates "faith." What is more, he draws a connection between their action and the meaning of faith: this story reveals that faith "means trusting that God can help through Jesus and doing all that is necessary to secure that help."[47]

Like Tannehill, Elaine's perceptive reading pointed to how the friends' conduct embodied faith. But unlike Tannehill or indeed any of the other scholars discussed here, her reading also expressed a clear awareness of the humorousness of that conduct and revealed the power of the friends' actions to transform the words on the page into an event that pulls the reader into the story world. It is worth noting that her interpretive strategy may be labelled literal, since she used the concrete elements of the story to make sense of the story—her close reading of the conduct of the friends led to her interpretation of that conduct. At no point did she assess the story for its historical viability. Rather, her concern was with making sense of the narrative.

Summary

This chapter has explored some of the chief aspects of the imagination as a reading strategy, based on the study's findings. By imagining the contents of Luke, the readers participated in the construction of its narrative world in

43. Johnson, *Luke*, 93, 95; Nolland, *Luke 1—9:20*, 235.
44. Evans, *Saint Luke*, 301; Morris, *Luke*, 129; Nolland, *Luke 1—9:20*, 234–35.
45. Craddock, *Luke*, 75.
46. Marshall, *Gospel of Luke*, 213.
47. Tannehill, *Luke*, 105–6.

dialogue with the text. This imagining also enabled them to make sense of the narrative world. They used their imaginations to read Luke literally—that is to interpret Luke's narrative world through its contents. What the readers knew about Luke was at least partially a product of how they imagined it and they retained this understanding through the memories created by their imaginative engagement. This imaginative engagement generated an experience that could potentially become part of the readers' own world.

The imagination functioned as an important instrument in the readers' participatory reading toolkit. In the next chapter, I examine another key tool: empathy.

Chapter 9

Reading through Empathy

Jenny: I read because of "affection for the characters. I want to find out what happens to them."

Hannah C.: "The way that [the characters] are acting and how they are feeling creates an image of the person."

Introduction

The interview script included a number of questions about the readers' views of the characters in Luke, but the readers discussed the characters repeatedly throughout the interviews in response to other questions as well. Marguerat and Bourquin assert that "characters are all gates by which the reader can enter the world of the narrative."[1] It soon became evident that the characters were indeed one of the child readers' key entry points into the world of Luke, and that the readers made sense of that world at least partially via its characters.

The children's approach to Luke's characters may be referred to as empathetic reading. Emotive language frequently surfaced in the interview discussions about the characters. In their quest to work out what drove the characters' conduct, the readers attributed emotions, motives, and attitudes to the characters. It could be said, with reference to E. M. Forster's designations of flat versus round characters,[2] that one of the readers' assumed roles was to add emotional depth to flat characters, and another assumed role was to determine motives and attitudes for rounded characters when the characters' conduct appeared to be ambiguous.

To follow up on the interview findings, I tested for empathetic reading in the RVGs using the Luke 10:38–42 story of Mary and Martha. Using only

1. Marguerat and Bourquin, *How to Read*, 65.
2. Forster, *Aspects of the Novel*, 67–78.

one passage limited the results, which may be relevant only to this story. Nonetheless the results appeared to confirm the findings of the interviews. After hearing this story, 81% of the respondents claimed to imagine how Martha felt, suggesting that affect contributed to their interpretation. The participants also identified in some way with the characters, with 50% claiming to relate to Mary and 33% claiming to relate to Martha. Less than 5% claimed that they did not relate to any of the characters in this story.[3] The latter result may indicate that this small percentage of respondents did not read empathetically, or it may merely show that they did not or could not empathize with any of the story's three characters. Overall the RVG findings point to a strong tendency towards empathetic reading among the participants.

This chapter explores the role of empathy in the children's readings. I begin by discussing the main characteristics of empathy that were evident in the readings. Next I discuss the relationship between empathy and perspective, and then I look at the types of relational bonds formed by the readers with the characters. I conclude by probing how empathy was used by the readers to work out the sense of the text.

The Characteristics of Empathy

When I asked Stephanie about the Luke 14:15–24 parable of the Great Feast, she immediately began to talk about the host: "I felt sorry for the person who was making the feast. It was like they're all a bit arrogant and think they'll get invited loads more times so they can just not come to this one." This reader did not explain her view of the parable by discussing its events. Instead, she focused upon its characters. Her approach did not leave her detached from the story. Instead, she evaluated the characters as if they were people with whom she was familiar and she expressed feelings of compassion for the host and an aversion to the conceit of the guests.

Stephanie's reading of this parable provides a good example of the effect of empathy as a reading strategy. But before going further, I need to clarify my use of the term empathy.

Defining Empathy

In her landmark empirical research on empathy and the novel, Suzanne Keen aims "to take seriously" the readings of the "average reader" and

---

3. See Table 6 in chapter 6 for a full breakdown of the results.

distinguishes the experience of such readers from that of critics, classifying them into two categories: empathetic reading and analytical reading, respectively.[4] Keen believes that empathy explains some of the responses to literature that have been experienced by readers but neglected by scholars. Her categorization echoes Lewis's looking *along* versus looking *at* analogy, while not, within the context of this discussion, being identical to it since she narrows all participation in a narrative world to empathy.

Keen defines empathy broadly as the act of "feeling *with* another person" or character.[5] Empathy, at heart, is an emotion-based reading of the text. My study's findings suggest that this "feeling with" depended upon the reader attributing an emotion, whether positive or negative, to a particular character or narrative scenario. The source of this attribution was usually the reader's recognition of an emotion operative in the text, or the reader's own emotive response to the situation presented in the text. Stephanie, for instance, responded to the rejection of the host in the parable with a feeling of compassion.

The emotions generated by empathy were part of the epistemological package that comprised how the readers *knew* Luke: what the readers knew had affective dimensions. On the most basic level, empathy drew the readers into the narrative world by adding an emotive layer to their reading experience, making it more holistic. Oatley asserts that emotion "is that process in life by which events become meaningful to us."[6] The readers repeatedly expressed their interest in the emotional effects of Luke's stories: humor, sympathy, excitement, horror, sadness, frustration, and elation were all discussed in the readings.

It is important to add that empathy also incorporates cognitive elements. Keen indicates that, "[m]emory, experience, and the capacity to take another's perspective (all matters traditionally considered cognitive) have roles in empathy."[7] The children's empathetic readings usually developed in tandem with their cognitive engagement with the text. Stephanie evaluated the conduct of the guests in the parable and labelled them as arrogant due to their refusal of the host's invitation.

Empathy is not the same as sympathy.[8] Empathy is experiential and concerned with projecting into another person's situation in order to un-

---

4. Keen, *Empathy*, x.

5. Ibid., 45, xxi; italics in the original.

6. Oatley, *Such Stuff as Dreams*, 115; see also my discussion in chapter 3 under "Children Reading Narrative."

7. Keen, *Empathy*, 27.

8. This is *contra* Rosenblatt who uses the two terms interchangeably. See Rosenblatt, *Literature as Exploration*, 37.

derstand that situation. Sympathy, in contrast, means feeling in support of another person.[9] Sympathy is an expression of compassion for another person's situation and does not necessarily entail personal experience of that situation. Sympathy is narrower than empathy and is usually elicited in response to the problems of others while empathy may be relevant to any scenario.[10]

Empathy is relational and connects the reader to the world of the text. This connection usually occurs through a character. Mikkelsen's definition of empathy emphasizes this relational aspect: empathy is "[d]iscovering something about a character that connects to the reader's own life; a natural ability readers have to understand what others are feeling or experiencing that draws them into [the] text."[11] Stephanie's response of compassion to the host aligned her with him, and against the guests.

The readers' interpretations of Luke were at least partially contingent upon the characters with whom they empathized. This finding reflects that of Powell, who, in his survey of clergy and laity readings of the Gospels, found that these two groups of readers tended to empathize with different characters in the same passage and produced divergent readings as a consequence.[12] Stephanie's empathetic responses to the host and against the guests were in alignment with the perspective in the text and opened her up, at least theoretically, to the parable's representation of God.

To summarize, empathy is an affective tool with cognitive features. For the purposes of this study, I define empathy as:

> The affective reading of a character or situation that connects
> the reader experientially to the narrative world.

Since affect is a personal response, it augments the reader's participation in the reading dialogue.

Empathy and the Imagination

I need to address briefly the relationship between empathy and the imagination as reading strategies. My findings indicate that, in the context of this study, these two reading strategies were often used in close conjunction. A key difference was their subject matter: the readers appeared to use

---

9. Keen, *Empathy*, 4–5.

10. Diffen, "Empathy versus Sympathy."

11. Mikkelsen, *Powerful Magic*, 4; Mikkelsen refers to this as "empathetic/personal literacy."

12. Powell, *Chasing the Eastern Star*, 38–39.

empathetic reading with the characters in Luke and imaginative reading with the all of the contents of the text including the characters. The question, then, is how did these two reading strategies influence each other with reference to characters?

This question is worth raising since a number of scholars either do not distinguish between the two reading strategies or else make one subsidiary to the other. Keen subsumes the imagination under empathetic reading, treating the imagination as a tool of empathy rather than as a partner in the reading process.[13] Other scholars take the opposite approach and subsume empathy under the imagination. McIntyre for example discusses empathy as a product of the imagination,[14] while Hart describes the empathetic construction of a character as a task of the imagination.[15]

It is not necessary for the purposes of this study to unravel the relationship between empathy and the imagination. But it is worth noting that the findings suggest that there was not a clear hierarchy in which one was secondary to the other. At times, a reader's empathy for a character appeared to stimulate imagining. Hannah C. believed that her understanding of the characters' conduct and emotions in Luke led to her visualization of these characters: "The way that they're acting and how they are feeling creates an image of the person." For the Luke 8:42–48 story of the Bleeding Woman, Hannah C. thought that her image of the woman grew directly out of the character's attitude: "The personality creates an image. And for the woman, I imagined her—like it says she's desperate and really wants healing." She accordingly visualized the woman as small, old, frowning, and "in a really big hurry." Here, empathy provided insight into the nature of a character, and fueled the reader's imagination.

In other readings, imagining a character appeared to stimulate empathy. In Lisa's reading of the Luke 18:31–34 story in which Jesus Predicts his Death, she imagined a few specific elements of the story and used that to work out the disciples' reaction. She initially envisaged Jesus "standing up and speaking to them all." Lisa noted that the disciples did not question Jesus and visualized them in confusion thinking, "what?" and then "oh well," as they capitulated to their ignorance. Lisa's imagining led her to contemplate the disciples' perplexed but quiescent response, and she concluded that they were naïve and somewhat oblivious characters.

My analysis of the readings led me to conclude that empathy and the imagination were usually inextricably intertwined. It is perhaps best to view

---

13. For example Keen, *Empathy*, vii, 27–28, 99.
14. McIntyre, *Faith Theology and Imagination*, 74.
15. Hart, "Imagination and Responsible Reading," 323.

empathy and the imagination as complementary tools in the readers' armory of reading strategies. Both served the common cause of participation in the narrative world.

Empathy and Perspective

It is important to stress that the readers' empathetic reading strategy was not imposed upon the text. Luke appeared to invite it. The Gospel of Luke makes space for empathetic reading by offering only occasional insights into the thought world of its characters. As is often observed by scholars, the synoptic Gospels, like ancient narratives in general, "reveal little information about inward motivations" so that a character's internal motives must be discerned via their "external situations."[16] Alter, in his discussion of the Hebrew Bible, suggests that a key way of working out the internal world of biblical characters is through their speech and actions. He makes the useful point that the biblical reticence about the characters' internal world opens the door to a wide variety of interpretations.[17] Many of the child readers used empathy to walk through that door. For just a few of the child readers, this absence of information about the characters' internal motives had the opposite effect and discouraged empathetic reading.

The findings of this study suggest that a key discourse device, perspective, also opened the door to empathy. Luke's use of perspective seemed repeatedly both to elicit and to guide empathetic reading. While the readers were not beholden to the perspectives provided by the text, many of them aligned with these perspectives or even devised a perspective of their own which generated empathy. This section looks at the relationship between empathy and perspective using two of the categories established in chapter 7 under my discussion of perspective: seeing with the narratee and seeing with a character. I also consider what happened when a character's perspective was not provided by the text but was assumed by a reader.

Empathy and the Narratee

As discussed in chapter 7, the narratee's perspective positions the reader outside of the narrative world. For Luke's micro-narratives and parables, when the readers aligned with this perspective, their empathy was usually

---

16. Gowler, *Host, Guest, Enemy and Friend*, 312. See also Tannehill, "Freedom and Responsibility," 268, but the point is widely made.
17. Alter, *The Art of Biblical Narrative*, 114, 119.

elicited through observations about the situation of a character. The readers remained external to the story and tended to interpret the character's situation through an analogy or comparison with the reader's world.

Sophie M. built her reading of the parable of the Good Samaritan in Luke 10:25–37 around a personal comparison with the beaten man. She compared his plight to an experience she had when her wrist was broken: "My bag dropped off my back as I was walking to school and I couldn't get it back on with my broken wrist. And the priest, who was my next door neighbor, walked past me and he didn't stop to help." Sophie M. stated that her experience helped her to make sense of the parable.

While Sophie M. used her own experience to work out the meaning of the parable, the parable also led her to reflect back on that experience: "I wouldn't have cared who helped me get the bag back on my back, but you think that a priest is a good person who would help me." Her personal reflection connected with the parable's reversal of expectations about neighborliness. Sophie M.'s reading foregrounds what Johnson considers one of the shocks in the parable: the frustration and disappointment generated by a religious leader esteemed for his "place in the people and dedicated to holiness before the Lord" not even stopping to look.[18] The reader forged an empathetic bond with the beaten man around their common experience of being disregarded.

As I discussed in chapter 7, Luke's teaching sections use second person pronouns, thereby aligning the narratee and the reader. These sections do not have focal characters and sometimes this lack of characters appeared to impede empathetic reading. A number of readings provided a character for the text by turning the narratee into a character. This character, in turn, elicited the readers' empathy. For instance in the Luke 6:43–45 Tree and Fruit saying, verse 44 in the GNB states that "you do not pick figs from thorn bushes or gather grapes from bramble bushes." Michael interpreted this statement by imagining "somebody trying to pick figs from a thorn bush and grapes from a bramble bush. I imagined them being frustrated trying to get grapes on a bramble bush." The reader felt the frustration of this character and this emotion was part of the interpretive mix.

Many readers assumed the role of the narratee with these passages. For the Tree and Fruit saying, Zak put himself into the scene, alongside other people. He said: "I imagined each one of us are like a plant. If we do good things and think about good things, we produce good harvest. But if you do bad things to people, you won't get good things back." Zak's empathy here is comprehensive and personal. His assumption of the perspective of the

---

18. Johnson, *Luke*, 174–75.

narratee means that he hears Jesus' teaching as directed to himself along with all those who keep company with him.

"I Imagine Myself as Her"

The other main type of perspective in Luke is that of the characters. When the readers assumed the perspective of a character, their empathy with that character appeared to direct their interpretation of a passage. In Kit's reading of the parable of the Rich Man and Lazarus in Luke 16:19–31, Kit worked out the dynamics of the parable by donning the mantle of Abraham, who arbitrates between the two contrasted characters at the heart of the story. Although the parable presents the rich man and Lazarus in parallel, the character voices it includes are those of the rich man and of Abraham. Lazarus is a passive character whom Abraham defends. When asked how he viewed himself relative to the rich man and Lazarus, Kit replied: "I think of myself in between." He was neither poor nor rich, but like Abraham, he defended Lazarus and viewed the parable through that defense.

Accordingly, Kit's reading firmly took the part of the poor. He said of Lazarus: "He was sitting really close to God up there." Tannehill points out that Abraham plays a "prominent role" in this parable, and that the parable demonstrates "God's concern for the poor." [19] Kit's reading echoes that of Tannehill. The reader declared that he liked this parable because "it showed how much God cares for even the nobodies." Tannehill adds that while the parable "may comfort the poor," it is "primarily designed to challenge the rich."[20] Comparatively, Kit concluded that it is harder for the rich to get into heaven because they think, "If I pray to God, I'll lose all my popularity. And I'll lose all my stuff."

Sometimes alignment with a character's perspective led to role-playing by the reader. For the Luke 15:8–10 parable of the Lost Coin, Grace became the searching woman: "When she's on her own I imagine myself as her." The reader experienced the narrative's tension by enacting the actions of the parable: "I imagine myself looking everywhere." Green points out that the parable's description of the woman's search highlights the urgency of that search: "she lights a lamp, sweeps the house, and searches carefully."[21] Grace's reading steeped the situation in emotion. The heightened anxiety of the search paved the way for greater elation at the finding of the coin and Grace expressed excitement at the coin's discovery. Her reading was primar-

---

19. Tannehill, *Luke*, 251–52.
20. Ibid.
21. Green, *Luke*, 576.

ily experiential and included little reflection upon the parable's theological implications. The reader's experience of the story simply pointed towards what the parable suggests about God's search for humanity.

Grace's approach to empathy is *contra* Hart who claims that as "we read, we effectively leave our 'selves' behind in suspended animation and move out to become, in our imagination, someone other than ourselves."[22] Grace's empathy involved the taking of a role but not the full surrender of identity. Her role playing may be more aptly described using Gerrig's performance metaphor of reading:[23] Grace drew on her own experience to live out the character whose position she assumed, much like an actor interpreting and performing a dramatic role.

No Perspective, No Empathy?

The Gospel of Luke, like any narrative, does not provide a perspective at all times for all of its characters. But a lack of perspective did not always equate to an absence of empathy in the readings. Indeed sometimes the readings used empathy to supply an omitted perspective. The readers repeatedly brought up in the interviews, for instance, the absence of the disciples' point of view in many of Luke's micro-narratives.

B.C.'s reading specifically filled in how the disciples might have felt about travelling with Jesus: "Some of the disciples when they were going along were like, {speaking in a whiney voice} 'When are we going to get there? Where are we?' Like kids do." He imagined each disciple carrying a mobile phone and texting Jesus, who eventually became annoyed with their conduct. B.C. determined the disciples' attitude by drawing parallels with his experience of family trips. It is worth noting that he cast Jesus in the parental role while the disciples functioned as children. B.C. aligned himself with the perspective of the disciples and assumed that their response would be similar to his own as a child travelling with his parents.

On the other hand, the text's omission of a character's perspective sometimes appeared to block empathy. Robyn found that Luke's paucity of details about the disciples inhibited her empathy: "I just didn't engage, because I didn't know what they were." She felt that the text "told you who they were at the beginning, and that was it. Then you were like, 'Well, who?'" The disciples appeared to function as a faceless group with little agency and Robyn could not work out their identity or motives. This inability to

---

22. Hart, "Imagination and Responsible Reading," 316.

23. Gerrig, *Experiencing Narrative Worlds*, 17; see also my discussion in chapter 3 under "Children Reading Narrative."

empathize distanced her from these characters. Consequently, she did not develop a favorable view of the disciples and engaged minimally with the parts of Luke in which they featured.

Relational Reading

Empathy usually depends upon the reader connecting with a character in the text. The nature of the empathy, accordingly, reflects the type of connection the reader forges with that character. Mikkelsen describes empathy as an "active involvement with the story-character" which constructs a relationship with that character.[24] It is important not to make assumptions about this relationship. Empathy does not depend upon the reader either liking or sympathizing with a particular character. In the readings, the nature of the relationship between the readers and the characters varied, and I discuss here the most prominent types of relationship: companionship, identification, and ambivalence.

"The Characters Become My Friends"

A common approach to the characters in Luke was that of empathizing with them as one might empathize with a companion. Such readings usually took the narratee's perspective and treated the characters as distinct agents with their own identities. As Sophie M. stated, "the characters become my friends and so in a way it's like they're telling me the story." Seeking to know about these character-companions appeared to be an important incentive for participating in the text-reader dialogue. The readers followed a story by following a character's plights, deeds, and words. When asked what kept her reading a story, Jenny replied, "affection for the characters. I want to find out what happens to them." She described herself as getting "to know" and becoming "attached" to characters. This companionship empathy often seemed to generate feelings of fondness for the characters and added a relational layer to the readings.

Due to taking the narratee's perspective, the readers viewed the characters externally but sought to understand them internally, much as they might approach a companion. Hannah C. described herself as looking at the Lukan characters "from the outside in," seeking to penetrate their interior lives. She pondered for instance the emotive responses of "the people who did wrong" and especially "how they felt to have all the attention from

---

24. Mikkelsen, *Powerful Magic*, 40, 41.

Jesus," given her own surprise at Jesus' generosity towards and unlikely relationship with such characters. Her empathy personalized these characters, turning sketches on the page into more holistic portraits.

The companionship bond did not depend upon the readers linking their own identities to those of the characters. Tatar makes the useful point that child readers "may empathize with characters and still not necessarily live through them or identify with them." Instead they may "see the characters as role models and companions rather than second selves."[25] This is evident in Rachel's approach to Jesus. Rachel declared that her favorite aspect of Luke was what it revealed about Jesus' personality: "He isn't polite and nice to everyone. He doesn't just follow the rules." She admired Jesus for his independent approach to the constraints of his social environment, and appeared amused by his failure to conform to the expectations projected upon him by religious piety. Rachel enjoyed her encounter with Jesus through Luke, and explored Jesus' identity without direct reference to her own.

"I Relate to Him"

The readers frequently forged connections with the characters through comparison: they compared themselves in some way to a character. This approach tended to be personal and drew the readers further into the world of the text. The comparison process, which I refer to as identification, usually involved the reader identifying some personal point of commonality with a character or a character's situation, and constructing a reading that aligned the reader and character around that common point. This process occurred both when the readers assumed the narratee's perspective and when they assumed a character's perspective. Tannehill describes identification as one of the key ways that a narrative may impact a reader.[26] In the findings of my study, identification often had implications not only for the fleshing out of the character, but also for the life of the reader.

Sometimes the characters served as personal models for the readers. Elaine, Ebby, and Zak identified with Jesus' experience of being questioned about what he believed because they too had experienced questioning about their beliefs. Zak reflected on the contrast between Jesus' response and his own: "If somebody throws something at Jesus and tries to trick him into something, he just wriggles out of it. If somebody caught me like that, I would just stand there, 'Uhhhh, is this a trap? Is this a trick question?'

25. Tatar, *Enchanted Hunters*, 18.
26. Tannehill, "Freedom and Responsibility," 272.

{exaggerates a confused voice}. It makes you want to be like him." Due to this point of identification, Jesus' conduct provided these readers with a model for dealing with difficult questions.[27]

James S., on the other hand, identified with Peter's penchant for making errors: "Peter says, 'I will never deny you Lord.' And it turns out he does, then he realizes his mistake. The mistakes [Peter] makes helps me to relate to him." Peter's weakness formed a point of contact between the reader's experience and the narrative world. Like Jesus in the previous reading, Peter served as a model, but whereas Jesus' model generated aspiration, Peter's model produced assurance of God's acceptance.

Identifying with a character frequently led the readers to wrestle personally with the text. John identified with Martha in the Luke 10:38–42 story of Mary and Martha: "I could imagine myself in Martha's position, and I would be like, 'Right!'" Taking on this role evoked the reader's emotions: "I personally would be really annoyed. I almost didn't like Jesus at that point." His empathy led to a critique of the story's contents and John positioned himself firmly against what he deemed to be sibling injustice. This reaction was confirmed repeatedly in the RVGs. One RVG participant raised his hand and declared of Martha: "I feel like this and it's as if my brother is Mary—I do the work." Another stated strongly: "It's not equal rights!" Note that John, in his reading, focused on his own reaction to Jesus' statement about the sisters' conduct. John did not attribute his own response to Martha, although he did ponder what that response might be.

Such readings challenge Darr's assertion that "the reader's relationship to a character is a totally verbal experience, somewhat detached and intellectual."[28] Darr uses reader response theory to analyze how readers respond to characterization in Luke, but Darr's "reader" is very different from those in this study. He uses the text to work out the traits of Luke's so-called "first" readers, which he admits limits his interpretive field of view to a "specific time and place." His key question is: "What did a reader have to bring to [Luke] in order to actualize it competently?"[29] That is, he begins with the text in order to analyze the first readers so that his reader is essentially a construct derived from literary devices. His study seeks to show real readers what they ought to take from Luke, rather than asking how real readers do, in fact, engage with Luke. He does not consider how empathy, such as that shown in John's and James S's readings, might influence his first

---

27. In chapter 11 I discuss in more detail the readers' identification with Jesus over the experience of being questioned. See the section "People Question Me Too."

28. Darr, *Character Building*, 47.

29. Ibid., 26, 36.

readers' interpretation of Luke. Perhaps unsurprisingly, Darr's first readers take an analytical approach to the text not dissimilar to his own.

My findings also do not support Tannehill's claim that social roles augment the process of identification. Tannehill asserts, by way of example, that women are more likely to identify with female characters, and those who are rich with wealthy characters.[30] The findings suggest that Tannehill's position is too limiting. The points of identification evident in the findings varied considerably and were not limited to social roles. John's identification with Martha centered on a demand for justice in the delegation of household tasks. In this reading, a young male teenager identified with an adult female character.

"Even as a Kid"

Tannehill's assertion nonetheless raises the question, "were the child readers inclined to identify with the children in Luke?" Luke's narrative world does not include many children, leaving the readers with few young characters with whom to identify. This did not prevent the readers from relating to Luke's characters. Even in the stories that included children, the child characters were not always the ones that generated empathy. For the Luke 18:15–17 story of Jesus Blessing the Children, Jack identified with the disciples, a group of adult males, rather than the children. He was curious about the disciples' reason for excluding the children, realized that their conduct was deemed inappropriate by Jesus, and surmised that this conduct was motivated by a blameworthy emotion. Jack concluded that the disciples' conduct was driven by "jealousy," an emotion which he too had experienced in clashes with other people.

The key exception to Luke's lack of child characters is the Luke 2:40–52 story of the Boy Jesus in the Temple in which the twelve-year-old Jesus is the central character. The age of the boy Jesus was close or even identical to the age of the readers and some of them took particular notice of this story. The story piqued Vanessa's interest in Jesus: "I wished they'd described that more because I only know about Jesus as a man and I don't know him really as a child. So I would have liked to hear more of that." This reading suggested a desire on the part of the reader to "know" the character better. This knowing appeared to be relational in orientation: the reader particularly wanted to encounter Jesus as a boy and thereby to gain a fuller picture of him as a person.

---

30. Tannehill, "Freedom and Responsibility," 272.

Some readers looked for points of identification between themselves and the boy Jesus. Both Ebby and James S. admired the young Jesus' ability to hold his own with a group of adult teachers, a scenario that any child may find intimidating. Ebby exclaimed: "I really like the part where they accidentally left him behind in Jerusalem and he was teaching all the teachers ... how Jesus was involved in teaching people even as a kid is so inspiring." This reading cast Jesus as a child hero who surmounted the daily trials of every school child.

Grace said she was drawn to this story because "as children you want to know what Jesus was like at your age, so you can say, 'I recognize that in me.'" Her identification with Jesus hinged on their similarity in age; they were both twelve years old. But she did not treat Jesus as a model to aspire to, as may be expected of her by the adult gatekeepers who use this story as a moral example.[31] Instead, she wanted to associate herself with Jesus and to form a bond that helped her to understand both herself and him.

"I Don't Like Him"

If empathy is, by definition, affective reading, then it may incorporate a wide range of emotions. Not all of the empathetic readings of Luke involved positive emotions. Some of the readers could even be described as enjoying the experience of disliking some of the more unpalatable characters. This was clearly evident for those characters that the readers viewed as villains: the religious leaders, Judas, Pilate, Herod, and Satan. Zak laughed as he described the religious leaders' verbal impotence relative to Jesus, Kit called Pilate names, and Hannah M. declared emphatically that she "didn't like" Herod. The readers experienced elation whenever such characters encountered obstacles or defeat. The readers' empathy accrued not from feeling *with* but from feeling *against* such characters.

Empathy therefore may not be reduced to identification. Empathy encompasses but is also broader than identification and is not contingent upon it. Such reductionism is evident in Rosenblatt's discussion of the role of literature as an emotional outlet for the reader. In this discussion, she collapses identification and empathy into one another, treating them as interchangeable. She refers to empathy as a "tendency toward identification" and defines this tendency as the ability to "feel ourselves into" another object or person;[32] that is, empathy produces identification. In contrast, this

---

31. For a full discussion of the moral and educational purposes to which this story is often put, see Briggs, "The Word Became Visual Text."

32. Rosenblatt, *Literature as Exploration*, 37–38.

study found that identification functioned as a subset of empathy. While all identification was empathetic, not all empathetic responses could be labelled as identification. For instance, the readers tended to respond to Jesus' enemies emotively, but with aversion: Luke's villains generated negative affect towards themselves.

What is more, some of the characters presented an ambiguity which challenged the readers' empathy and the readers struggled with their emotive responses to these characters. From his examination of the construction of characters in the Hebrew Bible, Alter concludes that the "narrative art of the Bible . . . is more than an aesthetic enterprise" for the biblical characters embody a complexity that reflects the biblical view of humanity. Alter thinks this complexity "leads to multiple or sometimes even wavering perspectives on the characters."[33] Such ambiguous characters provide readers with the opportunity to grapple with the complexity of human nature.

The characters' ambiguity sometimes led to ambivalent readings. Grace struggled with the presentation, in Luke 23:39–43, of the criminal on the cross who views his death sentence as just but Jesus' sentence as unjust:

> In a way, he's bad because he's a criminal, but he still understands better. I don't like him especially, cause when you say "criminal" you think of a person with scratches all over. But actually this one—it doesn't tell you the name, it doesn't tell you what he was, it only says "criminal." But then it says quite a nice thing that he says. So I think that's quite good.

Because the character does not have a name, but only a label, Grace had to view him through that label and her associations with that label were all negative. She imagined criminals as defaced and damaged. Yet this character unexpectedly showed understanding of Jesus' identity. Tannehill describes the second criminal as recognizing what the other human beings around Jesus did not: Jesus' offer of salvation is not nullified by his death and Jesus' Messiahship is connected to a future kingdom.[34] Grace's reading recognized such insight in the criminal.

Yet for Grace, the character was fundamentally contradictory: the criminal's words to Jesus were at odds with the reader's image of a criminal. A conflicted empathy developed as the reader embraced the words of a character from which she would otherwise distance herself. Grace did not draw on her own experience to work out the criminal's motives. Instead the character interrogated her experience. Tannehill observes that this criminal

---

33. Alter, *The Art of Biblical Narrative*, 126, 130.
34. Tannehill, *Luke*, 343.

is one of the many outcasts in Luke to whom Jesus' ministers.[35] Grace's candid yet perceptive reading went beyond Tannehill's observation and added into the narrative mix a tension that derived directly from her ambivalent response to this character, a response that may be deemed fitting within the context of the narrative world. Her conflicted empathy challenged her prejudices and expanded her thinking.

Empathy and the Pursuit of Meaning

One of the key functions of empathy in the readings was the pursuit of meaning. Jenny, for instance, specified that working out a character's motives helped her to reflect on the meaning of a story. Keen corroborates this finding in her discussion of a study that demonstrated that empathy enhanced comprehension of a text for both child and adult readers.[36] In my study, this meaning-making took two forms: empathy enabled the readers to think about the meaning of the narrative world via its characters; empathy also enabled the readers to interpret the narrative world experientially. In both cases, empathetic reading functioned as form of textual interpretation. These two forms of meaning-making were of course inextricably linked, but for the sake of clarity I look at them separately.

"It's about Having Faith"

Empathy seemed to stimulate the readers to interpret Luke's narrative world. Nicholas Wolterstorff notes the importance for interpretation of the reader indwelling "the world which the [text] projects."[37] Although Wolterstorff's discussion is concerned primarily with the role of the imagination for indwelling a text, a similar point may be made concerning empathy. Empathy enables an indwelling of the narrative world which facilitates interpretation.

The readers frequently interpreted the meaning of a story by indwelling its characters. Elaine interpreted the Luke 18:9–14 parable of the Pharisee and the Tax Collector by acting out the role of each character:

> The Pharisee goes, "Thank you that I am not like that sinner person over there. Hooray!" {stretches body and arms out victoriously}, all loud for all to hear. And the Tax Collector says, "I'm

---

35. Ibid., 343.
36. Keen, *Empathy*, 87–88, discussing Bourg, "The Role of Emotion."
37. Wolterstorff, "A Response to Trevor Hart," 335.

going to be quiet" {scrunches body down small, head down, hands clasped}.

In the parable, the characters' attitudes are expressed through their conduct and words. The Pharisee stands apart and gives thanks for his superiority while the Tax Collector keeps his distance, bows his head, beats his breast, and pleads for mercy.[38] Darr notes that the "body language" of the characters "is indicative of their hearts."[39] Elaine's reading embodied those attitudes, using actions to give them physicality and shape. What the parable meant for this reader emerged through what the characters felt: the Pharisee felt victorious in his religiosity while the Tax Collector felt humble in his sin. The speech that her reading attributed to the characters, "hooray!" and "quiet," respectively, indicated the reader's personal understanding of the emotions underlying these attitudes.

After acting out the attitudes of both characters, Elaine embraced the attitude of the Tax Collector. She thought of the Pharisees as "a bit pompous. They are clever and they know it." What is more, she believed that they represented the destiny of the disciples without Jesus' intervention: "I think [the Pharisees] were what the disciples would have been if Jesus had gone sooner, because the disciples had to learn how Jesus wanted them to act and behave." Green makes a similar comparison in reference to this parable: the "disciples [were] always in danger of Pharisaic behavior . . . having already demonstrated comparable self-possession."[40] The young reader arrived at the same conclusion as Green, via the route of empathy.

Reading through empathy sometimes stimulated direct theological reflection, as may be seen in Rachel's reading of the Luke 11:5-8 parable of the Friend at Midnight. Rachel initially assumed the position of the sleeping friend: "If someone is asking you for bread and you've gone to sleep . . . But they just keep asking, then eventually you'll give it over. You'll give in because they're pestering you." The reader identified with the character's reluctance to get out of bed because it would be her own reaction in similar circumstances. Empathizing with the sleeping friend enabled Rachel to make sense of the parable's portrayal of the relationship between God and his people: "It's about having faith that God will provide for you" rather than being "a big God up there who you have to worship or else." Her incisive reading cast God as a friend who responds to the needs of those who seek

---

38. Gowler indicates that the actions included in the text are fundamental to understanding the parable, but he discusses only the actions of the tax collector; see Gowler, *Host, Guest, Enemy and Friend*, 268.

39. Darr, *Character Building*, 114.

40. Green, *Luke*, 646.

him out, rather than being a distant deity who only makes demands of his followers.

Rachel's reading did not attribute the sleeping friend's reluctance to God but rather showed awareness that the parable was a "how much more" similitude about God. Her interpretation reflects the parable's categorization by scholars like Tannehill and Craddock.[41] Tannehill asserts that the parable "cannot be understood allegorically as a depiction of God."[42] Rachel did not read this parable allegorically, but she did work out the parable's import by placing herself in the role of the sleeping friend and comparing God to that role. Her empathy led the reader to ponder what the parable had to say about God.

"Now I See"

Empathy gave the readers a type of personal experience with the narrative world. Referring back to both Lewis's epistemological argument, experiential learning equates to learning about something through a direct encounter with it: that is, knowing something through an experience of that thing.[43] The readers' understanding of the contents of Luke appeared to grow through their empathetic encounters with Luke. Zak's innovative reading of the Luke 5:17–26 story of the Healing of the Paralyzed Man provides an example:

> I definitely remember imagining the paralyzed man going through the roof. I remember them going up there onto the roof and then them tearing into the roof {acts out tearing} so that the guy who owns the house must be looking up, like, he's going to kill the guy who comes through {laughs}. I actually pictured the Pharisees in the corner {points at corner and speaks *sotto voce*}, there in the shadow.

This reading supplied not only a house owner, who is absent in the text, but also this character's motives. The house, after all, must have had an owner who would have had an opinion on the dismantling of his roof. The supplied character foregrounded the unexpectedness of the actions of the paralyzed man's friends, actions driven by faith. Ironically, the paralyzed man was not killed by the owner but was healed by Jesus. Part of the

---

41. Craddock, *Luke*, 154; Tannehill, *Luke*, 189.

42. Tannehill, *Luke*, 189.

43. Lewis, "Meditation in a Toolshed," 53. See also my discussion in chapter 2 under "An Experiential Epistemology."

meaning for the reader emerged through the response of the house owner who enacted the irony Zak detected in the story, an irony that captured the humor of the event while also expressing the unexpectedness of its result.

Zak acted out much of his reading and his actions had two effects. First, they added emphasis to each point he made. Secondly, they revealed Zak's immersion in the story world. The sense he made of the story was contingent upon this empathetic inside position. He rejoiced in the triumph of the friends, laughed at the irony of the healing, and pointed at the Pharisees accusingly. As far as Zak was concerned, the Pharisees were some of the key villains of Luke and his reading depicted them symbolically: they lurked in a corner and were swathed in shadow, signifying their threatening role.

Gowler emphasizes the importance of narrative experience for characterization: "Character analysis, when characters are ripped from text and context, is woefully inadequate. All cannot be explained; the text itself has to be experienced by the reader."[44] Zak experienced the power of the friends' faith and the intractability of the Pharisees. The meaning he took from this story derived not from an abstraction about the importance of faith for seeking Jesus (such abstractions are often the thrust of lessons about this story). Instead, Zak's empathetic reading generated for him an experience of the effect of faith upon those who have it and upon those who get in its way.

The readers' empathetic encounters with Luke appeared at times to foster spiritual insight. Michael was particularly moved by the account of Jesus' crucifixion. He aligned with the perspective of the crowd in Luke 23:27-38 and watched Jesus dying: "When there was a crowd around Jesus, when he's dying, I felt like one of them." This reader's empathy with the crowd gave him a glimpse of their experience: "I felt like I could see Jesus there. I wanted to get close to him but the Roman soldiers were stopping me. I imagined lots of people weeping around me, crying, and calling out, 'Lord!'"

Like the crowd, the reader's focus was drawn to Jesus: "I was mainly looking at Jesus. Jesus had the crown of thorns and the nails in his hands too. The nails were painful." His inside-experience led Michael to contemplate Jesus' words: "When he was dying, he said, 'Father forgive them. They don't know what they are doing.' And that takes a lot of courage, to say that, while they've put him on a cross." As a result, Michael described Jesus' death as "moving" and "quite sad." Michael's emotive response to Jesus' crucifixion was evoked by Jesus' suffering which in turn gave him insight into Jesus' act of forgiveness.

Michael went on to state that reading all of Luke had changed his view of Jesus. Prior to reading Luke, he thought that "Jesus was telling everybody

---

44. Gowler, *Host, Guest, Enemy and Friend*, 182.

what to do." Reading Luke generated an alternative view: "But now I see that Jesus is repenting them, he's giving them miracles, he's saving them, and he is making things right for the everyday normal person." For Michael, Jesus was no longer a distant moral authority. By in-dwelling the narrative world, he gained new insight into Jesus as a caring, self-sacrificial leader, someone who was concerned for normal people, like the crowd and the reader.

Summary

Empathy appeared to be fundamental to the readers' encounters with Luke. This reading strategy provided the readers with an experiential foothold in the narrative world through the characters, as the readers worked out the characters' emotions, attitudes, and motives relative to the narrative events. The character with whom a reader empathized was often, but not always, determined by a perspective in the text. Empathy forged a relationship between the reader and the character, although the nature of this relationship ranged from close identification to ambivalence. The readers used empathy to interpret Luke so that the meaning they attributed to the text derived at least partially from their affective experience of the narrative world.

In my discussions of both imagination and empathy, I have touched upon the readers' pursuit of the sense of the text. I focus on this third reading strategy more fully in the following chapter.

Chapter 10

Sense-Orientated Reading

Jake: "Whenever I read something, I remember, 'Oh, that's with that.' I have a mental picture of these things just gluing together."

B.C.: I read that way "so I could understand Luke and so that it could relate to me."

Introduction

The study's findings suggest that the pursuit of Luke's meaning was a fundamental part of the children's reading experience. This pursuit was a process that took various forms and the contents of Luke were the focus of this pursuit. The children's interpretation of those contents, and Luke's plot in particular, were at the heart of what the overall narrative *meant* for the readers and is the subject of the following chapter. Here I concentrate upon the process: the pursuit of meaning as a reading strategy.

The IFGs narrowed this reading strategy down to two key forms, represented by two code categories: "reading by puzzle-solving" and reading by asking "how does Luke relate to me?" These categories were also articulated by Allie in her interview. She stated that she read Luke by asking two questions: "What's going on there?" and "How does that relate to me?" Referring to the first question, the readers appeared to expect the text to make sense *as* a text and part of their transaction with Luke involved working out the meaning of the narrative world relative to itself. This approach may be referred to as literal reading. The second question suggests that the readers wanted Luke to mean something to them. The meaning of the text rested not just in its internal coherence but also in its interface with their world. Thus the readers interpreted Luke with reference to both the world of the text and the world of the reader.

This chapter examines these two pursuits of the sense of the text. I begin by clarifying the terminology. Then I discuss the readers' pursuit of the meaning of Luke as a text. This section has three parts: the role of the overall narrative in this pursuit, the readers' sense-seeking process, and the epistemological implications of this sense-seeking. The next section examines the role of the readers' worlds in their sense-seeking. The chapter closes with a discussion of what happened when sense-seeking failed.

Clarifying the Terms

I have deliberately avoided using the term "meaning" as the focal concept for this chapter because of the theoretical baggage attached to the word. "Meaning" has been the focus of considerable debate in the field of biblical hermeneutics.[1] Some scholars point out that, in the context of reading a text, the use of the term "meaning" is often nebulous due to slippage between the different theoretical interests and experiential concerns that readers bring to a text. The meaning one interpreter attributes to a text will differ from that of another due to their difference in starting points.[2] Fowl suggests that the solution to this issue is to eliminate theoretical discussions of "meaning" altogether and to foreground interpretive interests instead, which has the benefit of revealing what a reading of a text seeks to achieve.[3]

On the other side of the debate are those who seek to retain the concept of meaning as a way of keeping the focus on the biblical text.[4] Moberly, for example, points out that Fowl's concern is primarily with the character of the reader.[5] Fowl's position is particularly pertinent for readers who are looking *at* the text relative to a particular critical perspective. Briggs adds that the debate, at least in part, arises from the need for referents for the term "meaning": when the term is used in an abstract sense to refer to meaning in general, confusion results due to the differences in interpretive interests. But when the term is used in reference to a particular word, statement, or passage, then the connotations of that word, statement, or passage

---

1. For a summary, see Spinks, *The Bible and the Crisis of Meaning*.

2. For further discussion, see: Fowl, "The Ethics of Interpretation"; Holland, *Five Readers Reading*; Fish, *Is There a Text in This Class?*; Stout, "What is the Meaning of a Text?"

3. Fowl, "The Ethics of Interpretation," 386.

4. This is a traditional conservative approach in biblical studies. Vanhoozer offers one of the best defenses of it. See Vanhoozer, *Is There a Meaning in this Text?*

5. Moberly, *The Bible, Theology, and Faith*, 40.

can be pursued.⁶ Discussing the meaning of a particular biblical passage is not the same as discussing the interpretive interests of those interpreting that passage, although both have their contribution to make.⁷

What happens when the role of the reader relative to the text is participative? The readers in my study pursued meaning as a way of following the narrative trajectory. They used the terms "interpretation" and "meaning" in their interviews but always in a non-technical way. Interpretation for them was a heuristic act. They read Luke to find out what happened, and to do this, they had to make sense of the text as they progressed through it. Returning once again to the literal reading model, the readers' approach to meaning was via specific textual elements. Meaning was, for them, not a theoretical concern but a way of making sense of the concrete components of the text.

In this chapter I seek to use the term "meaning" in the way that it was used by the readers. By meaning, I refer to the understanding of particular parts of Luke that the readers constructed through their interaction with those parts. Of course, the readers brought their own interpretive interests to Luke but they were not concerned with declaring their particular meaning as the "right" one; that concern was never in view. In order to emphasize the readers' approach to meaning, I foreground a different term that the readers used: the "sense" of the text. The readers' pursuit of meaning often concluded when they reached a coherent view of a passage. Once they worked out a way of looking at a saying, parable, or micro-narrative, they moved on. The term "sense" implies this orientation towards coherence.

This coherence had its own referents. The readers sought to comprehend portions of Luke relative to the overall narrative and relative to their world. The term "sense" has the benefit of incorporating both the text's and the readers' input into the interpretive process. Fokkelman helpfully notes that the "use of the word *sense* in English shows an ambiguity which aptly illustrates the reader-text relation. You can say: this text . . . makes sense . . . as well as: we try to make sense of this text." Using this term highlights that meaning "originates on both sides" of the text-reader dialogue.⁸

The readers repeatedly used terms like "sense," "meaning," "understanding," and "interpret" to explain their transactions with Luke, and they usually expressed these concepts in conjunction with some form of verb: "it makes sense of . . ."; "it helps to understand . . ."; "work out the meaning . . .";

---

6. Briggs, "How to Do Things with Meaning"; Briggs draws on J. L. Austin for this point. See Austin, "The Meaning of a Word."

7. Briggs, "How to Do Things with Meaning," 157.

8. Fokkelman, *Reading Biblical Narrative*, 24; italics in the original.

and "in my way of interpreting . . ." The pursuit of meaning was for them an activity, a way of participating in the reading game. The emphasis of this chapter, then, is not upon the particular sense that the readers made of their engagement with Luke but upon how they played the game.

Seeking the "Big Picture"

Perhaps the most significant locus of meaning in Luke for the readers was the overall narrative. Most of the readings treated Luke as more than a string of unrelated episodes and approached it through what the readers referred to as its "big picture." While the readers regularly pondered the meaning of specific parts of Luke, their point of reference for these parts was usually the parts' relationship to the whole. The readers appeared to expect Luke to have a narrative synthesis, a big picture that made the whole narrative meaningful.

One of the readers' motives for seeking the big picture was obvious. Since none of them had ever read the entirety of Luke prior to the study, in their reading they sought an overview of the text. Trevor's description of his reading process was illuminating: "When you're actually reading through a whole book [like Luke], you find yourself thinking, 'Okay, where does that fit in with what's just happened?'" This reading assumed that the various parts of Luke cohere around the plot and that the plot makes sense. Many of the readings similarly assumed that the whole narrative was built on an internal logic. The readers' pursuit of this logic was tantamount to pursuit of how the narrative world *works*.

This search for a narrative synthesis aligns with Oatley's finding that child readers form mental schemata of how a narrative coheres.[9] The readers' "big picture" may be comparable to a mental model of how Luke fits together and what this fitting together signifies. Narrative criticism utilizes a comparable reading strategy since it treats the Gospels as "coherent narratives" and seeks to interpret "individual passages . . . in terms of their contribution to the story as a whole."[10] This pursuit of narrative coherency, by both child readers and narrative critics, is no doubt due to how narrative worlds are constructed.

As I discussed in chapter 2, one of the hallmarks of a narrative world is internal coherence. In his analysis of fairy stories, Tolkien asserts that a narrative creates a world which the reader's "mind can enter," enabling the

---

9. Oatley, *Such Stuff as Dreams*, 17; see also my discussion in chapter 3 under "Children Reading Narrative."

10. Powell, *Narrative Criticism*, 7.

reader to take a mental place "inside" that world.[11] This entrance is made possible through what Tolkien calls the narrative's "inner consistency of reality."[12] This consistency is achieved through "laws" which shape and govern the narrative world so that every element is "true" within the context of that world.[13] Even nonsense realms such as Lewis Carroll's *Wonderland* have their own internal logic, even if that logic is deliberately to defy the logic of the primary world.[14]

The reader's pursuit of this logic was tantamount to pursuit of Luke's theological worldview.[15] As Tannehill points out, because of its narrative form, Luke influences its readers "in a much richer way than through theological statements, which might be presented in an essay." This influence derives at least in part from the "values and beliefs" out of which Luke's worldview is constructed.[16] These values and beliefs are forms of Tolkien's "laws." A reader may mentally assume Luke's theological worldview when she or he engages with Luke's narrative world, and may accept Luke's value system within the context of that world. This acceptance is for the pursuit of meaning within the narrative world and does not require the reader to transfer that acceptance to the primary world.

The children's readings repeatedly pursued the logic of Luke's narrative world in order to make sense of a particular story or saying. An example may be seen in Sophie A.'s reading of the Luke 7:36–50 story of the Sinful Woman. Initially, she visualized the scene: "I liked the way that the woman was so humble right at the beginning, washing Jesus' feet and then drying it with her hair. I mean, you get a very vivid image of that." Next Sophie A. pondered the woman's motives: "She knows what she is and she knows that Jesus knows what she is. But she doesn't care. She goes anyway." Empathy, however, was not Sophie A.'s final interpretive move for she then compared the story to the Luke 15 parables of the Lost Sheep and the Lost Son. This reference to the bigger picture as an interpretive guide led her to conclude that together these three stories show that "it's never too late to turn back" and that this turning back is "a cause of celebration."

In the final part of her reading, Sophie A. moved beyond story events into theological concepts. The meaning she attributed to these stories, that forgiveness is always possible and that repentance should be celebrated,

11. Tolkien, "On Fairy-Stories," 60.
12. Ibid., 68.
13. Ibid., 60.
14. See Carroll, *Alice's Adventures in Wonderland* and *Through the Looking Glass*.
15. See my discussion in chapter 2 under "Luke's Narrative World."
16. Tannehill, *The Narrative Unity of Luke-Acts*, 1:1, 8.

expressed a theological understanding of the Gospel. Interestingly, Sophie A. had minimal previous exposure to Luke, suggesting that the connection she made between these stories was her own. Her interpretation appeared to result at least in part from reading Luke as a whole narrative.

Reading by "Puzzle-Solving"

How the readers' pursued Luke's internal logic often appeared to equate to a puzzle-solving process. This reading strategy was not unique to the children. In his discussion of interpreting the Gospel of Mark, Kermode highlights a similar process and calls it "a basic principle of interpretation-theory."[17] Hart describes the process well: "We consider the shape of the whole text by relating its parts, and make sense of the parts in terms of the shape of the whole."[18] This process was a cognitive activity and could be described as a form of inductive reasoning.

The readers used puzzle-solving terminology to express the process. Allie declared that the whole Gospel was "like a big puzzle." Other readers talked about "building a picture," and "piecing" or "putting together" the various story elements. In the RVGs, 79% of the respondents described the Luke 6:43–45 Tree and Fruit saying as having a "hidden meaning" that had to be worked out and one participant stated that she imagined this saying in order "to put together the pieces like a jigsaw." The IFGs placed "puzzle-solving" second on the list of their most common reading strategies.

Luke, for its part, invites this approach. Maxwell specifies that in a narrative such as Luke's, discourse devices like "metaphors, riddles, fables, and parables provide the audience with puzzles to complete."[19] The readers responded accordingly and assumed the role of puzzle-solvers. Jenny said of the metaphors in Luke: "It was fun to try and work out what they meant." Positive responses like Jenny's substantiate Gerrig's assertion that making an effort "to find solutions to textual dilemmas" intensifies readers' enjoyment of narrative.[20]

This puzzle-solving tended to be an iterative process that involved cross-comparing parts of the narrative. Hannah M. explained this reading

---

17. Kermode, *The Genesis of Secrecy*, 5, 9. Much of the argument of Kermode's book hinges upon his description of the Gospels as "opaque narratives," which require interpretation to draw out their latent, or spiritual, meanings. He contrasts this with the Gospels' "primary sense," which he believes is straight-forward and superficial. The child readers, in contrast, used the puzzle-solving process for all forms of reading.

18. Hart, "Imagination and Responsible Reading," 330.

19. Maxwell, *Hearing Between the Lines*, 77.

20. Gerrig, *Experiencing Narrative Worlds*, 239–40.

strategy: "It was all together. So one bit helped you understand the next bit, instead of just reading that one bit and not really understanding it very well." Determining the meaning of one part of Luke functioned as a tool for working out the meaning of other parts. Vanessa pointed out that the Pharisees "don't treat tax collectors very well" which meant that they did not listen to Jesus' saying in Luke 6:27–36 to Love Your Enemies. For her, the Pharisees' rejection of Jesus' teaching contributed to their tension with Jesus, an important element in the plot.

Luke's big picture was the primary referent for the puzzle-solving process. Jake explained how the process helped him to work out the sense of the whole text: "It's all pieced together more. Whenever I read something, I remember, 'Oh, that's with that.' I have a mental picture of these things just gluing together." Conversely, the absence of an overall synthesis appeared to inhibit meaning. James A. described the effect of his previous encounters with isolated passages in Luke, prior to reading the whole text. He stated: "When I read little bits, it didn't make that much sense cause you couldn't follow what would happen next, like if there're any other connections." This reading treated the logic of the overall plot as the key referent for making sense of the different parts of Luke.

The puzzle-solving process stimulated reflection on Luke. As Hannah C. stated, "I liked it quite a lot because it made you understand Luke more, because if you think then you sometimes come to an answer." Note that her reading expected the puzzle-solving to reach a resolution, an answer to the meaning of a part of the text. This process may be fundamental to how a text shapes the reader into someone who fits the model reader of the text, as described by Eco.[21] Puzzle-solving may lead to an understanding of the text which in turn may expand the reader's thinking. The reader may then return to the text with new questions or discover in it other puzzles to solve.

Knowing *through* the Narrative

The readers' pursuit of meaning was invariably shaped by an epistemological framework, even if that framework was not one that they had overtly chosen or could consciously articulate. As I discussed in chapter 2, all forms of interpretation are implicitly governed by an epistemology of how to know the text.[22] The theory arising from my findings is that the readers' epistemo-

---

21. As discussed in Marguerat and Bourquin, *How to Read*, 134; see Eco, *The Role of the Reader*, 200–260; see also my discussion in chapter 2 under "In Search of a Theory."

22. Schneiders, "The Gospels and the Reader," 104; see also my discussion in

logical framework was experiential: they came to know Luke through their participation in the reading game. Their sense-seeking could be classified as participation by puzzle-solving and what the readers were seeking to know through this puzzle-solving was the logic at work in Luke's narrative world.

According to Alasdair MacIntyre, narrative is the means by which experience is ordered and understood.[23] In his examination of the relationship between epistemological crises and progress in the philosophy of science, MacIntyre concludes that narrative enables knowing and epistemological development occurs through "the construction and reconstruction of more adequate narratives."[24] MacIntyre cites literary narratives as models and his discussion has ramifications for the epistemological role of written narrative in general. By engaging with a narrative, a reader may come to know not only the narrative but also *through* the narrative.

This effect of knowing through a narrative may be seen in John's reading of the Luke 14:15–24 parable of the Great Feast. John empathized with the host in the parable, whose conduct he considered "amazingly thoughtful." The reader explained that had he been in the host's situation, he would have tried to cajole the original invitees into attending the feast: "I'm not sure I would invite the blind, the cripple. I just thought that was something ingenious, almost inspired, to do." According to Craddock, this parable delivers a jolt when the host extends invitations to people from outside of the social circle of the original guests.[25] John's comparison of himself to the host suggests that he experienced this jolt. John then made sense of the host's conduct by considering what it revealed about God: the parable showed that "God will invite everyone in. He wants you to come." The reader's interpretive strategies, empathy and sense-seeking, disclosed his values and expanded his view of God. *What* John knew had to do with these values and theological insight; *how* John knew was through the dialogical experience.

The readers' experiential epistemology incorporated not only the readers' interactions with Luke, but also what the readers' brought to that interaction, that is, their personal experience. Sophie M.'s reading of the Luke 19:1–10 story of Zacchaeus provides an example. Initially she identified with Zacchaeus due to his stature: "I've always been small and I could feel his annoyance at not being able to see [Jesus]." Her reading made sense of Jesus' response to Zacchaeus by comparing it to the familiar scenario of teenage social pressure: "Like in school, some people don't mix with people

---

chapter 2 under "In Search of a Theory."

23. MacIntyre, "Epistemological Crises," 140.

24. Ibid., 142.

25. Craddock, *Luke*, 179.

who they think are below them. But Jesus will talk to anybody whether they're popular people or the non-popular people." Green also believes that Zacchaeus' "chief characteristic" is being "a social outcast,"[26] a status comparable to Sophie M.'s relegation of Zacchaeus to the position of an unpopular teenager. The meaning the reader derived from the story interrogated her school social hierarchies, for she concluded that her response to people like Zacchaeus should be "to help that one person." Since she identified with Zacchaeus, Jesus' charitable response to this character became a model for her own conduct with marginalized people in her social context.

This reader came to know Zacchaeus' situation, in part, through empathy. Having seen his plight from the inside, she extrapolated its implications to her own conduct. Her epistemology has a clear personal orientation and illustrates Polanyi's argument that what is known is partially a product of the position of the knower.[27] Polanyi contends that epistemology relies on a variety of sources that are implicated in what is known without necessarily being the focus of this knowing.[28] In this case, the Gospel of Luke was one of the sources of Sophie M.'s knowing but not her final focus. She was able to think about the ethical quandaries of her social world through her dialogue with the text.

"How Does That Relate to Me?"

While the key referent for the readers' sense-seeking was the logic of the narrative world, their sense-seeking also had another referent. Making sense of Luke meant working out a sense that was coherent for the reader. That is, sense was not only text-dependent, but also reader-dependent. Making sense of Luke meant making sense of it from the position of the reader, the position from which Luke's narrative world was viewed.

This position was primarily a product of the reader's context. To the text-reader dialogue, the reader brought her or his understanding, experience, and personal world, all of which were components of the reader's context. As Searle states, "All human beings are inevitably shaped by their historical, cultural and social context, rendering it impossible to come to any text with a *tabula rasa*, morally or intellectually."[29] Accordingly, the readers often discussed Luke in terms of its impact upon them. Sometimes this impact derived from their vicarious experience *of* the contents of Luke

---

26. Green, *Theology*, 86.
27. Polanyi, *Personal Knowledge*, vii–viii.
28. Scott, *Michael Polanyi*, 52.
29. Searle, *The Eyes of Your Heart*, 111n14.

and sometimes it had more to do with the personal implications which they derived *from* Luke.

This section considers how the readers' contexts functioned as reference points for working out meaning. First I look at how the readers used analogies to pursue the sense of Luke. Then I consider three types of readings that came out of the readers' juxtaposition of text and context, and that represent key codes validated by the focus groups, including: ethical readings, teen readings, and personal readings. Finally, I discuss the ways in which the readers critiqued Luke based on their context, and their context based on Luke.

Reading by Analogy

Numerous readings made sense of Luke by drawing an analogy between the reader's world and the narrative world. This reading strategy aligns with Applebee's finding that young adolescents determine meaning not by working out abstract conceptions of a story, but by comparing the situations in a narrative to situations from their personal experience.[30] Reading by analogy is also one of the hermeneutical rules that Charles Cosgrove identifies in his discussion of the hermeneutics of moral debate. He argues that reasoning by analogy serves as a method of bridging the gap between the ancient world presented in the Bible and the contemporary world of the reader. For reading by analogy to be effective, like has to be compared to like.[31]

In Cosgrove's discussion, biblical scenarios serve as the paradigm cases for solving the ethical dilemmas of contemporary situations. In the children's readings the reverse often occurred: contemporary situations were used to work out scenarios in the text. Hannah C. made sense of the conduct of the woman in the Luke 8:42b–48 story of the Bleeding Woman by comparing the woman's conduct to the conduct of a fan at a pop concert that the reader had attended. For Hannah C., the woman's "desperate" pursuit of healing was like that of the fan: she "burst out of the crowd" to touch "the famous person," Jesus, jumping the "bars" to do so. The strength of determination shown by the fan enlarged upon Hannah C.'s understanding of the woman's determination to reach Jesus.

Green's discussion of this micro-narrative further illuminates the reader's comparison of like to like. He describes the woman's touch as "irregular" for it broke Jewish purity rules, much as the fan at Hannah C.'s concert

---

30. Applebee, *The Child's Concept of Story*, 115. See also my discussion in chapter 3 under "Developmental Theories of Reading."

31. Cosgrove, *Appealing to Scripture in Moral Debate*, 52–53.

illegally broke through the police barriers. According to Green, the woman crosses "the borders of legitimate behavior to gain access to divine power." Hannah C.'s reading expressed the woman's attitude, in part, through the fan who risked arrest in order to access the music celebrity whom he may have deemed an elite member of society. Green believes that the woman's touch is interpreted as "an act of faith" by Jesus.[32] Hannah C., through her analogy, appeared to gain insight into the effort the woman expended to reach Jesus and thus into the faith which motivated that effort.

It is worth noting that the readers used analogy rather than allegory to make sense of Luke. Hannah C.'s reading compared like to like but did not map specific aspects of the biblical story onto the fan's conduct, or vice versa, as an interpretation method. Elements of the story that could potentially be allegorized, such as the woman's bleeding and Peter's statement, received no attention in the reading. Analogy allowed the reader's experience to play a role in the interpretation process. Allegory, in contrast, is a form of symbolic reading that could potentially distance the interpretation from the reader's experience.[33]

The children's readings sometimes constructed analogies between Luke's world and the readers' world by modernizing the text. Lawrence argues for the value of such contextual reading because it generates "new perspectives" on the text and it may enable people to "inhabit and live by" the biblical story so that it is actualized in their contexts.[34] This actualization may be seen in B.C.'s inventive approach to Luke's characters. In order to understand Luke's key characters, he cast them in roles that merged aspects of the narrative with his own socio-cultural context, a university town. The disciples acted like university students, the soldiers like policemen, and the Pharisees like young graduates who thought that they already knew everything. These characters wore contemporary clothes and used accoutrements that corresponded to their role, although their conduct followed the actions in Luke. B.C.'s modernization was a form of interpretation of those actions. When I asked B.C. about his modernization, he explained that it was "so I could understand Luke and so that it could relate to me." Notice that B.C.'s purpose was two-pronged: modernizing the characters helped him to follow the narrative but it also created an interface between Luke and his world.

---

32. Green, *Luke*, 346–49.

33. Therefore the children's readings were not merely a less sophisticated version of patristic allegorical readings.

34. Lawrence, *The Word in Place*, 121.

Ethical Readings

Reading ethically was a common theme in the interviews and most of the readers mentioned at some point the moral implications of Luke for their personal lives. Abby referred to Jesus' teaching as "useful" life "lessons." Percy found that reading Luke led him to evaluate his conduct. He exclaimed, "Hey! What's my life like? Hey! I need to wake up. Hey! I need to do something good." The RVGs confirmed this ethical orientation. When asked about the import of the Luke 6:43–45 Tree and Fruit saying, 64% of the respondents opted for an ethical response. When asked what the Luke 15:1–7 Lost Sheep parable was about, 72% of the RVG respondents indicated "saying sorry," an answer that had moral implications even if the interpretation was primarily theological.[35]

Many of the readers seemed to expect Luke to provide them with moral guidance. This expectation appeared to derive from an ethically-driven model of biblical interpretation that the children brought to their reading.[36] Trevor's reading exemplified this view: the "Bible is about how you should live your life." This reader specified that he learned this view of the Bible from his church. Stephanie and Jack likewise asserted that they had expected Luke to be a moral guidebook due to the teaching of their churches. Readers such as Kit and Rachel expressed surprise at the ways in which Jesus' behavior diverged from their church's views of appropriate conduct.

Yet the ethical readings were not just a product of this external model of interpretation for Luke itself also seemed to stimulate ethical reflection. Luke's teaching sections generated ethical readings no doubt due to their content but also perhaps partially due to their merging of the reader's perspective with that of the narratee. For the Luke 6:37–38 saying on Not Judging, Lisa read the saying as if it addressed her: "It's saying the way you treat others is how God is going to treat you. That really makes you think, 'Well actually, maybe I should treat others a bit better.'"

Luke's micro-narratives and parables likewise generated ethical readings. In their discussion of the role of narrative in ethics, Stanley Hauerwas and David Burrell specify that character development in a story offers "insight into the human condition" making narrative "a form of rationality especially appropriate to ethics."[37] This effect is evident in Robyn's reading of the Luke 15:11–32 parable of the Lost Son. Robyn interpreted the role of

---

35. See Table 6 in chapter 6 for a full breakdown of the results.
36. See my discussion in chapter 4 under "Children and the Bible."
37. Hauerwas and Burrell, "From System to Story," 179–80.

the younger son ethically, as driven by greed, and declared that the parable "really got to me" because it "made me feel like I should not be so greedy sometimes." The parable appeared to impact the reader's self-perception, not through a summarizing moral but through the unfolding of the life of the younger son.

The dialogue between the ethics of the text and the situation of the reader was not unidirectional: it led at times to a sober critique of both. James A. found Jesus' injunction in Luke 6:27 to "love your enemies" personally challenging and exclaimed, "it's quite hard to do that." When probed about his reason for this assertion, he replied, "sometimes my brother annoys me and I don't really forgive him." Holding a personal mirror up to the saying provided instructive reflections on both the demands of the text and the short-comings of the reader. By considering the implications of Jesus' saying for his on-going interaction with his sibling, this reader recognized the difficulty of implementing its ethical demands.

The ethical readings sometimes corresponded with a clear location on Kohlberg's scale of moral reasoning.[38] Jenny asserted that the morals in Luke were simply "right." She believed that the ethics in the text were reliable because they aligned with the rules at work in her world, such as prohibitions against stealing. This reader appeared to be operating at Kohlberg's level of conventional morality since she did not question the morals of her context but used them instead to evaluate the ethics of Luke. Her stage of moral reasoning, within this level, was evident in some of her other readings. Jesus' healings, for instance, made her realize, "I really don't value my life very much," and motivated her to treat what she had with more respect. The reader evaluated Jesus' healings relative to her own life, indicating stage 3 reasoning which makes ethical judgements by comparing the self to others.

Teen Readings

The key social context which shaped how the readers interpreted Luke was perhaps unsurprisingly that of a middleclass British teenager. Lingo from this context peppered the interview readings with words and phrases like "popularity," "bullying," "peer pressure," "teacher," "school," and "friendship." These readings frequently made sense of Luke with reference to various facets of a teenage social world. This alignment of the world of the text with the

---

38. See my discussion in chapter 3 under "Childhood Development."

world of the reader could be described as a form of contextual reading, since the readers' social contexts orientated their reflections.[39]

I tested for teen readings in the RVGs with mixed results. On the response sheets, 40% of the respondents agreed that the lost sheep of the Luke 15:1–7 parable was comparable to someone who was not popular at school. This figure represents less than half of the respondents, but it also reflects the reading of only one parable. Perhaps more significantly, in a previous question, nearly one third of the respondents had indicated that the character in the parable that was most like them was the lost sheep, a response that may have inclined many of them not to classify the lost sheep as unpopular in the subsequent question.[40] However, in the oral parts of the RVGs, various participants raised their hands to assert that the parable was about: "taking care of friends," "someone who doesn't follow the crowd," and "a social outcast." These oral teen readings were broader and more prevalent than the response sheet allowed. Such readings point to an issue with the response sheet: its equation of the lost sheep with an unpopular person was too narrow. Therefore while the findings of the RVGs may not substantiate the findings of the interviews, they may also not be said to contradict those findings.

My selection of the Lost Sheep parable for use in the RVGs came directly out of the interviews. A number of readings approached this parable with a teenage lens, interpreting it from the perspective of a teen social situation. Allie read this parable through the lens of bullying at school and declared loudly: "It's not fair! I want a banquet too!" She empathized with the ninety-nine sheep that remained in the pasture, which she believed Jesus ushered into heaven with bland remarks: "You're a nice person. Okay. You can go in." Her reading contrasted this dull treatment with the treatment received by the lost sheep: "A really horrible person who's picking on you at school can get in and they'll be like, 'Wow. I love you.' And they'll throw a banquet." The reader, as a good pupil, identified with the obedience of the herd while she viewed the lost sheep as a school bully.

Due to the reader's empathy with the herd, the actions of the shepherd appeared unjust rather than merciful. Like the religious leaders in the framing verses, Luke 15:1–3, she grumbled at Jesus' attention to the bully/lost sheep. Yet Allie was also unlike the religious leaders in that what she appeared to desire was not the exclusion of those who were difficult but comparable treatment for herself. In his discussion of this parable, Bailey

---

39. See Riches, *Contextual Bible Study*, 5; see also my discussion of Contextual Bible Study in chapter 4 under "Real Readers of the Bible."

40. See Table 6 in chapter 6 for a full breakdown of the results.

draws on Middle Eastern community life to explicate the joy at the heart of the story.[41] Allie recognized this joy and wanted it to extend to her. Reading the parable through the lens of bullying turned the parable on its head, making the obedient herd into the characters in need of rescue. By viewing herself as a victim of the bully/lost sheep, she added a relational layer to the reading that is not present in the narrative.

Pike raises the concern that secular social culture dominates how children use reading to interpret their lives.[42] While Allie's reading supports this assertion, other readings suggest a more complex interchange. Sometimes when a reading juxtaposed Luke with a teenage context, the result was a mutual interpretation of text and context. This interpretive transaction can be seen in Lisa's reading of the Luke 9:23–26 teaching on Gaining the World. Her reading initially focused on the saying's discussion of gaining and losing which she interpreted to mean: "You can have the whole world but if you don't have God, you still won't be happy." Notice her use of the second person pronoun. She personalized the teaching and pondered its implications relative to her personal sphere.

Lisa then claimed that the teaching made her smile because it showed that "it doesn't matter if I don't have something. It really doesn't. It puts it all in perspective." She described the teaching as "real reassurance" for her in the midst of a teenage culture obsessed with owning the latest gadgets and sporting the trendiest fashions. Lisa's reading narrowed the sense of the passage down to its relevance for her context. But her interpretive process also enabled the saying to change Lisa's perspective on that context.

Personalized Readings

Participatory reading by definition depends upon the reader's involvement. Sophie M. explained why this was important to her: "If you make your own decisions and come to your own conclusions, it'll mean a bit more to you. You don't feel like you've been forced into thinking that." Because she discerned Luke's meaning herself, this reader appeared to be willing to embrace that meaning. Such self-involvement gives the reader a sense of ownership in the reading game, as Sophie M. so clearly articulated. This self-involvement also gave a personal orientation to many of the readings.

This personalization of the readings often generated meaning that influenced the reader in some way. Johnson asserts that a narrative world

---

41. Bailey, *Poet and Peasant* and *Through Peasant Eyes*, 149–50, 153–54.
42. Pike, "Transactional Reading," 85; see also my discussion in chapter 3 under "Children Reading Narrative."

may shape the reader if the reader accepts the premises of that world as valid.[43] The text's internal logic makes sense both *of* the narrative world and *in* the reader's world. Rachel's reading of the Luke 10:38–42 story of Mary and Martha demonstrates the potential result of the text's logic being appropriated for the reader's personal circumstances. Rachel's reading initially concentrated upon the narrative world, contrasting the actions of the two sisters: "When it's saying about Martha being all upset about having lots of work to do, you can just imagine her rushing around doing stuff, and Mary there, just sitting with Jesus." The reader used this contrast to evaluate Jesus' statement: "You can imagine Jesus saying to Martha, 'Mary's got it right. Just sit down.'"

Spencer notes that this story's reception history often treats the sisters as models of two forms of spirituality: Martha's "active works" versus Mary's "contemplative faith."[44] Rachel's reading drew similar interpretive conclusions but with a twist. Rachel imagined herself having to make a choice between the models of the sisters, but with this choice pertaining to the reader's own lifestyle. The reader surmised that Martha's actions represented the busyness of life but that based on the text, "Jesus does want me to sit down and just be with him." The story granted her permission to emulate Mary despite the pressures of her personal context which pressed her towards imitating Martha. Notably, some of the other interviewees as well as a number of RVG respondents resisted Jesus' assertion and preferred Martha's model. Jesus' commendation clearly guided Rachel's reading but may not have been the sole determinant of her response. The reader discovered in the story grounds for resisting the demands of a busy lifestyle in preference to relationship.

Some of the personalized readings treated Luke not so much as a dialogue partner as a springboard for self-reflection. Percy said that the Luke 10:25–37 parable of the Good Samaritan "reminded me a bit about myself, how I can be kind. But I can also be cruel like the men who walked on the other side of the road." His veritable Jungian reading configured the entire parable as a representation of his inner nature. Percy empathized with the conduct of the Samaritan as well as with that of the priest and Levite. He viewed himself as having a good side and a dark side that were in tension, and expressed the need to bring balance to that tension by giving the good side priority. The reversal of expectations in the parable was lost in this reading, which treated the Samaritan as a model of good conduct but did

---

43. Johnson, "Imagining the World Scripture Imagines," 166.
44. Spencer, *Salty Wives*, 173.

not contemplate the implications of an enemy providing this model.[45] Such wholesale personalization obscured some of the facets of the parable.

Critiquing Text and Context

The interaction between text and context in the readings invariably led to mutual critique. The text contributed to the reader's evaluation of her or his context, and the context contributed to the reader's evaluation of the text. It is worth noting that the findings of my study do not support Fowler's assertion that a Gospel narrative causes the reader to function as a "credulous narratee" relative to the world of the text.[46] Reading Luke experientially did not cause the readers to approach the narrative world with credulity. Indeed, the overwhelming evidence from this study points to the readers wrestling critically with Luke's world.

The readers' contexts were often marshalled in critique of the text. Some readers showed awareness of the historical and socio-cultural differences between their contexts and that of Luke. Elaine pondered how to modernize the Luke 8:4–8 parable of the Sower and Seeds, asserting that the model of sowing seeds "wouldn't really work today" in her city. She believed that Jesus "was probably only saying this kind of thing because of the context back then. If he had been around nowadays he would have said something completely different, like starting a branch of shops."

The readers also used contemporary values to critique Luke. Fishy was not pleased with Jesus' parable of the Dutiful Servant in Luke 17:7–10. According to his reading, the parable demonstrated that if the servant "does what his master says, he still doesn't deserve his thanks, cause all he is doing is his job." As a result of this interpretation, the reader reacted against the parable. Fishy declared that it was a part of Luke that he "didn't think was right" and protested, "I think the servant should be treated well." The reader applied his contemporary views of social equality and employer-employee civility to the narrative world and declared the parable wanting. Fishy's lack of awareness of Luke's socio-historical context left him to interpret the parable based on the values of his own context.

Just as often, Luke stimulated critique of the reader's world. Trevor brought to his reading a view of Jesus that had been developed through many years of church attendance. Reading Luke caused him to re-negotiate this pre-established view:

---

45. See Tannehill, *Luke*, 184; Johnson, *Luke*, 175.
46. Fowler, *Let the Reader Understand*, 78.

> I found myself pondering what Jesus is actually like. Because I found there was a lot of contradiction between what's been drummed into me for ages at church, like, "Jesus was amazing. Jesus was perfect," then what I've read, it's really different. There's a lot in there where you think, "actually that probably wasn't the perfect Jesus that I've had drummed into me."

Trevor's church-derived view kept Jesus at a distance by portraying Jesus as primarily divine and morally perfect. Through reading Luke, Trevor discovered "that Jesus was a human" too and that Jesus was sometimes even "really rude, like when he pushes the tables over. It makes you think, 'Oh, it's okay to get angry sometimes.'" The reader found himself unexpectedly identifying with the Jesus of Luke and even embraced him as a model. His former, saintly view of Jesus proved thin and was replaced by a more complex version with which the reader could empathize. Ironically, Trevor stole past the watchful dragons of church piety by reading the text itself.[47]

When Sense-Seeking Fails

What happened when a reader was not able to make sense of the text? Sense-seeking tended to fail whenever the readers encountered a part of Luke that they deemed incompatible either with other parts of the text or with the overall narrative synthesis. Lisa was confused by Jesus' injunction to the 72 disciples in Luke 10:6 to "take back your greeting of peace" because it seemed to contradict the angels' declaration in Luke 2:14 that Jesus' birth brought "peace on earth." B.C., in reference to the Luke 6:43–45 Tree and Fruit saying, bemoaned, "I was a bit confused by it because I didn't see why it had to link in with the rest of the book." He could not work out the role of the saying in the overall narrative with the result that his reading of the saying was incomplete.

Marguerat and Bourquin claim that "the more implicit the message [of a passage], the more the participation of the reader in the act of reading must be an active one."[48] My findings support this assertion, but with a caveat: although difficulty with determining meaning sometimes appeared to enhance a reader's participation, it also frustrated that participation if meaning proved elusive. Hannah C. stated that when she could not make sense of a passage, "sometimes I carry on because I really don't want to keep on that bit." However, she preferred to wrestle with meaning as much as possible: "Some bits I do try and come up with a conclusion because it really

---

47. Cf. Lewis, "Sometimes Fairy Stories," 47.
48. Marguerat and Bourquin, *How to Read*, 120.

pesters me." The inability to construct meaning also led to non-participation. Jack and Jake both admitted to skipping sections of Luke that they did not understand.

Reading through an Imposed Grid

The most common source of abortive readings, however, was externally imposed reading grids which stymied the readers' pursuit of sense by sending them down an interpretive cul-de-sac. An example of this may be seen in Stephanie's inability to produce a full reading of the Luke 20:9–18 parable of the Tenants in the Vineyard. Stephanie visualized many of the elements of this parable, including the vineyard, the vineyard owner, and the tenants. But she could not work out the action in the parable: "I was just so confused about it that I didn't really imagine it." The causal links between the different story components eluded her and she could not make sense of the plot.

The source of Stephanie's confusion was her assumption that the parable should be read as a model of morality since it was part of the biblical canon: "I thought it was written how Christians were supposed to behave." She brought to Luke an already established interpretive grid which led her to seek morals for Christian living in the parable. But since the vineyard owner kills his wicked tenants, the conduct that seemed to be advocated in the parable was killing people. This reading caused her cognitive dissonance since she could not reconcile the vineyard owner's conduct with the morals she associated with the Christian faith. In the end, she abandoned the parable as incomprehensible. Her imagination could only get her so far before being stymied by the conflict between the plot and her moral expectations.

Due to this externally imposed grid, Stephanie did not interpret the parable with reference to the narrative world. A narrative-orientated approach may have served her better. Richard Hays uses this parable to argue for the importance of reading the Gospels within the matrix of canonical narrative. Such reading, he points out, gives "both hermeneutical guidance and theological depth" to interpretation.[49] Even without a whole canon perspective, a perspective which the participants in this study could not be expected to bring to their reading of Luke, it is possible to make sense of this parable using Luke's overall narrative world. Rowe refers to this parable as "an allegory for the larger story of the Gospel."[50] Within the world of Luke, the parable functions as a prophecy by Jesus of his death at the hands of the religious leaders, and his vindication through resurrection.

49. Hays, "The Canonical Matrix of the Gospels," 54.
50. Rowe, *Early Narrative Christology*, 167.

Externally imposed reading grids also diminished the readers' experience of the narrative world because they positioned the readers outside of the text. When I asked Jack how he would describe the Gospel of Luke, he stated glumly, "it's a set of rules that I have to obey in life." According to Jack, this view of the Gospel came from his church. It is not going too far to say that whenever Jack's reading in the interview was constructed out of externally imposed ideas, his energy level plummeted, he slumped in his chair, became passive, and dully repeated national curriculum and Sunday School lessons by rote.

In contrast, whenever Jack imagined the contents of a story or empathized with a character, his whole demeanor changed, he sat up, and he became animated. For instance, Jack liked the Luke 19:11–27 parable of the Gold Coins and became positively excited when discussing it, partially because of its promise of a reward, but primarily because, "I wanted to see the look on this guy's face when he sees his master and he heard the other two people had made money and he hadn't" {giggles}. Working out the emotive response of the servant who hid his coin transformed the narrative world into a place with which Jack could interact, as opposed to a set of rules to which he had to submit. For Jack, making sense of Luke depended upon being able to hold a genuine dialogue with it.

These findings, needless to say, interrogate the school religious education and church programs which impose external grids upon the interaction of child readers with the Bible. The moral, historical, and symbolic agendas discussed earlier in chapter 4 may distance readers from the text, disrupt the reading game, and rob readers of a narrative experience. The result may be an incomprehension which turns the Bible into an inaccessible tome, as was evident in Stephanie's reading, or a conception of the Bible as an oppressive artefact, as was evident in Jack's reading.

Summary

The child readers pursued meaning in two key ways: by making sense of the narrative world as a narrative world, and by relating the narrative world to their worlds. For the first form of pursuit, the readers used a puzzle-solving reading strategy whereby they worked out the big picture of Luke using its parts and made sense of the parts of Luke relative to that big picture. A key method for the second form of pursuit was reading by analogy, a form of interpretation which drew parallels between the world of the text and the world of the reader. Some of the key types of readings produced by the pursuit of contextual meaning were ethical readings, teen readings, and personal readings. The juxtaposition of text and context often led to their mutual critique. Externally-imposed reading grids sometimes prevented the readers from working out the sense of the text. When the readers could not make sense of the text, their reading experience was stymied.

I have, until this point, avoided direct discussion of the contents of the overall narrative picture as expressed in the readings. In the final analysis chapter, I examine this big picture. Most of the readings constructed very similar big pictures of Luke, pictures which took shape around the plot of the Gospel.

Chapter 11

Plot-Driven Reading

Lisa: "I've heard the story of him being crucified before. But I think after reading the whole thing, [because] it's built up, then he gets crucified, you feel more of a connection."

Robyn: "Some people hated [Jesus] and the people who hated him were really bad people. Jesus was the goodie who everyone has to love."

Introduction

The plot of Luke was the main reading incentive for most of the participants: they read to find out what happened. Culler refers to plot-driven reading as "epistemophilia" or the "desire to know" the end of the story as well as the truth of the story.[1] Despite its episodic structure, the readers viewed Luke as plot-based. Indeed, many of their complaints about Luke pertained to its juddering presentation of the plot. Lucy declared the episodic structure "dismissive" of topics and said she would have preferred a smoother flow between stories. Although Luke's micro-narratives appear on one level to be self-contained, the readers recognized that the macro-narrative knits them together. The macro-narrative functioned as the interpretive frame of reference, or big picture, for the readers. Green affirms this approach, indicating that each episode "must be read with reference to its narrative location" so that "Luke's staging of events in their narrative sequence is a primary control on determination of meaning."[2]

This staging of events in a sequence is a fundamental component of plot. Brooks defines plot as the "organizing line, the thread of design, that

1. Culler, *Literary Theory*, 91.
2. Green, *Luke*, 11.

makes narrative possible" because a plot is finite and comprehensible.[3] Through the plot, the narrative world exists as a dynamic yet coherent place. Fokkelman helpfully describes plot as "a course that is run."[4] The function of the plot, according to Brooks, is to move a narrative "forward" so that the reader seeks "a line of intention and a portent of design that hold the promise of progress toward meaning."[5] A narrative's big picture is not a single image, like a painting, but rather a series of inter-twined and developing units, more like the images in a film. In the readings, the plot centered on Jesus' life trajectory. In Luke, this trajectory is essentially linear, beginning as it does with the infancy stories and concluding with Jesus' death, resurrection, and ascension. The readings constructed Luke's big picture by following the trajectory's forward movement, so that what Luke meant was, at least partially, a matter of how the plot developed.

It is important to note that the readings treated Luke's plot and characters as inter-related. In his essay "The Art of Fiction," Henry James famously states: "What is character but the determination of incident? What is incident but the illustration of character?"[6] James' concern is with the writer's art, especially with the construction of a novel, and his discussion focuses on how a narrative communicates through the organic connection between characters and action. Luke is neither a novel nor fiction; but it is a narrative and as such its actions and characters coalesce to guide its reader along its narrative trajectory. Accordingly in the readings and in this chapter, action and characters are inextricably linked.

The centrality of plot to interpretation, as well as the mutual inter-working of action and character, may be seen in Lisa's insightful reading of Jesus' crucifixion. Reading the whole Gospel forged a bond between Lisa and Jesus which heightened her immersion in the crucifixion story. She illustrated the impact of this immersion by comparing it to her response to the plight of television characters: "It was like if you watch on t.v. a program for the first time and you see someone get killed, you don't feel that emotional about it. But if you watch, say, six episodes and then they get killed, then you feel the connection, then it's more emotional." Lisa's encounter with Luke's overall plot altered how she interpreted an already familiar event in that plot, the crucifixion.

Using her television analogy, Lisa described her previous, repeated encounters with the crucifixion story as isolated "episodes" which elicited little

---

3. Brooks, *Reading for the Plot*, 4.
4. Fokkelman, *Reading Biblical Narrative*, 77.
5. Brooks, *Reading for the Plot*, xiii.
6. James, "The Art of Fiction," 55.

empathy. But placed in the context of the whole plot, the crucifixion came near the end of the "series" allowing space for her to form an empathetic bond with Jesus as the central character. Lisa explained: "I've heard the story of him being crucified before. But I think after reading the whole thing, [because] it's built up, then he gets crucified, you feel more of a connection." Due to this bond, Lisa found that Jesus' death was "quite powerful." The reader's bond with Jesus gave new clarity to Jesus' death as a key plot twist near the end of the story.

In this chapter, I discuss the plot of Luke's macro-narrative as articulated in the readings and how that plot shaped the readers' experience of the Gospel. Whereas in the previous chapters I structured my analysis around an elucidation of the key findings from the children's readings, the nature of the topic in this chapter requires a slightly different approach. The structure of this chapter is essentially an outline of the children's understanding of Luke's big picture. First I look at the different elements of the plot, beginning with the main characters discussed in the readings. I then explore the readers' conception of the plot as a conflict, consider the weapons the readings attributed to the characters, and conclude with a discussion of the plot's resolution.

Reading Jesus as the Hero

When I asked Lucy what Luke was about, she exclaimed, "about Jesus!" and laughed at my apparent obtuseness. For all of the readers, Jesus was the hero of the Gospel. This was due not simply to his veritable ubiquity in the text, but also to the role the readers' perceived him to play in the plot. This label, "hero," needs some clarification. In his seminal work on the mythology of heroes, Joseph Campbell examines the similarities between multiple hero "myths" through the centuries, including the story of Jesus as interpreted by the Christian church.[7] His definition of hero is a summary of the hero's functions: "A hero ventures forth from the world of common day into a region of supernatural wonder; fabulous forces are there encountered and a decisive victory is won"; the hero returns "with the power to bestow boons" on other people.[8]

Although his treatment of the hero role is decidedly Freudian, Campbell's definition is salvific in orientation. The functions which comprise his definition provide clues to some of the expectations that the readers appeared to bring to Luke, particularly the hero engaging in a series of conflicts

---

7. Campbell, *The Hero with a Thousand Faces*, viii.
8. Ibid., 30; original italics removed.

and securing a victory over hostile forces. Almost all of the readings deemed Jesus to occupy the type of hero role associated with salvific narratives. Michael called Jesus a "hero" and then explained, "a hero is someone who does good and saves the world." This hero role is familiar within popular culture and the readings compared Jesus to Harry Potter, Aslan, Superman, and James Bond.

As Michael stated, a hero is expected to do good. In salvific narratives, doing good is not only about specific meritorious acts, but also and especially about acting on behalf of the commended side in the conflict at the heart of the narrative. In these narratives, the narrative world is a moral place, usually divided between good and evil, and the hero occupies a moral position relative to this world. Robyn summed this up for Jesus' role in Luke: "Some people hated [Jesus] and the people who hated him were really bad people. Jesus was the goodie who everyone has to love."

That the readings viewed Jesus as a hero dovetails with Appleyard's "Reader as Hero or Heroine" reading role.[9] This reading role is a means of participating in the narrative world through close alignment with the protagonist in the midst of the protagonist's struggles. Tannehill describes Luke as a "system of influence" that leads its readers "to believe or to reaffirm their belief in the central character, Jesus."[10] Tannehill's description of Luke supports the viability of the readers viewing Jesus as the hero of Luke and aligning with him in the narrative world.

According to Appleyard, the reader in this reading role regards the protagonist as a "powerful or clever hero or heroine."[11] The readings certainly expressed high views of Jesus, repeatedly declaring him "good" and describing him as: "clever," "a take-charge leader," "connected with God," "mysterious," "a powerful personality," "loving," "knowledgeable and passionate," "caring and forgiving," "strict but nice," "commanding," and "wise." Jack stated that Jesus was "not boring," a vital trait in a hero for an eleven-year-old boy. Kit, B.C., and Allie's readings all compared Jesus to various types of superhero. But not all of the traits attributed to Jesus were positive: Trevor called him "rude" while Stephanie deemed him a "know-it-all." These negative traits were nonetheless considered befitting of Jesus' status, for, as Stephanie clarified, "he probably does [know everything], but he's not being subtle about it."

---

9. Appleyard, *Becoming a Reader*, 15; see my discussion in chapter 3 under "Children Reading Narrative."

10. Tannehill, *The Narrative Unity of Luke-Acts*, 1:8.

11. Appleyard, *Becoming a Reader*, 59.

Appleyard's Reader as Hero or Heroine role is particularly concerned with "the motif of character defined by struggle."[12] Such a motif runs like a thread through Luke, for even Luke's infancy narratives foreshadow the struggles awaiting Jesus.[13] The readings repeatedly articulated this struggle, characterizing Jesus' life as a series of conflicts. Vanessa's visualization of Jesus was indicative: "He had the eyes of an army man . . . when you're in battle, you always have to be alert, and you always have to watch your own back. It was like that for Jesus." According to this reading, Jesus' life situation demanded constant vigilance and included the threat of attack. This was because, as Robyn explained, "someone was after him, like plotting after him." The hero had enemies who wanted to take his life.

The "Bad Guys"

Most heroes have enemies to face. As Vanessa declared, "there is always a bad guy." Campbell symbolizes such enemies as a "monster avid for the greedy rights of 'my and mine'" which leads the hero into tragedy.[14] The relationship between the hero and these enemies is invariably confrontational, and the readings viewed Jesus as engaging in an escalating conflict with the religious and political authorities of his world; that is, Jesus was embroiled in controversy with those in power. Anthony Le Donne concurs that the Gospels are stories of conflict and points out that the reader "should expect that Jesus' 'enemies' will enter and act within this story accordingly."[15] Although the readings classified a variety of characters as enemies, most of the readings perceived Jesus' primary opponents to be the religious leaders who repeatedly questioned and sought to kill him.

In reference to these religious leaders, the readings rarely distinguished between the Pharisees, teachers of the law, priests, and other Jewish leaders, although they did frequently refer to all of these groups using just one of these labels. As Michael clarified, "I thought they were all the same." The child readers' handling of these characters is validated by Kingsbury's point that, although these different religious groups were diverse historically, "within Luke's story world" they "stand out as a group character." He explicates that the role Luke attributes to this group "is distinct: They are the stereotypical opponents of Jesus, those with whom he becomes locked in controversy and who see to it that he is put to death." The religious leaders

---

12. Ibid., 61.
13. Cf. Gowler, *Host, Guest, Enemy and Friend*, 179–80.
14. Campbell, *The Hero with a Thousand Faces*, 15, 28.
15. Le Donne, "Jewish Leaders," 206.

"are second only to Jesus as the ones who influence most the plot of the story."[16] Gowler's analysis of the Pharisees adds a few helpful nuances to this concept of a group character. He describes them as stylized and closed, with little possibility of development. The group character has one central function: to be Jesus' opponent.[17]

Since the readings consistently treated the religious leaders as a group character, in this chapter, in order to convey the readings accurately, I use the term "religious leaders" to refer generically to Jesus' religious opponents. I specify a particular group of religious leaders or a different opponent only when this is appropriate to a reading. This gains particular pertinence in the discussion of the readings of Jesus' trials and death, since the Pharisees are absent from this part of the narrative. Most of the readings showed little or no awareness of this absence.[18]

A good guy versus bad guy distinction thus pervaded the readings. The religious leaders were not seen merely as a group of people who disagreed with Jesus. They were, in the words of Percy, the "bad guys" of the text. Le Donne believes that the Gospels deliberately foreground the differences between Jesus and the religious leaders and cast them in "a good guy/bad guy scenario." Jesus' enemies are "painted darkly" while Jesus is "seen as the hero."[19] One reader envisaged a group of religious leaders lurking in the shadows, while another imagined them wearing long black hooded cloaks. Both of these visualizations symbolically cast the religious leaders on the side of evil. Although some of the readers stated that they brought a negative view of the religious leaders to the text, many of them also expressed surprise at the pervasiveness of the religious leaders' opposition. Vanessa, who comes from a high church tradition, was particularly taken aback to discover that Jewish priests helped to perpetrate Jesus' death.

---

16. Kingsbury, *Conflict*, 21–22.

17. Gowler, *Host, Guest, Enemy and Friend*, 306, 313.

18. It is worth noting that although Gowler classifies the Pharisees as closed characters whose primary role in the narrative is to oppose Jesus, he separates them out from the other Jewish leaders in the Gospel since they disappear from the narrative after Jesus reaches Jerusalem, and because they have a different role in Acts. He asserts that the Pharisees play "an intermediary role in Luke-Acts" and "should not be lumped together with the other Jewish leaders." But this is to read back into Luke a development that takes place in Acts. The readers in this study were concerned only with Luke. See Gowler, *Host, Guest, Enemy and Friend*, 311. Kingsbury believes that despite the disappearance of the Pharisees from the narrative, it would be "erroneous to think that Luke is thereby exculpating them from guilt for Jesus' death or picturing them as less opposed to him than the other groups." Kingsbury, *Conflict*, 22.

19. Le Donne, "Jewish Leaders," 199, 207.

Yet the readings did not treat the religious leaders as mere cardboard cut-out enemies, the orcs of the Gospel world, for one of the readers' common empathetic maneuvers was working out the religious leaders' motives. Hannah M. thought they were "people who always think they're right" and consequently were "always trying to find out bad things about other people." Another reader, Boris, asserted that the religious leaders were "not listening" to Jesus and should have "thought about it a bit harder." Hannah C.'s reading labelled the religious leaders as "judgmental" people who refused to "give Jesus a chance" and were motivated instead by a desire to conform to those who held the reins of power in Jerusalem. Grace's reading described them as not being able to understand Jesus which led them to assume that "if we can't understand him, then no one else can," rendering Jesus' ministry pointless in their eyes.

The readings' category of "enemy" also stretched to any character who opposed Jesus. Satan, Pilate, Herod, and the crowds who called for the release of Barabbas all received censure in the readings. Zak summed up well when he stated that the characters he did not like included "the Romans, Pharisees, and Judas . . . [anyone who was] involved in getting Jesus killed." Outside of the religious leaders, the main figure who earned the readers' disapprobation was Judas. As one of the original disciples, his betrayal was viewed with considerable scorn. Elaine exclaimed that he "smelled" while Sophie A. declared his conduct "repulsive," and both readers added a nasty face for emphasis. The readers expended considerable effort trying to work out the motive behind Judas' betrayal as well as the implications of his role. Grace wondered "if Judas Iscariot hadn't been chosen would Jesus have still been betrayed?"[20]

"Finding Out What Happens"

When I asked James S. what kept him reading Luke to the end, he responded, "finding out what happens." The readers particularly wanted to find out what happened to the hero, Jesus. As Michael stated, "I was more interested in what Jesus did instead of what Jesus told." Numerous other readings also asserted a strong preference for the action in Luke over its teaching sections, and some readers even complained about the teaching. James A. thought the teaching sections "went on a bit long" and Boris thought they did not "help the story along." Jack even suggested ways to re-write parts of Luke in order to instill the narrative with more action.

20. Grace's question puts her in company with an array of theologians. See in particular Karl Barth's discussion of Judas' election: Barth, *Church Dogmatics*, II/2:458–506.

The readings expected "what happened" to equate to a coherent plot. Trevor explained this view: reading all of Luke helped me to "understand how it is actually a book. How it all links together, how the beginning links to the end and the end links to the beginning. How it's actually got a running storyline through it, a running plot." This plot propelled the narrative forward from the story of Jesus' birth to his ascension and clarified the causes of his death. Jake added that the plot was constructed around a tension: Luke "is telling us the idea that Christianity is a good thing and Jesus is correct. Yet the story still tells of these Pharisees who don't believe in that." Note that this reading incorporated into the plot the roles of both Jesus and the religious leaders. Both are fundamental to what happens in Luke.

This section examines the readings' treatment of Luke as a conflict-driven plot, the readings' interpretation of that conflict, and the readers' tendency to take sides in the conflict.

The Conflict

As far as the readings were concerned, what happened in Luke was a conflict between Jesus and his opponents. Lisa explained: "You saw all the good work that Jesus did. Then you saw gradually people were turning against him." Kingsbury concurs, stating that the driving element in Luke's plot is this conflict.[21] Oral discussion in the RVGs confirmed this finding with participants stating that the conflict "builds up tension" and shows that "something else will happen later" in the narrative. Jesus' opponents foment a mounting struggle that advances the plot towards its climax. Elaine described these opponents as "villains" specifically because "they are fighting against Jesus and his good news." Jesus' opponents seek to thwart his mission and silence his message. But they are repeatedly foiled by the hero. Fishy declared that the religious leaders repeatedly tried to "trap" Jesus, but "it didn't work."

Kit's reading of the Luke 20 debates between Jesus and the religious leaders provides an intriguing symbolic portrayal of this conflict. Luke 20 consists of a series of dialogues in which Jesus is tested by the religious leaders. Kit's reading followed the text and situated the debates in the temple:

> Jesus was standing before all the Pharisees and the people of the temple. They were all questioning him, and he was just standing there looking up at them. I pictured them in seats, like stadium

---

21. Kingsbury, *Conflict*, 34.

seating, in a row {acts this out in great detail}. They're on this side and he's standing on a little block.

Configuring the temple as a stadium with Jesus on center stage expressed not only Jesus' centrality to the debates, but also his success. The religious leaders, in contrast, were arrayed en masse in the stadium seating, indicating that they did not merit a hearing in the way that Jesus did.

In his discussion of Luke 20, Green observes that "Jesus cannot afford a laissez-faire attitude toward the temple, but must engage it directly," in particular because the religious leaders who oppose Jesus legitimate their status through "their relationship to the temple."[22] Kit's reading echoed Green's assertions about the power struggle within the temple precincts and added in a symbolic representation of that struggle. His temple-stadium symbolized the magnitude of the encounter between Jesus and the religious leaders as well as the status of both sets of characters relative to the temple. On another level, this symbolism reflected the reader's view of Jesus as the hero at the center of the Gospel with the religious leaders as the antagonists who question his importance.

The reading went a step further and branded the religious leaders as unappealing not only in conduct but also in essence. Kit imagined them robed them in apparel which he associated with high church leaders and which he deemed as rather odd, Kit being from a free-church tradition: "They're each wearing these funny outfits, you know, like those bishop ones, except a lot more weirder." The reader could identify neither with the use of such apparel nor with the beliefs and attitudes represented by the apparel. Kit's visualizations symbolized his dissent from the religious leaders.

Readings such as this interrogate the attempts of commentators like Nolland[23] and Craddock[24] to defend the status of religious leaders like the Pharisees within the narrative world. It is not just due to Luke's critical comments[25] that readers develop a negative view of these characters. It is also due to the plot, which presents Jesus as the hero and the religious leaders as those who array themselves against him.

---

22. Green, *Luke*, 697–98.
23. Nolland, *Luke 1—9:20*, 233.
24. Craddock, *Luke*, 74.
25. Nolland, *Luke 1—9:20*, 233.

The Battleground

A conflict has a focus, something that is fought over. One of the RVG participants pointed out that "Jesus was in conflict because he needed to make a point, not for the sake of conflict." The readings viewed the conflict in Luke as being over a number of issues, but the heart of this conflict was a power struggle: Jesus and the religious leaders tangled over which of them had the authority to speak for God. Jenny thought that the religious leaders "were trying to keep other people away from the truth so that they could still remain in charge." This view of the conflict is upheld by various scholars, including Kingsbury who states that the conflict is particularly over "the critical question of who will rule God's people."[26] The readings consistently backed Jesus' right to rule and several readings attributed Jesus' authority to his identity, referring to him as "Son of God" and "the Savior."

A number of readings cited the Luke 5:17–26 story of the Healing of the Paralyzed Man as an example of the power struggle. The first clash in the Gospel between Jesus and the religious leaders occurs in this story and its portrayal of them verbally crossing swords sets the tone of their relationship for the remainder of the narrative. In response to the Pharisees and teachers of the Law questioning his declaration of forgiveness, Jesus asserts, "I will prove to you, then, that the Son of Man has authority on earth to forgive sins," and heals the paralytic. The readers consistently aligned with Jesus in this story and against his questioners, a participative move which positioned the readers to agree with Jesus' claim to authority. James S., for instance, disparaged the religious leaders and approved of Jesus' decision to "put to them that he has the right to heal."

Elaine paraphrased the dialogue in the story so that it climaxed with Jesus' vindication:

> Jesus is like, "Oh yes. I'm going to heal this person."
>
> All the Pharisees are like, "No, you're not. You can't do that."
>
> And he's like, "Yes I can. And I can forgive his sins too. So there."
>
> Then he gets up and shows them who's boss.

The final "he" in this reading is ambiguous. It may refer to the paralyzed man, so that his healing demonstrates Jesus' authority, in close parallel to the passage. But this interpretation requires an abrupt alteration of active subject from Jesus to the paralyzed man in the final line. A more natural approach assumes that the reading maintains consistency in its use of

---

26. Kingsbury, *Conflict*, 82; see also Le Donne, "Jewish Leaders," 204, 205.

pronouns and the final "he" refers to Jesus, while the actions, getting up and showing, emphasize his authority. This latter interpretation maintains Jesus as the defiant agent of the story.

Assuming Jesus' authority in this story still left the readers puzzling over the answer to Jesus' question in verse 23: "Is it easier to say, 'Your sins are forgiven you,' or to say, 'Get up and walk'?" The commentators also fix upon this question. Johnson believes that physical healing and spiritual forgiveness emanate from the same divine power making them equal expressions of that power; Green, comparably, holds that the purpose of the question is to draw an equation between the two acts.[27] Elaine found the question perplexing but also thought that Jesus was deliberately connecting his abilities to heal and to forgive. This connection made her ponder their overlap and she drew an astute theological conclusion: "Forgiveness is a kind of healing of the soul."

Some of the readings evaluated Jesus' and the religious leaders' counter-claims to authority. In her reading of the Luke 14:1–6 story of the Healing of the Man with Dropsy, Abby weighed up the argument and agreed with Jesus: "I think he's absolutely right there." She could not accept the religious leaders' position on the Sabbath: "I understand that they respect this day and that they say you shouldn't do any work on it. But I don't think healing is some kind of work. It's a great thing." After analyzing the two positions, she concluded that "it was stupid how the teachers of the law and the Pharisees criticized Jesus for healing people on the Sabbath." This reader did not appear to align with Jesus simply because he was the hero but because of her intellectual assent to his position. Her reflections echoed the debate in the text.

The readings repeatedly connected Jesus' miracles to his authority, as is evident in the above readings of the healings of the paralyzed man and of the man with dropsy. Such miracles were seen not only as exertions of Jesus' power but particularly as verifications of his authority. Grace even seemed to think that a reason for the inclusion of miracles in the narrative was to gain the reader's attention: "I think if Jesus couldn't perform miracles but only preached about God and the things that you should do, I don't think [Luke] would have been as good as it is." Then again, perhaps Grace is right: why should ordinary readers be interested in a hero with verbal eloquence but who cannot alter his world?

---

27. Johnson, *Luke*, 95; Green, *Luke*, 242.

Taking Sides

The readers tended to respond to the conflict by aligning themselves with one side of that conflict, that of Jesus. This was also evident in the RVG results. I tested for plot-driven reading in the RVGs using the Luke 20:19–26 story of Paying Taxes to Caesar. Using only one passage limited the implications of the results to this passage. For this story, 66% of the respondents believed that Jesus and the religious leaders were in conflict, while 80% believed that the religious leaders used difficult questions in their attempt to trap Jesus.[28] The responses to the oral questions added an interesting nuance to these results. A total of 96% of the RVG participants raised their hands to indicate that they wanted Jesus to win this conflict, while 2 % wanted the religious leaders to win and the final 2% were uncertain. Even if not all of the participants would classify this story as a conflict, almost all of them were willing to take sides.

Aligning with one side of the conflict caused the readers to experience the narrative world from that position. As I discussed in chapter 2, narrative worlds tend to be governed by value systems which instill them with significance. Alignment with one side of a conflict leads the reader to embrace the value system of that side. Such values are often implicit so that the reader has to assume them in order to look *along* the narrative path. Zak, aware that he gleaned ideas from Luke's narrative world, explained: You are "so excited and caught up with the story that you wouldn't think that it was teaching you anything." This reading suggests that one of the roles of the plot was to impart to the reader the theology of the narrative world. Appleyard adds that a heroic narrative suits the way child readers "view the world" because it provides a simple way of distinguishing between "good and evil."[29] The values associated with good are condoned while those associated with evil are denounced.

The children's readings associated Jesus' values with good and those of the religious leaders with evil. This distinction was often expressed through contrasts, one of which was between humility and pride. Michael thought that Jesus taught his followers "to be humble" while the religious leaders declared: "We are good men. We are God people. We are better than you." Another contrast was between courage and self-preservation. James S. described Jesus as having "courage" in the face of opposition while the religious leaders sought to avoid being "put to shame." Other readings juxtaposed truth and deceit. Sophie A. labelled the religious leaders as "lying

---

28. See Table 6 in chapter 6 for a full breakdown of the results.
29. Appleyard, *Becoming a Reader*, 64.

and deceitful" in contrast to Jesus. Some readings focused on the tension between belief and hypocrisy. Trevor contrasted those who believed what Jesus said with the "hypocritical" religious leaders. Therefore as part of their narrative alignment, the readings upheld values such as humility, courage, truth, and belief, and renounced displays of pride, self-preservation, deceit, and hypocrisy. A number of the former values overlap with Luke's values of God's Kingdom, as discussed in chapter 2.

Against the Bad Guys

The readers' alignment was bound up with their empathetic responses to the conflict. As discussed in chapter 9, an important function of enemies in a narrative is to generate negative empathy or antipathy, and the readers' most salient response to the religious leaders was affective: they disliked them. Vanessa declared of the religious leaders after one of their disputes with Jesus, "I could understand their point. But it didn't make me like them any better." Even those readers who struggled at times to understand Jesus compared themselves to the disciples in their confusion rather than to the religious leaders in their antagonism. This finding does not support Le Donne's assertion that a key role of the religious leaders in the Gospels is to show readers "how *not* to act."[30] Le Donne assumes that a didactic aim undergirds the text's representation of the conflict. But the readings never viewed the religious leaders as a model of any sort.

Instead, a key role of the religious leaders appeared to be to provide characters for the readers to react against thereby strengthening the readers' bond with Jesus. Some of the readings expressed a desire for Jesus' success. Rachel stated: "You knew that Jesus was going to win because you just know that he's going to have a good answer. But you want him to have a good answer." This reading suggests that the reader aligned firmly with Jesus and experienced tension over how Jesus would best his opponents. Many of the readings expressed delight in Jesus' triumphs. When I asked Elaine what she liked about the Gospel, she immediately replied, "I liked the way Jesus is constantly getting the better of all these people who are asking him tricky questions. That's funny." Her explanation left her giggling.

The readers also appeared to take pleasure in denigrating the religious leaders. Zak expostulated: "They're supposed to be religious people and they're the ones that are causing all this trouble. It really makes me mad." Then he smiled. Sophie A. exclaimed that she "despised" the religious leaders and wanted, metaphorically, "to kill them." Her assertion made her

---

30. Le Donne, "Jewish Leaders," 199; italics in the original.

giggle, perhaps partially out of embarrassment at the strength of her statement. Ebby liked the religious leaders' consternation at being foiled: "They always end up embarrassed and scowling at themselves. I think that's funny." These denouncements of Jesus' enemies reveal not only the readers' alignment with Jesus but also their enjoyment of being on what they perceived as the winning side.

The Weapons

A conflict is carried out with weapons and the readers took a keen interest in the weapons wielded by Jesus and the religious leaders. The readers viewed Jesus' miracles as a powerful weapon which confounded his opponents and proved his authority, at least to his followers. But miracles were clearly not a weapon which Jesus' opponents could wield in opposition, and the battle was more closely joined using an entirely different type of weapon but one appropriate to a textual format: words.

The readings repeatedly referred to Jesus' opponents as attacking him with words, so that the conflict was often conceived of as verbal combat. As Elaine explained, the religious leaders "were not going to go around shooting people. They are villains with their mouths and their tongues." Le Donne supports this view of the conflict, describing the dialogue between Jesus' and the religious leaders as "combative speech."[31] The religious leaders used words, according to Allie, to "try to trick Jesus," for "arguments," and for interrogation: the leaders "tried to catch [Jesus] out with difficult questions." The readings interpreted this verbal conflict as central to Jesus' life. Rachel summarized the period of Jesus' ministry as, "he went through people questioning him."

The religious leaders' verbal attacks were not without purpose. Their aim initially appeared to be, in the words of Trevor, "to get Jesus to say something wrong." Had he done so, Jesus would have come down to their level and been less of a threat. As the narrative progressed, their verbal attacks were intended, Jeremy believed, to "find something out about him that could lead to his arrest." A number of the readings held that the verbal battles eventually reached a point where the religious leaders no longer engaged with Jesus substantively. Rather, as Percy stated, they became "so fixed on catching Jesus in something wrong that they don't really care what he says to them, even if it's a really valid point." The only verbal response that the religious leaders wanted from Jesus was an error.

31. Ibid.

"Clever Comebacks"

Jesus parried these attacks with what both Zak and John called "clever comebacks." Jesus countered words with words. Many of the readers openly admired Jesus' verbal prowess. Ebby liked how Jesus "had a quick fire answer for every evil thing [the religious leaders] tried to put on him." The readings expressed confidence in Jesus' verbal indomitability and he was seen as equal to any attack. Tarquin perceptively articulated a "law" of the narrative world: the religious leaders "asked Jesus all these tricky questions and he managed to answer them all, and left them speechless." Jesus' verbal skill not only won the skirmishes, but also disarmed his opponents. In this form of warfare, to be speechless is to be weapon-less.

Jesus' words proved his cleverness, a trait the readers also admired. Elaine thought that the religious leaders "were quite clever and cunning, but not cunning and clever enough to catch Jesus out." In the battle of wits, Jesus proved the sharper contender. John said that Jesus' "clever responses" were one of his favorite parts of the Gospel. He was particularly enthusiastic about the Luke 20:19–26 story of Paying Taxes to Caesar because Jesus' opponents "sent the cleverest people to try to trap him and yet they couldn't do it." In this reading, Jesus' intellectual wit surpassed the craftiness of his opponents.

The readings also viewed Jesus as taking the offensive in the verbal conflict. Percy's reading of the Luke 6:6–11 story of the Healing of the Man with the Paralyzed Hand highlighted Jesus' deliberate provocation: "He knew the Pharisees were looking for a way to accuse him, and he even went further to bring the man to the front, and to heal him in front of them." Gowler states that this story creates "the heroic image of Jesus standing defiant in front of those who would accuse him."[32] Percy's reading focused on this courageous defiance: Jesus used the healing to "criticize" the religious leaders "knowing what they could do to him, even knowing that they wanted a reason to do terrible things to him."

Jesus was not perceived as a passive hero. Even in the encounters which began with Jesus on the defensive, he often maneuvered into an offensive position. Both Tarquin and John discussed how Jesus' response in the Luke 20:19–26 story of Paying Taxes to Caesar turned the tables on his questioners. Percy pointed out the irony in such tactics: Jesus "often criticizes what [the religious leaders] did when they were actually trying to catch him out, and criticize him, and arrest him." Not only were the religious leaders'

---

32. Gowler, *Host, Guest, Enemy and Friend*, 212.

attempts to check Jesus unsuccessful but these attempts also caused them to lose ground, metaphorically, in the conflict.

"People Question Me" Too

One of the readers' key points of identification with Jesus was their mutual experience of verbal conflict. The readers were familiar with the use of words as a weapon and many of them identified with the experience of being questioned. In the RVG sessions, over 80% of the participants raised their hands to indicate that they had experienced fighting using words; in one session, all of the participants raised their hands in agreement. When asked if anything in Luke reminded him of his own life, Kit promptly responded, "people question me about my faith." The readings repeatedly compared the verbal attacks on Jesus to the readers' experiences of being questioned by their peers. Elaine stated, "People try and ask me clever questions about God that I can't really answer [just as] Jesus was being asked difficult questions." She stressed her relative short-comings: "The difference is that Jesus had an answer. I have to go with what I know and use my initiative and copy Jesus." This reading treated Jesus both as a hero who knew how to defeat those who attacked him but also one whose verbal skills could be emulated.

Jesus' conduct in the midst of antagonism also served as a model for the readers. Jesus' courage inspired Percy: it "showed me that I could stand up to things if I want to." For James S., Jesus demonstrated the importance of perseverance, particularly when "you know you're not doing anything wrong." Hannah M. read Jesus' experience of antagonism as analogous to her own experience of teenage social maneuvering. Grimacing and ducking her head in a moment of personal discomfort, she wondered, "How did he feel when people were horrible to him and they didn't like him?" She viewed Jesus as someone who would understand her distress, and her teen reading probed the effect of animosity upon Jesus' self-perception.

As I discussed in chapter 3, Erikson's developmental model of personal identity indicates that teenagers are attracted to heroes who both help them to work out their identity and serve as a person or idea in which they may have faith.[33] The readings above suggest that Jesus as hero may do both. The readers' identification with Jesus, over being questioned and even ridiculed, allowed Jesus to serve as a model for dealing with conflict. This model challenged both Percy and James S. to reflect upon their identity in the midst of conflict and motivated them to stand up for themselves. Jesus' conduct

---

33. Erikson, *Identity*, 128–29. See also my discussion in chapter 3 under "The Stage Theorists."

served as a focus of faith for readers like Elaine and Hannah M. who found in Jesus a hero who went through similar experiences and came out the other side.

Reading for Resolution

A plot builds towards resolution, a resolving of the tension which propels the story forwards. The resolution constitutes what ultimately happens in the narrative.[34] In the readings, Luke's resolution had to do not only with the outcome of the conflict between Jesus and his antagonists, but also with the fulfilment of Jesus' purpose, or his hero quest. The readings viewed Jesus' quest as greater than merely triumphing verbally over the religious authorities. The purpose of the quest, according to many of the readings, was salvific. A number of scholars also argue that salvation is central to the Gospel. Marshall for instance asserts that "the idea of salvation supplies the key to the theology of Luke."[35]

Michael summarized Jesus' quest as "he comes into the world" and tells everyone, "'you're going to be the world that I save. I'm going to resurrect and you're not going to believe it until you've seen it and heard it.'" This reading suggests that, while the early parts of Luke adumbrate Jesus' quest, the full purpose of the quest only becomes apparent in the narrative world through its fulfilment. Fokkelman upholds this view, specifying that Jesus' quest is to establish the reign of God but the true nature of the quest, and thus the nature of the reign of God, becomes clear through Jesus' death and resurrection.[36]

I discuss the resolution of Luke's plot, as expressed in the readings, in two parts: Jesus' submission to his opponents and the fulfilment of his quest.

"Refusing to Answer the Questions"

Resolution of the plot invariably involved resolution of the conflict between Jesus and his opponents. The verbal battle needed to be resolved. Tarquin believed that the religious leaders "don't like Jesus because he's better than them. So they try to make him answer something wrongly so they can arrest him." In this they fail, for as Michael stated the religious leaders did

---

34. Prince, *Dictionary of Narratology*, 84.

35. Marshall, *Luke: Historian and Theologian*, 92. Marshall is debating the view of salvation in Luke held by Conzelmann. Cf. Conzelmann, *The Theology of Luke*.

36. Fokkelman, *Reading Biblical Narrative*, 193.

eventually trap Jesus, but "not with words." Jesus' opponents had to resort to other tactics in order to defeat him. John considered these tactics underhanded: they "can't beat him. In the end the only way he is beaten is by betrayal. It's quite interesting how it's actually just betrayal which beats him. It's not sheer force or might." Jesus' one area of weakness, it appeared, was his followers and the religious leaders found an ally in one of them.

Vanessa described Judas' betrayal as the key turning point in the plot: through it, the religious leaders gained an advantage over Jesus. Elaine pointed out that it meant they joined ranks with Satan. The betrayal enabled the religious leaders to stop Jesus' ministry by putting him to death. Ebby summarized this plot development as, "all the religious teachers wouldn't believe Jesus so they killed him for it." The religious leaders' treatment of Jesus demonstrated the need of the Jewish nation for radical intervention. This intervention was made possible by Jesus' submission to his enemies.

Jesus' submission necessarily included his speech. Prior to his betrayal and arrest, Jesus repeatedly bested his opponents with words, as the readings persistently asserted. But afterwards, Jesus' speech patterns changed so that he allowed his opponents the advantage. Trevor pointed out that "Jesus, when he's faced by Pilate, refused to answer the questions that he's being asked." Dinkler's analysis of Jesus' conduct affirms Trevor's reading. This scholar points out that Jesus' responses to the questioning of his opponents shifts over the course of the trials leading up to his death: before the Jewish Council, he foregrounds the pointlessness of answering their questions and supplies only indirect responses; he reduces his speech to blatant ambiguity in response to Pilate; his approach finally climaxes with complete silence before Herod.[37]

Up to this point, Jesus' voice had dominated the narrative world. Now that world is dominated by other voices. In terms of the plot, Jesus put down one of his chief weapons. Dinkler indicates that Jesus' silence was not passive: he chose "to remain silent" and not to exercise his authority.[38] Sophie M. described this as an act of submission: "He chose to die." Jesus' silence before his opponents was part of the path to his death, which as far as his opponents were concerned was the ultimate means of silencing him.

Up to this point in her argument Dinkler follows the narrative closely, but when she seeks to explain why Jesus embraced silence, she steps outside of the narrative world to look for answers. This may be a misstep. She concludes that Jesus' change of speech pattern in the trial scenes has two functions: to expose the "hard-heartedness" of Jesus' opponents thereby

37. Dinkler, "Telling Silences," 5.
38. Ibid., 3.

providing "a counter-example for Lukan readers"; and to impel Jesus' followers to speak on Jesus' behalf subsequent to his death and resurrection.[39] In short, Dinkler does not interpret Jesus' silence in keeping with the plot. The children's readings, however, interpreted Jesus' silence with reference to the narrative world. Prior to the trial scenes, a key "law" of the narrative world had already been established, as articulated in the reading by Tarquin: silence in the midst of verbal combat equated to defeat. In order to die, Jesus had to stop speaking.

"Jesus Changed Everything"

According to the readings, Jesus submits to his opponents and ultimately to death in order to fulfil his quest. Kingsbury concurs, pointing out that although Jesus is "seemingly being stripped of all authority by being put to death," his death paves the way to triumph in the conflict with his opponents.[40] An interesting variant between the readings was their specification of which event particularly fulfilled the quest and resolved the plot: Jesus' death, resurrection, or ascension.

Jesus' death was viewed by some as a twist in the plot. Fishy asserted: "I thought Luke read like a story. You get the starting and you get the middle bit where it starts to go wrong. Then the end where it all goes right but you think it's wrong, but it's not." This reading suggested that the effect of Jesus' death took the reader, not to mention the characters, by surprise for although Jesus' death appeared to lead to defeat, it actually enabled victory. Powell's description of the story lines of the Gospels as "built upon extended ironies" corroborates this reading. Powell states that through Jesus, God's rule arrives in a way "that people do not expect."[41] Jesus triumphs over his opponents by submitting to their power.

In a number of the readings, the plot's resolution hinged upon Jesus' death. According to Kit, "the most important thing about [Luke] is when Jesus was killed." He described Jesus' death on the cross as "the whole story." In this reading, the narrative trajectory culminates in Jesus' death. Percy added a theological nuance to this view: Luke "is the story of Jesus' death and how he saved us." Percy's soteriological reading maintained that Jesus' death was central to Luke and particularly stressed Jesus' salvation of humanity. Karris asserts that Jesus' death expresses "with-ness, not separation."[42] Percy's

39. Ibid., 6–7.
40. Kingsbury, *Conflict*, 35.
41. Powell, *Narrative Criticism*, 31.
42. Karris, *Luke*, 121.

reading reflects Karris' position: salvation in Luke is about uniting people to God.

Jesus' resurrection was also hailed as resolving the plot. In one of the RVGs, a participant asserted orally that "the religious leaders look like they win then Jesus resurrects." Elaine specified cogently: Jesus "comes to earth and he goes completely against what everyone expects. It's about how he lives and how he dies and how he lives again. The whole thing basically builds up to the resurrection." The resurrection, by bringing victory over everything opposed to Jesus and his people, was the key turning-point in this reading of the macro-narrative. Elaine declared that the resurrection was "the whole point of the book."

Elaine's reading was theological and had overtones of the *Christus Victor* view of the atonement. She believed that Jesus gained "control over the devil and death" through his death and resurrection. The *Christus Victor* view holds that in the resurrection Jesus triumphs over the powers holding humanity in bondage, including what Martin Luther called the "unholy trinity," the powers of sin, death, and the devil.[43] Seen through this lens, Jesus' quest was about defeating evil and it opened up new possibilities in the world, or as Elaine declared, Jesus' resurrection "completely changed everything."

In some of the readings, the ascension functioned, not so much as the resolution of the plot but as its epilogue. It is, after all, the final event in the narrative and brings closure to Jesus' life on earth. Green suggests that God's action at the ascension reverses the verdict of Jesus' enemies: they condemned and executed him but God elevates him and endows him with royal power.[44] Ebby similarly described the ascension as the moment when Jesus "lifted off" into heaven and he drew a picture of it which depicted God "reaching out to welcome his son back home again." In Ebby's reading, Jesus' life came full circle and he returned to the heavenly home from which he originated. Tannehill also points out the connections between the ascension account and the opening section of the whole narrative, and states that through these connections the "narrative achieves a sense of closure."[45]

The ascension caused a few readers to view the macro-narrative as open-ended. The story continues since, at its conclusion, Jesus is alive but departs while his disciples remain in Jerusalem praising God. James S. mused: "Jesus went up into heaven. It would be quite nice to know what

---

43. See the classic argument in Aulén, *Christus Victor*, 20; see also Boyd, "Christus Victor View," 29; Wright, *Evil and the Justice of God*, 59.

44. Green, *Luke*, 861–62.

45. Tannehill, *Luke*, 364.

happened after that, so I'm quite interested to read on, to see what happens." The ascension serves as what Powell calls, "a bridge between the two books," Luke and Acts,[46] and its open-endedness could potentially prompt readers like James S. to pick up Luke's next volume.[47]

This open-endedness led to theological ponderings about the interface between the narrative world and the readers' world. Sophie A. showed considerable theological insight when she declared: "It's past time uncompleted. It doesn't really finish, I mean, with Jesus going up to heaven. It continues because that's what the church is. And you want to carry on being a part of that and making it carry on happening." The story carries on in the church, of which this reader is a part, and thus it carries on through her.

Summary

In the children's readings, Jesus was the hero of Luke. This view of Jesus did not reduce to a divine but rather loquacious being who delivers moral platitudes. Nor did it reduce to a perfect man whose untarnished life should serve as a model for all good readers. Jesus was a hero of action involved in a divine plot to save the world. He engaged in conflict, stood for good, fought verbal battles, attacked with sharp wit, repeatedly trounced his opponents, asserted his authority, and benefitted the people around him. Like a true hero, he achieved his final victory in an unexpected but irreversible way.

The readers consistently sided with this hero. Consequently, they found themselves aligned with all that Jesus represented and cheering for his success. They particularly empathized with his verbal clashes and looked to him for a model for handling their own experiences of conflict. Reading Jesus as the hero of Luke gave the readers an understanding of Luke's vision of life with Jesus.

---

46. Powell, *What Are They Saying about Luke?*, 75. Powell is discussing Mikeal Parsons' interpretation of the ascension in Luke-Acts; see Parsons, *The Departure of Jesus in Luke-Acts*.

47. I recommended *Acts* to any of the readers who asked about what happened next.

Chapter 12

Conclusion

Sophie A.: Reading Luke was "like when you've just run a massive cross country thing. At the end you feel really good and you want to get out there and do some more."

Returning to the Question

This study has arrived at the following answer to the question of how this particular group of children read the Gospel of Luke: by engaging in reading strategies which gave the children experience of Luke's narrative world. I refer to this form of interpretation as participatory reading because the children's interpretation developed out of active engagement with the text. Gobbel and Gobbel might say that the readers interacted with the Lukan "playground" in order to gain understanding of it.[1] The readers, however, used a different analogy to express their participation. Both Sophie A. and Jenny compared their experience with Luke to the experience of running. Sophie A. stated that the effect of reading Luke was "like when you've just run a massive cross country thing. At the end you feel really good and you want to get out there and do some more." These young teenage girls felt that reading Luke had stretched them while also impacting their lives in a positive way.

This final chapter briefly reiterates how the readers participated in the activity of reading Luke. I then consider the implications of this participation for the academic fields pertinent to my study. The chapter concludes by emphasizing the limitations of my study and suggesting paths for further research.

---

1. Gobbel and Gobbel, *The Bible: A Child's Playground*, 47; italics in the original. See my discussion in chapter 4 under "Experiencing the Bible."

Accepting the Invitation

Maxwell asserts that when reading Luke, a "passive audience may remain untouched, but active hearers who help the proclaimer create the story in their own minds come away from that encounter formed and changed, continuing the story in their own lives."[2] Although Maxwell's concern is with the role of the ancient audience, my findings suggest that the child readers took just such an active approach. Maxwell goes on to query how the Lukan invitation to audience participation "might be issued in modern settings," deeming this an area for further research.[3] My study supplies an example of that research and shows how one group of child readers responded to Luke's invitation.

The children's readings point to a consistent acceptance of the invitation on the part of the readers. Sophie M. explained the result of her acceptance: "I felt like I knew Jesus a bit better. The more stories you read with the same character, the more you feel like you're their best friend. So it was a bit like that." Note that Sophie M.'s reading describes her participation as leading to knowing, and her descriptors of knowing are relational and affective. She did not come to know the protagonist better either by conducting a semiotic analysis of the text or by investigating the social world of first-century Galilee, though doubtless both of these activities would have added to her understanding of Jesus' world. Her knowing derived neither from seeking in the pages of the Gospel a moral to live by, nor from handling Luke like a historical document, the approaches that adult gatekeepers may have expected of her or even imposed upon her. Sophie M. knows Jesus a little better by encountering him in the pages of his story and interacting with his life and world.

Acceptance of the invitation led the readers to participate in a reading dialogue with Luke using five key reading strategies. First, the readers approached Luke as a narrative and the text's discourse directed their interpretation through literary devices such as genre, perspective, voice, and sequence. Secondly, they used their imaginations to "see" metaphorically the contents of Luke, sometimes simply to observe but usually in order to make sense of the text. The readers' memories often served as a starting point in this process. Thirdly, empathetic reading enabled the readers to connect emotively with the narrative world through its characters. As Sophie M.'s reading indicates, this affective engagement was relational and seemed to be partially contingent upon the perspectives in Luke.

---

2. Maxwell, *Hearing Between the Lines*, 180.
3. Ibid.

Fourthly, the readers pursued the sense of the text, a reading strategy that took two different yet inter-connected forms. The first of these forms entailed working out how Luke made sense as a text, and to this end the readers engaged in puzzle-solving, a cognitive activity that enabled them to determine how the various parts of the narrative fit together into a big picture. For the second form of this reading strategy, meaning was pursued in reference to the readers' contexts. This form of sense-seeking often constructed analogies with the readers' worlds, and generated ethical, teen, or personal readings. The big picture had Luke's plot at its center and the readers' fifth reading strategy entailed following the narrative trajectory to find out what happened. At the heart of the plot was Jesus' conflict with his opponents, a battle waged particularly through words. The readers aligned with Jesus, the hero, in this conflict. Jesus eventually submitted to the weapons wielded by his opponents and the plot was resolved through an ironic twist in which the hero secured victory by following the path of defeat.

By accepting the invitation, this group of readers gained, in Lewis's words, "inside-experience" of Luke's narrative world.[4] The reading strategies they brought to the task enabled them both to make sense of the story world and to connect that world to their worlds. In Luke's world, the readers found a hero whose struggles at times resonated with their personal experience and whose triumphs proved motivational. But most of all, they found a hero whom they could get to know, at least a little.

Considering the Implications

If participatory reading is a viable approach to engaging with the Gospel of Luke, then it raises a number of questions for the fields undergirding this study. These fields include biblical studies, children's literature theory, and practical theology particularly in its use of the Bible with children. I look at each of these in turn.

Studying the Bible

As I discussed in chapter 2, much of biblical scholarship depends upon analytical approaches to the Bible, approaches which seek to keep separate the worlds of the text and the reader in a display of appropriate critical distance. Although such distance provides useful perspectives on the text, the findings of this study suggest that it may not be conducive to a holistic reading of

---

4. Lewis, "Meditation in a Toolshed," 50–54.

the Bible. A scholar who seeks to know the text only from an external position and sidesteps textual directives, preferring to discuss them rather than to follow them, may overlook the impact of those directives. How then can that scholar's discussion be complete? Multiple scholars note the oddity of the first two locations of the lamp in Luke 8:16, but John, who assumed the perspective of the narratee, foregrounded the humor at work in the saying.

Some of the findings even suggest that interpretations that are solely analytical may misfire. Allie responded to the Luke 6:41–42 Speck in the Eye saying with personal contrition about her conduct, in direct opposition to the reader response predicted by one scholar. While biblical scholars look outside of Luke's narrative world in order to explain Jesus' silence during his trials, the child readers interpreted this silence in keeping with the logic at work in the narrative world. As Tarquin made clear, Jesus' silence equates to putting down one of his chief weapons, his words. Both Allie's and Tarquin's readings add an interpretive angle that interrogates the readings of their scholarly peers.

One of the dangers of relying exclusively upon critical approaches to interpret the Bible is that scholars may make readers out in their own image without acknowledging that they are doing so. Darr posits that the first readers of Luke used an analytical strategy not dissimilar to his own.[5] Tannehill asserts that readers will identify with characters in Luke who are socially similar to themselves.[6] Tannehill, as an adult male, has plenty of characters to choose from, but what are child readers to do if his assertion is correct? My findings suggest that young readers may actually empathize with characters across the social strata.

As Lewis warns, critical approaches utilize one form of knowing, the analytical. Inside-experience draws another epistemological seat up to the interpretive table. To use another analogy, a critical approach is comparable to watching a film with the director's commentary on. The viewer hears an analysis of how the film was made along with a series of historically relevant anecdotes, all the while seeing the film but not experiencing the story. The experiential approach, in contrast, is like watching the film as a film, without commentary, so that the viewer engages first and foremost with the story.

My discussion in chapter 9 of Grace's reading of the criminal on the cross provides a salutary example. Grace experienced internal conflict as she found herself approving the conduct of the criminal, a character from whom she preferred to distance herself. The meaning of this story, for her,

---

5. Darr, *Character Building*, 26, 36; see my discussion in chapter 9 under "Relational Reading."

6. Tannehill, "Freedom and Responsibility," 272; see my discussion in chapter 9 under "Relational Reading."

was neither a one-dimensional observation about the configuration of its contents, nor was it an abstraction about salvation. Instead meaning resided in the tension generated for her by the criminal's words, which led to an expansion of Grace's view of the human potential for salvation. Making space at the hermeneutical table for such experiential knowing may enrich biblical interpretation.

The implications of participatory reading may go beyond children's engagement with Bible stories. Two of the key developmental theories of reading hold that the reading strategies developed in childhood continue in use throughout adulthood, relative to the type of text with which a reader engages.[7] Adults may read experientially too. The research of the cognitive psychologists substantiates this point. Gerrig argues that adults read by immersing themselves in the narrative world and use their personal experience to construct that world.[8] Harris adds that a standard feature of adult reading is the reader's use of the imagination to construct a mental model of the narrative world.[9] Oatley's findings indicate that both children and adults use their imagination and empathy to make sense of a narrative.[10] The findings of these researchers highlight the potential universality of the children's reading strategies. This being the case, participatory reading should not be relegated to the child-only corner of the biblical studies workroom.

Children as Readers

Turning to the fields of children's literature theory and cognitive psychology, all five of the reading strategies evident in the findings are described in this literature. Applebee's study suggests that thirteen-year-olds approach a story *as* a story, pursue the cause and effect of the plot, and interpret stories by seeking their overall coherence.[11] Appleyard found that adolescent readings are often affective, pointing to empathy as a reading strategy.[12] Oatley

---

7. Applebee, *The Child's Concept of Story*, 114, 125; Appleyard, *Becoming a Reader*, 15; see my discussion in chapter 3 under "Developmental Theories of Reading."

8. Gerrig, *Experiencing Narrative Worlds*, 17, 66–67; see my discussion in chapter 3 under "The Cognitive Process."

9. Harris, *The Work of the Imagination*, 192; see my discussion in chapter 3 under "The Cognitive Process."

10. Oatley, *Such Stuff as Dreams*, 77, 115, 119; see my discussion in chapter 3 under "The Cognitive Process."

11. Applebee, *The Child's Concept of Story*, 109, 115, 118; see my discussion in chapter 3 under "Developmental Theories of Reading."

12. Appleyard, *Becoming a Reader*, 101; see my discussion in chapter under "Developmental Theories of Reading."

adds that imaginative mental activity enhances a reader's understanding of the narrative world.[13]

Participatory reading as a model is also suggested, but not developed, in the literature. Appleyard characterizes adolescent reading as an experience of immersion in a narrative.[14] Gerrig describes this immersion as being "transported" by the story into the narrative world, opening the door to experience of that world.[15] Tatar refers to child readers as "witnesses" of the narrative world,[16] since they observe and even experience the events of that world. What is missing in the literature is a cohesive model drawing all of these elements together. My study proposes an epistemological framework for that model: participatory reading generates an experience of the narrative world and child readers come to know the narrative world through that experience.

This study also has implications for a few specific theories within the field of children's literature. My findings substantiate Appleyard's Reader as Hero or Heroine reading role. As discussed in chapter 3, this role was initially theorized through Appleyard's analysis of fictional texts written for primary school-aged children.[17] My findings provide empirical evidence for the assumption of this role by real readers. As it stands, Appleyard's theory may simply indicate that children assume this role because it is the one provided for them in narratives written for children, but the findings suggest that child readers have a narrative orientation towards reading with a hero or heroine. The Gospel of Luke, after all, is not normally touted as an action-based hero story and certainly was not presented to the readers in this way in the empirical work, as may be seen by a perusal of the interview script (see Appendix A). The adoption of this reading role originated with the child readers.[18]

While the findings suggest that Appleyard's Reader as Hero or Heroine role is valid, the evidence comes from a slightly older age group than that

---

13. Oatley, *Such Stuff as Dreams*, 115, 119; see my discussion in chapter 3 under "The Cognitive Process."

14. Appleyard, *Becoming a Reader*, 101; see my discussion in chapter 3 under "Developmental Theories of Reading."

15. Gerrig, *Experiencing Narrative Worlds*, 66–67; see my discussion in chapter 3 under "The Cognitive Process."

16. Tatar, *Enchanted Hunters*, 19; see my discussion in chapter 3 under "The Literary Process."

17. Appleyard, *Becoming a Reader*, 60–64; see my discussion in chapter 3 under "Developmental Theories of Reading."

18. Indeed it came as a surprise to me, the interviewer. I was amazed by the number of readers who approached the narrative in this way.

suggested by Appleyard. The assumption of this role by an older group may simply be evidence for Appleyard's theory that a reading role, once developed, is a strategy that may continue in use throughout a person's lifetime. Appleyard also makes clear that such reading roles may be as much a factor of cultural influence as they are any form of innate developmental phase.[19] This distinction was not a focus of my study but it is worth noting that some of the most significant cultural influences upon the children's readings of Luke, particularly the institutions of school and church, tend to present neither Jesus as a hero, nor the Gospels as conflict-centered stories. Although the readers were clearly surrounded by hero tales in contemporary culture, Jesus' life story does not generally feature as one of those tales.[20]

The theory developed through my study also has implications for Mikkelsen's "field of literacies," as discussed in chapter 3. It will be recalled that Mikkelsen utilizes eight literacies to analyze the children's readings in her study. Some of her literacies overlap significantly with the reading strategies discussed in this study, particularly reading by imagining and empathetic reading. Yet Mikkelsen does not provide an explanatory framework for her literacies and her application of them often appears unsystematic. My study suggests that participatory reading may be the organizing principle around which many of Mikkelsen's literacies may potentially cohere. Mikkelsen found that children use a complex matrix of reading strategies,[21] and my study takes the next step and theorizes about that matrix.

The Bible and its Real Readers

Another set of implications coming out of this study pertains to how real readers, and child readers in particular, engage with the Bible. In chapter 4, I highlighted how empirical research in the field of the Bible and practical theology is relatively new. My study could provide an investigative model for further research in this field. Its qualitative methodology could be used with readers of a variety of ages and its methods replicated in a variety of contexts.

---

19. Appleyard, *Becoming a Reader*, 15; see my discussion in chapter 3 under "Developmental Theories of Reading."

20. On the other hand, elements of Jesus' life story are often reflected in contemporary narratives as part of their representation of a hero. Dying to save other people, for instance, features in the *Harry Potter* series, in *Doctor Who*, and in the BBC's *Sherlock*, to name but a few.

21. Mikkelsen, *Powerful Magic*, 5; see my discussion in chapter 3 under "The Literary Process."

It will also be recalled from chapter 4 that a number of theoreticians advocate that children be given the space to interact with the Bible[22] while others call for a holistic approach to using the Bible with children.[23] My study's empirical methodology aligned with the view of the former and enabled child readers to interact with the Gospel of Luke. The results, in turn, aligned with the approach proposed by the latter: interaction with Luke led to holistic participation. This finding substantiates the theoretical model proposed by Gobbel and Gobbel, while going beyond their model. Gobbel and Gobbel's driving argument is for children to be given experience of the biblical text so that they may, in turn, interact with the Bible in a developmentally appropriate way.[24] My study provides a description of that interaction.

My findings run counter to the dismissal of children's readings of biblical narrative because they may be classified as "literal."[25] If by "literal," scholars mean that a reading interprets a story using the story's contents, then this label has merit. It may then refer to experiencing a narrative world *as* a narrative world. This form of literal reading is orientated towards the literary elements of the text. But it does not also indicate what conclusions about the primary world a reader may draw from that engagement. For the Luke 5:17–26 story of the Healing of the Paralyzed Man, Zak's and Elaine's readings focused on the actions of the characters and interpreted them empathetically. Neither reading probed the story for its historicity. Instead Zak experienced the power of faith at the heart of the story, while Elaine reflected theologically upon the connection between healing and forgiveness.[26]

Scholars like Loman and Francis equate literal reading with the pursuit of historicity.[27] But the findings of my study align more readily with Pyper's assertion that children do not approach biblical narrative primarily asking questions about its factuality, but about the viability of its narrative world.[28]

---

22. Pike, "Belief as an Obstacle to Reading the Bible," 161; Cox, *Using the Bible*, 15. See my discussion in chapter 4 under "What the Child Might Make of the Bible."

23. Nipkow, "Elementary Encounters," 164; Van Ness, *Transforming Bible Study*, 45; Gobbel and Gobbel, *The Bible: A Child's Playground*, ix, 8; see my discussion in chapter 4 under "Experiencing the Bible."

24. Gobbel and Gobbel, *The Bible: A Child's Playground*, ix, 8; see my discussion in chapter 4 under "Experiencing the Bible."

25. For example Goldman, *Religious Thinking*, 227; Loman and Francis, "The Loman Index," 135–36. See my discussions in chapter 4 under "Reading Literally" and "Measuring Biblical Interpretation."

26. See my discussions in chapters 9 and 11.

27. Loman and Francis, "The Loman Index," 135, 136; see my discussion in chapter 4 under "Measuring Biblical Interpretation."

28. Pyper, "What the Bible Can Do to a Child," 148; see my discussion in chapter

As Trevor asserted, the key question guiding his reading of Luke was, "how does each story fit in with what has already happened?"[29] Children focus on the elements of a narrative world in order to make sense of that world. Using historicity as an evaluative tool appears to be a strategy they learn from their adult guides.

My findings likewise run counter to presenting the Bible to children primarily as a moral guide, an approach that appears to be common in both school and church.[30] As Stephanie's abortive reading of the Luke 20:9–18 parable of the Tenants in the Vineyard makes clear,[31] readers who have learned that they need to seek a moral in every biblical story rapidly run aground. This hermeneutical grid keeps the reader positioned firmly outside of the story world and reduces the child reader's interaction with the story to the question, "how should I live?" My findings even suggest that the imposition of a moral framework may be superfluous, since many of the readings generated a moral understanding of the text as a by-product of reading experientially. At the heart of Kit's reading of the parable of the Rich Man and Lazarus in Luke 16:19–31 was his empathy with Abraham, which led him to think about the plight of the poor.[32] If moral guidance is all that biblical narrative has to provide child readers, then children may outgrow the text as they outgrow the guidance of the adults who impose this framework.

The plot-driven reading strategy delineated in this study, on the other hand, provides readers with an interpretive framework that allows the narrative to function as narrative. Lisa's response to Jesus' crucifixion, after reading the whole Gospel, exemplifies the value of this strategy.[33] Although she had heard the account of Jesus' death on many previous occasions, this reader's immersion in Luke's narrative world allowed a bond to form between her and the protagonist that brought Jesus' crucifixion to life both within its narrative context and for her world.

---

4 under "What the Child Might Make of the Bible."

29. See my discussion in chapter 10 under "Seeking the 'Big Picture.'"

30. Copley, "Young People," 259; Cox, "Using the Bible with Children," 42; see my discussions in chapter 4 under "Reading for Values and Morals" and "What the Child Might Make of the Bible."

31. See my discussion in chapter 10 under "When Sense Seeking Fails."

32. See my discussion in chapter 9 under "I Imagine Myself as Her."

33. See my discussion in chapter 11 under "Introduction."

Using the Bible with Children

Not all children, of course, will be able or willing to read the entirety of a biblical book like Luke. Indeed many children cannot or do not read at all. The findings of my study may nonetheless have implications for how Bible stories, whether entire books or particular passages, may profitably be approached with children. As I discussed in chapters 3 and 8, Meek stresses the importance of oral and cultural exposure to a narrative as a means of entrance into its story world.[34] The exposure that even very young children have to Bible stories may contribute towards their interpretation of those stories. The key may be *how* they are exposed to those stories. If they are taught to view biblical narrative through a moral grid, for example, then future engagement may eventually be curtailed. On the other hand, if children gain a narrative-based experience of the biblical world, for instance through story-telling, by enacting it through drama, or by encountering it through an open-ended medium like Godly Play,[35] then that experience may engage their imagination, empathy, sense-seeking, and desire to know what happens. They may even view that world as a place to which they would like to return.

If the Bible is approached experientially, then those who work with children may prepare differently for activities which focus on biblical narrative. Preparation would not require them first and foremost to "know" more than their young charges, but instead to work out how to explore the story alongside of them. Of course, the better informed the adults are about the narrative world, the better guides they may be in that exploration. But based on my findings, their activities may be more effective in the long term if the emphasis is placed upon mutual discovery rather than upon the delivery of information. There is, of course, a whole range of other ways of using the Bible with children in a variety of catechetical or pedagogical contexts, but the approach of allowing children to be free to engage with biblical narrative *as* narrative should be one of these.

The purposes of the Gospel of Luke include persuasion of its readers, an aim which may make some adult gatekeepers wary of the text. Yet if the Gospel is to be read, then engagement with it as narrative is a more accurate representation of the text than approaching it through a grid that relegates it, for instance, to a handbook of beliefs. At the center of its story stands Jesus as its hero. Although this view of Jesus may be partially a product

---

34. Meek, *How Texts Teach*, 22; see my discussion in chapter 3 under "The Literary Process."

35. A method used by Worsley, "How Children Aged 9–10 Understand Bible Stories," 206; see my discussion in chapter 4 under "Valuing the Child as an Interpreter."

of the child readers' developmental stage, it also comes close to expressing one of the fundamental purposes of Luke: testifying to the identity of Jesus. What then if the Gospel were approached with children as a hero tale? Such an approach may align the perspectives of the child and Luke, and open a dialogue between them.

Taking it Further

I conclude by highlighting the need for further exploration of my findings. Although this study has made some progress in answering the question, "how do children read the Bible?" there is still a distance to go. The study clearly has limitations. To begin with, it was of necessity quite small. The practical constraints of the empirical work required me to strike a balance between producing an effective piece of research and executing a workable piece of research. Further investigation of the findings would mean broadening the scope of the research, perhaps using some of the suggestions discussed below.

Another limitation was the homogeneity of the child participants. This homogeneity means that the findings can only be affirmed as relevant to a limited demographic. An effective way forward would be to conduct a similar study using participants with a different demographic, such as non-churched child readers or child readers from a more economically deprived area than the one represented by this study. If time and resources had permitted, I would have conducted the original study using two groups of participants from demographically diverse backgrounds and compared the results as a means of both validating and fine-tuning the findings. As it is, the focus groups served as a sufficient means of validating the findings, but the demographic they represent is comparable to that of the interviewees.

Also the study was carried out by only one researcher. Having other researchers involved in the project would have provided additional perspectives on the findings and a more rigorous analysis. As it is, the idiosyncrasies of my personal perspective have invariably permeated the findings. I have sought throughout to minimize this effect. In the empirical phase of the research, I used the same basic interview script with each interviewee,[36] and the same sets of questions and response sheets with the focus groups. Part of the analysis involved cross-comparing the findings with other relevant research in the fields of biblical studies, children's literature theory, and

---

36. The interview script underwent some modification as part of the research process recommended by grounded theory; see my discussion in chapter 6 under "The Interviews."

practical theology. Much of this research had findings that substantiate my findings.

Future studies may build on the findings in a variety of ways. Children of other age groups need to be studied. Although the experiential model may encapsulate the reading strategies of older children, the engagement of younger children with biblical narrative may need an entirely different approach. Those who are not fluent readers may still immerse themselves in a Bible story, but the medium by which they attain access to that story may differ significantly. Worsley's Bible Story Project may provide a useful conversation partner for working out a methodology for such research.[37]

Although my study began with the question, "how do children read the Bible?" it only investigates children's interaction with biblical narrative; in fact, it only investigates the readers' interaction with one book in the biblical canon. An obvious way forward would be to conduct a similar study using an entirely different narrative in the canon, such as the book of Esther which has a female protagonist and is part of Hebrew Scripture. It may also be less familiar to most child readers than the Gospel of Luke. A different genre of biblical literature could also be investigated, such as a Psalm or a set of Psalms.

Finally, the findings of this study could be assessed in an entirely different way. A pragmatic approach that seeks to implement the findings could prove an effective means of testing their viability. Those who work with the Bible and children may seek to implement the findings in their relevant contexts. The institutions of church and school would be good testing grounds for asking what happens when child readers grapple with the Gospel of Luke as a narrative and are encouraged to use the reading strategies delineated here.

I began this study by stating my desire to locate and describe a metaphoric "field": what happens when a particular group of children read biblical narrative. The empirical research suggests that this field contains narrative-based, imaginative, empathetic, and puzzle-solving reading tools that are implemented in order to make sense of the text and to find out what happens in the plot. The foundation of this field appears to be epistemological and to derive from inside-experience. The child readers came to know Luke's narrative world experientially, through their participation with it. But these are only broad descriptions and the field needs more exploration.

While such exploration may not be easy, its aim should be clear. It is to bring together the world of biblical narrative and the world of the child

---

37. Worsley, "The Bible in Family Context," 117; see my discussion in chapter 4 under "Valuing the Child as an Interpreter."

reader, which will in the process open up new avenues between them. This is a challenge, for the field is not static. A child is always developing and a narrative world is, after all, never complete. But the result may be a fruitful alliance, for, in the words of Sophie A., "every time you read something like Luke, you get a little bit more out of it."

Appendix A

Interview Script

Tell Me about Luke

1. Tell me what you thought about Luke. What was your reaction?
2. Tell me about anything you liked about this book. Favorite parts?
3. Tell me about anything you disliked. Parts that bored you?

    Did you skip parts? If so, which ones?
4. What made you keep reading this book to the end?

    If you gave up, where did you stop and what stopped you?
5. Tell me about anything that puzzled you or that you didn't understand.

    Anything that took you by surprise?
6. Tell me about any patterns or themes that you noticed within the book.
7. What is this book about? What is the basic plot?

    Did you think of it as a story when you read it?
8. What did the book make you think about? How did it make you feel?
9. When thinking about the book now, what is the most important thing about it for you?

    Was there any part of the book that made you think about your own life?
10. Read a cited passage aloud and discuss briefly using questions 2, 5, 7, and 8:

    (What did you like? What puzzled you? What's it about? What did it make you think about?)

11. When you were reading, did you see the story happening in your imagination?

    Have you ever seen a picture of this story?

12. Did you imagine yourself in any of the stories?

    Did you imagine yourself as any of the characters?

13. What did you think of the images used in the book?

    [read and discuss a short passage from a teaching section in Luke]

14. What did you think of the images used in the book?

    (Read and discuss a short passage from a teaching section in Luke.)

15. Based on this book, how would you describe Jesus?

    What does the author want you to think about Jesus?

    If you could meet Jesus, what would you like to ask him?

16. In this book, Jesus tells lots of stories, so that the book contains little stories inside a bigger story. Can you think of one of Jesus' stories? What do you think made him tell that story?

    (Read and discuss a parable.)

17. Were there any parts of Luke that were already familiar to you? How did you know those parts? (family/home, school, church, books)

18. What was the effect on you of reading the whole book through? Did it change your mind about those familiar stories, or any other parts of the book?

    Did your view of Jesus change?

19. If the author asked you what could be improved in Luke, what would you say?

20. Tell me what you thought when you saw the book. What did you think of the cover, page size, font, pictures?

21. Would you like to read Luke again some time?

    What questions remain unanswered as you close the book?

22. Is there anything else you would like to tell me? Anything you would like to ask me?

Appendix B
IFG Discussion Guide
Your Views on Reading Luke

1. *Participants' Views of Reading Luke*
   What do you think: what were the main ways that you all read Luke?
   Overall, what kinds of things did you find interesting?
   What kinds of things did you talk about?
   What kinds of things were important to you?

2. *Participants' Responses to the Emerging Theories:*
   Tell me: do these results sound familiar? Do they reflect what you recall from your reading of Luke?
   Do you agree or disagree with my conclusions? In what way?
   How does this compare to how you read other books?

   my conclusions about how you read Luke:

as a conflict	*plot-driven reading*
Jesus is human too	*he is not Mr Happy*
for the characters	*what motivates them & how they feel*
by imagining	
by puzzle-solving	*working out what it means*
by asking questions	
by asking how does it relate to me?	*personal significance*
by asking how should I act?	*moral guidance*
by wondering how it works for a teenager	

by comparing it to what I believe

Do you have any to add?

3. *After the interview:*

   Has reading Luke affected your interaction with the Bible in any way?

   Has your view of Luke changed in any way?

   Have you read Luke again, or any other part of the Bible, since the interview?

4. *Involvement in the research:*

   What did you think of the interview process: what was it like for you?

   Tell me about your experience of being involved in this research.

   Any other questions?

Appendix C
RVG Response Sheet for Session 6

Reading Luke

1. Gender: Female   Male

2. Birthday: _____
               month   year

3. Religion: Christian, Muslim, Jewish, Hindu, Sikh, none
               other: _____

   if Christian: Church of England, Catholic, Methodist, Free Church,
                   Orthodox, other: _____

Mary & Martha—Luke 10

4. When I hear this story, I imagine how Martha feels:
   Strongly Agree | Agree | Uncertain | Disagree | Strongly Disagree

5. I think Jesus is unfair to Martha:
   Strongly Agree | Agree | Uncertain | Disagree | Strongly Disagree

6. Which character in this story is most like you?
   Mary   Martha   Jesus   none of them

   This character is like me because: _____

The Lost Sheep—Luke 15

7. In this story, I am most like: (circle only one)

    the shepherd   the lost sheep   one of the ninety-nine sheep

    other: _____

8. This story makes me think about my own life:

    Strongly Agree | Agree | Uncertain | Disagree | Strongly Disagree

9. The lost sheep is like someone who is not popular at school:

    Strongly Agree | Agree | Uncertain | Disagree | Strongly Disagree

10. This story shows that you can get to heaven if you say sorry:

    Strongly Agree | Agree | Uncertain | Disagree | Strongly Disagree

11. If Jesus lived today, he would tell this story differently:

    Strongly Agree | Agree | Uncertain | Disagree | Strongly Disagree

12. This story is about: (circle only one)

    a lost sheep

    a lost person

    how each person is special

    how Jesus treats people who are not popular

    saying sorry

    other: _____

Bibliography

Abrams, M. H. *The Mirror and the Lamp: Romantic Theory and the Critical Tradition*. Oxford: Oxford University Press, 1953.
Adam, Jean-Michel. "Décrire des Actions: raconter ou relater?" *Littérature* 95, no. 95 (1994) 3–22.
Alasuutari, Pertti. *Researching Culture: Qualitative Method and Cultural Studies*. London: Sage, 1995.
Alderson, Priscilla. "Ethics." In *Doing Research with Children and Young People*, edited by Sandy Fraser et al., 97–112. London: Sage, 2004.
Alderson, Priscilla, and Virginia Morrow. *Ethics, Social Research and Consulting with Children and Young People*. Rev. ed. Ilford, UK: Barnardo's, 2004.
Alexander, Loveday. *The Preface to Luke's Gospel: Literary Conventions and Social Context in Luke 1:1–4 and Acts 1:1*. Society for New Testament Studies Monograph Series 78. Cambridge: Cambridge University Press, 1993.
———. "What is a Gospel?" In *The Cambridge Companion to the Gospels*, edited by Stephen C. Barton, 13–33. Cambridge: Cambridge University Press, 2006.
Alter, Robert. *The Art of Biblical Narrative*. New York: Basic, 1981.
Applebee, Arthur N. *The Child's Concept of Story: Ages Two to Seventeen*. Chicago: University of Chicago Press, 1978.
Appleyard, J. A. *Becoming a Reader: The Experience of Fiction from Childhood to Adulthood*. Cambridge: Cambridge University Press, 1991.
Ashton, Elizabeth. "Readiness for Discarding? An Examination of the Researches of Ronald Goldman Concerning Children's Religious Thinking." *Journal of Education and Christian Belief* 1, no. 2 (1997) 127–44.
Auerbach, Erich. *Mimesis: The Representation of Reality in Western Literature*. 1946. Translated by Willard R. Trask. Princeton: Princeton University Press, 1953.
Aulén, Gustaf. *Christus Victor: An Historical Study of the Three Main Types of the Idea of the Atonement*. Translated by A. G. Herbert. London: SPCK, 1931.
Austin, J. L. "The Meaning of a Word." In *Philosophical Papers*, 55–75. 3rd ed. Oxford: Clarendon, 1979.
Bailey, Kenneth E. *Poet and Peasant and Through Peasant Eyes: A Literary-Cultural Approach to the Parables in Luke*. Combined ed. Grand Rapids: Eerdmans, 1983.
Barbour, Rosaline. *Doing Focus Groups*. London: Sage, 2007.
Barth, Karl. *Church Dogmatics II/2: The Doctrine of God*. 1942. Translated by G. W. Bromiley et al. Edinburgh: T&T Clark, 1957.

———. "The Strange New World within the Bible." In *The Word of God and the Word of Man*, 28–50. London: Hodder & Stoughton, 1928.

Bartlett, Frederic C. *Remembering: A Study in Experimental and Social Psychology*. Cambridge: Cambridge University Press, 1932.

Barton, John. "Classifying Biblical Criticism." *Journal for the Study of the Old Testament* 29 (1984) 19–35.

Bauckham, Richard. *Jesus and the Eyewitnesses: The Gospels as Eyewitness Testimony*. Grand Rapids: Eerdmans, 2006.

———. *Scripture and Authority Today*. Grove Biblical Series B12. Cambridge: Grove, 1999.

Bauer, David. *The Structure of Matthew's Gospel: A Study in Literary Design*. JSNTSup 31. Sheffield, UK: Almond, 1988.

Bazeley, Pat. *Qualitative Data Analysis with NVivo*. London: Sage, 2007.

Bennett, Zoë. *Using the Bible in Practical Theology: Historical and Contemporary Perspectives*. Farnham, UK: Ashgate, 2013.

Benny, Mark, et al. "Age and Sex in the Interview." In *Interviewing*, edited by Nigel Fielding, 4:34–47. London: Sage, 2003.

Birnie, Ian. "Is Teaching the Bible Too Dangerous a Task for Schools?" *British Journal of Religious Education* 5, no. 3 (1983) 143–46.

Bottigheimer, Ruth B. "The Bible for Children: The Emergence and Development of the Genre, 1550–1990." In *The Church and Childhood*, edited by Diana Wood, 347–62. Studies in Church History 31. Oxford: Blackwell, 1994.

———. *The Bible for Children: From the Age of Gutenberg to the Present*. New Haven: Yale University Press, 1996.

Bourg, Tammy. "The Role of Emotion, Empathy, and Text Structure in Children's and Adults' Narrative Text Comprehension." In *Empirical Approaches to Literature and Aesthetics*, edited by Roger J. Kreuz and Mary Sue MacNealy, 241–60. Norwood, NJ: Ablex, 1996.

Boyd, Gregory A. "Christus Victor View." In *The Nature of the Atonement: Four Views*, edited by James Beilby and Paul R. Eddy, 23–49. Downers Grove: IVP, 2006.

Brierley, Peter. *Reaching and Keeping Tweenagers*. London: Christian Research, 2002.

Briggs, Melody. "The Word Became Visual Text: The Boy Jesus in Children's Bibles." In *Text, Image, and Otherness in Children's Bibles: What Is in the Picture?*, edited by Caroline Vander Stichele and Hugh S. Pyper, 153–72. Atlanta: SBL, 2012.

Briggs, Richard S. "How to Do Things with Meaning in Biblical Interpretation." *Southeastern Theological Review* 2, no. 2 (2011) 143–60.

Brooks, Peter. *Reading for the Plot: Design and Intention in Narrative*. London: Harvard University Press, 1984.

Bryman, Alan. *Social Research Methods*. 3rd ed. Oxford: Oxford University Press, 2008.

Burman, Erica. *Deconstructing Developmental Psychology*. London: Routledge, 1994.

Burridge, Richard A. *What Are the Gospels? A Comparison of Graeco-Roman Biography*. 2nd ed. Grand Rapids: Eerdmans, 2004.

Cadbury, Henry J. *The Style and Literary Method of Luke*. Cambridge, MA: Harvard University Press, 1920.

Campbell, Joseph. *The Hero with a Thousand Faces*. London: HarperCollins, 1949.

Carpenter, Humphrey, and Mari Prichard. "Fantasy." In *The Oxford Companion to Children's Literature*, 181–82. Oxford: Oxford University Press, 1984.

Carroll, Lewis. *Alice's Adventures in Wonderland*. 1865. Reprint, London: Puffin, 2008.

———. *Through the Looking Glass*. 1871. Reprint, London: Puffin, 1994.
Chambers, Aidan. *Tell Me: Children, Reading & Talk*. Stroud: Thimble, 1993.
Chapman, Stephen B. "Imaginative Readings of Scripture and Theological Interpretation." In *Out of Egypt: Biblical Theology and Biblical Interpretation*, edited by Craig Bartholomew et al., 409–47. Milton Keynes, UK: Paternoster, 2004.
Charmaz, Kathy. *Constructing Grounded Theory: A Practical Guide through Qualitative Analysis*. London: Sage, 2006.
Chatman, Seymour. *Story and Discourse: Narrative Structure in Fiction and Film*. Ithaca, NY: Cornell University Press, 1978.
Clark, Andrew. "Language, Embodiment, and the Cognitive Niche." *Trends in Cognitive Sciences* 10 (2006) 370–74.
———. "Material Symbols." *Philosophical Psychology* 19 (2006) 291–307.
Clines, David J. A. *The Bible and the Modern World*. Sheffield, UK: Sheffield Academic, 1997.
Cole, Arnold, and Pamela C. Ovwigho. "Bible Engagement and Social Behavior: How Familiarity and Frequency of Contact with the Bible Affects One's Behavior." Paper presented at Tel Aviv University. April 2009. Tel Aviv, Israel. http://www.backtothebible.org/files/web/docs/cbe/Bible_Engagement_and_Social_Behavior.pdf. Accessed February 6, 2017.
Coleridge, Samuel Taylor. *Biographia Literaria: Biographical Sketches of My Literary Life and Opinions*. Edited by George Watson. Rev. ed. London: Dent, 1960.
Conzelmann, Hans. *The Theology of Luke*. Translated by Geoffrey Buswell. London: Faber and Faber, 1960.
Copley, Claire, et al. *On the Side of the Angels: The Third Report of the Biblos Project*. Exeter, UK: University of Exeter School of Education Press, 2004.
Copley, Terence. *Echo of Angels: The First Report of the Biblos Project*. Exeter, UK: University of Exeter School of Education Press, 1998.
———. "Young People, Biblical Narrative and 'Theologizing': A UK Perspective." *Religious Education* 100, no. 3 (2005) 254–65.
Copley, Terence, et al. *The Speech of Angels: Ninety-Eight Young People Talk about the Bible: An Extension of the Third Report of the Biblos Project*. Exeter, UK: University of Exeter School of Education Press, 2006.
Cosgrove, Charles H. *Appealing to Scripture in Moral Debate: Five Hermeneutical Rules*. Grand Rapids: Eerdmans, 2002.
Cox, Rosemary. *Using the Bible with Children*. Grove Biblical B15. Cambridge: Grove, 2000.
———. "Using the Bible with Children." *Journal of Education and Christian Belief* 5, no. 1 (2001) 41–49.
Craddock, Fred B. *Luke*. Interpretation: A Bible Commentary for Teaching and Preaching. Louisville: Knox, 1990.
Creswell, John W. *Qualitative Inquiry and Research Design: Choosing among Five Approaches*. 2nd ed. Thousand Oaks: Sage, 2007.
Csanyi, Daniel A. "Faith Development and the Age of Readiness for the Bible." *Religious Education* 77 (1982) 518–24.
Culler, Jonathan. *Literary Theory: A Very Short Introduction*. Oxford: Oxford University Press, 1997.
———. *Structuralist Poetics: Structuralism, Linguistics and the Study of Literature*. Ithaca, NY: Cornell University Press, 1975.

Darr, John A. *On Character Building: The Reader and the Rhetoric of Characterization in Luke-Acts*. Louisville: Westminster John Knox, 1992.

Dawsey, James M. *The Lukan Voice: Confusion and Irony in the Gospel of Luke*. Macon, GA: Mercer University Press, 1986.

De Hulster, Izaak J. "Imagination: A Hermeneutical Tool for the Study of the Hebrew Bible." *Biblical Interpretation* 18 (2010) 114–36.

Diffen. "Empathy versus Sympathy." Diffen. http://www.diffen.com/difference/Empathy_vs_Sympathy. Accessed February 6, 2017.

Dinkler, Michal Beth. "Telling Silences: The Function of Ambiguities and Silences in the Gospel of Luke." Paper presented at the annual meeting of the Society of Biblical Literature. San Francisco. 20 November 2011.

Donaldson, Margaret. *Children's Minds*. London: Harper, 1978.

Dornisch, Loretta. *A Woman Reads the Gospel of Luke*. Collegeville, MN: Liturgical, 1996.

Eco, Umberto. *Interpretation and Overinterpretation*. Cambridge: Cambridge University Press, 1992.

———. *The Limits of Interpretation*. New ed. Bloomington: Indiana University Press, 1994.

———. *Reflections on the Name of the Rose*. London: Minerva, 1994.

———. *The Role of the Reader: Explorations in the Semiotics of Texts*. Bloomington: Indiana University Press, 1979.

———. *Six Walks in the Fictional Woods*. Cambridge, MA: Harvard University Press, 1994.

Eder, Donna, and Laura Fingerson. "Interviewing Children and Adolescents." In *Handbook of Interview Research*, edited by J. F. Gubrium and J. A. Holstein, 181–201. London: Sage, 2002.

Erikson, Erik H. *Childhood and Society*. Harmondsworth, UK: Penguin, 1950.

———. *Identity: Youth and Crisis*. London: Faber and Faber, 1968.

Evans, C. F. *Saint Luke*. 2nd ed. London: SCM, 2008.

Fee, Gordon D., and Mark L. Strauss. *How to Choose a Translation for All It's Worth: A Guide to Understanding and Using Bible Translations*. Grand Rapids: Zondervan, 2007.

Fewell, Danna Nolan. *The Children of Israel: Reading the Bible for the Sake of Our Children*. Nashville: Abingdon, 2003.

Fish, Stanley. *Is There a Text in This Class? The Authority of Interpretive Communities*. Cambridge, MA: Harvard University Press, 1980.

Fokkelman, J. P. *Reading Biblical Narrative: An Introductory Guide*. 1995. Translated by Ineke Smit. Louisville: Westminster John Knox, 1999.

Forster, E. M. *Aspects of the Novel*. New York: Harcourt, Brace & World, 1927.

Fowl, Stephen. "The Ethics of Interpretation or What's Left Over after the Elimination of Meaning." In *The Bible in Three Dimensions: Essays in Celebration of Forty Years of Biblical Studies in the University of Sheffield*, edited by David J. A. Clines et al., 379–98. JSOTSup 87. Sheffield, UK: JSOT, 1990.

Fowler, James W. *Stages of Faith: The Psychology of Human Development and the Quest for Meaning*. San Francisco: Harper & Row, 1981.

Fowler, Robert M. *Let the Reader Understand: Reader-Response Criticism and the Gospel of Mark*. Harrisburg, PA: Trinity, 1996.

France, Alan. "Young People." In *Doing Research with Children and Young People*, edited by Sandy Fraser et al., 175–90. London: Sage, 2004.
Francis, Leslie J. "Research and the Development of Religious Thinking." *Educational Studies* 5 (1979) 109–15.
———. "Who Reads the Bible? A Study among 13-15 Year Olds." *British Journal of Religious Education* 22, no. 3 (2000) 165–72.
Frei, Hans W. *The Eclipse of Biblical Narrative: A Study in Eighteenth and Nineteenth Century Hermeneutics*. New Haven: Yale University Press, 1974.
Fry, Donald. *Children Talk about Books: Seeing Themselves as Readers*. Milton Keynes, UK: Open University Press, 1985.
Genette, Gérard. *Narrative Discourse: An Essay in Method*. 1972. Translated by Jane E. Lewin. Ithaca: Cornell University Press, 1980.
———. *Paratexts: Thresholds of Interpretation*. 1987. Translated by Jane E. Lewin. Cambridge: Cambridge University Press, 1997.
Gerrig, Richard J. *Experiencing Narrative Worlds: On the Psychological Activities of Reading*. New Haven: Yale University Press, 1993.
Glaser, Barney G., and Anselm L. Strauss. *The Discovery of Grounded Theory: Strategies for Qualitative Research*. New York: de Gruyter, 1967.
Gobbel, Roger, and Gertrude Gobbel. *The Bible: A Child's Playground*. London: SCM, 1986.
Goldman, Ronald J. *Readiness for Religion: A Basis for Developmental Religious Education*. London: Routledge, 1965.
———. *Religious Thinking from Childhood to Adolescence*. London: Routledge, 1964.
Gooder, Paula. *Searching for Meaning: An Introduction to Interpreting the New Testament*. London: SPCK, 2008.
Gowler, David B. *Host, Guest, Enemy and Friend: Portraits of the Pharisees in Luke and Acts*. Eugene, OR: Wipf and Stock, 1991.
Green, Garrett. *Imagining God: Theology and the Religious Imagination*. Cambridge: Eerdmans, 1989.
Green, Joel B. *The Gospel of Luke*. New International Commentary on the New Testament. Cambridge: Eerdmans, 1997.
———. "Narrative Criticism." In *Methods for Luke*, edited by Joel B. Green, 74–112. Cambridge: Cambridge University Press, 2010.
———. *The Theology of the Gospel of Luke*. New Testament Theology. Cambridge: Cambridge University Press, 1995.
Green, Melanie C. "Transportation into Narrative Worlds: The Role of Prior Knowledge and Perceived Realism." *Discourse Processes* 38 (2004) 247–66.
Green, Melanie C., and Tim C. Brock. "The Role of Transportation in the Persuasiveness of Public Narratives." *Journal of Personality and Social Psychology* 79 (2000) 702–21.
Greene, Sheila, and Malcolm Hill. "Researching Children's Experience: Methods and Methodological Issues." In *Researching Children's Experience: Methods and Approaches*, edited by Sheila Greene and Diane Hogan, 1–21. London: Sage, 2005.
Greer, J. E. "A Critical Study of Thinking about the Bible." *British Journal of Religious Education* 5, no. 3 (1983) 113–55.
Greig, Anne, et al. *Doing Research with Children*. 2nd ed. London: Sage, 2007.
Harris, Paul. *The Work of the Imagination*. Oxford: Blackwell, 2000.

Hart, Trevor. "Imagination and Responsible Reading." In *Renewing Biblical Interpretation*, edited by Craig Bartholomew et al., 307–34. Carlisle, UK: Paternoster, 2000.

Hartin, Patrick J., ed. "The Bible, the Child, and Education." *Scriptura* 34 (1990) 1–47.

Hauerwas, Stanley and David Burrell. "From System to Story: An Alternative Pattern for Rationality in Ethics." In *Why Narrative? Readings in Narrative Theology*, edited by Stanley Hauerwas and L. Gregory Jones, 158–90. Eerdmans: Grand Rapids, 1989.

Hays, Richard B. "The Canonical Matrix of the Gospels." In *The Cambridge Companion to the Gospels*, edited by Stephen C. Barton, 53–75. Cambridge: Cambridge University Press, 2006.

Hennessy, Eilis, and Caroline Heary. "Exploring Children's Views through Focus Groups." In *Researching Children's Experience: Methods and Approaches*, edited by Sheila Greene and Diane Hogan, 236–52. London: Sage, 2005.

Hill, Malcolm. "Ethical Considerations in Researching Children's Experience." In *Researching Children's Experience: Methods and Approaches*, edited by Sheila Greene and Diane Hogan, 61–86. London: Sage, 2005.

Holland, Norman N. *The Nature of Literary Response: Five Readers Reading*. London: Yale University Press, 1975.

Holm, Jean L. "What Shall We Tell the Children?" *Theology* 76 (1973) 141–48.

Holmes, Robyn M. *Fieldwork with Children*. London: Sage, 1998.

Hume, David. *A Treatise of Human Nature*. 1739. 2nd ed. Oxford: Clarendon, 1978.

Iser, Wolfgang. *The Act of Reading: A Theory of Aesthetic Response*. Baltimore: Johns Hopkins University Press, 1978.

———. *The Implied Reader: Patterns of Communication in Prose Fiction from Bunyan to Beckett*. Baltimore: Johns Hopkins University Press, 1974.

James, Allison, and Alan Prout, eds. *Constructing and Reconstructing Childhood: Contemporary Issues in the Sociological Study of Childhood*. 2nd ed. London: Falmer, 1997.

James, Henry. "The Art of Fiction." 1884. Reprinted in *Literary Criticism: Essays on Literature, American Writers, English Writers*, 44–65. New York: The Library of America, 1984.

Johnson, Luke Timothy. *The Gospel of Luke*. Sacra Pagina 3. Collegeville, MN: Liturgical, 1991.

———. "Imagining the World Scripture Imagines." *Modern Theology* 14 (1998) 165–80.

Jowett, Benjamin. "On the Interpretation of Scripture." In *Essays and Reviews*, 330–433. 7th ed. London: Longman, Green, Longman, Roberts, 1861.

Kant, Immanuel. *Critique of Judgement*. 1790. Translated by J. C. Meredith. Oxford: Clarendon, 1964.

Karris, Robert J. *Luke: Artist and Theologian: Luke's Passion Account as Literature*. New York: Paulist, 1985.

Kay, W., and R. Wilkins. "Reading for Readiness." *Journal of Education and Christian Belief* 2 (1998) 65–69.

Keen, Suzanne. *Empathy and the Novel*. Oxford: Oxford University Press, 2007.

Kermode, Frank. *The Genesis of Secrecy: On the Interpretation of Narrative*. Cambridge, MA: Harvard University Press, 1979.

Kingsbury, Jack Dean. *Conflict in Luke: Jesus, Authorities, Disciples.* Minneapolis: Fortress, 1991.

Knight, Peter T. *Small-Scale Research: Pragmatic Inquiry in Social Science and the Caring Professions.* London: Sage, 2002.

Kohlberg, Lawrence. "Moral Stages and Moralization: The Cognitive-Developmental Approach." In *Moral Development and Behavior: Theory, Research, and Social Issues,* edited by Thomas Lickona, 31–53. New York: Holt, Rinehart & Winston, 1976.

Krueger, Richard A., and Mary Anne Casey. *Focus Groups: A Practical Guide for Applied Research.* 4th ed. London: Sage, 2009.

Kvale, Steiner. *Doing Interviews.* London: Sage, 2007.

Lakoff, George, and Mark Johnson. *Metaphors We Live By.* Chicago: University of Chicago Press, 1980.

Landy, Francis. "Do We Want Our Children to Read This Book?" In *Bible and Ethics of Reading,* edited by Dana Nolan Fewell and Gary A. Phillips, 157–76. Semeia 77. Atlanta: SBL, 1997.

Lawrence, Louise J. *The Word in Place: Reading the New Testament in Contemporary Contexts.* London: SPCK, 2009.

Le Donne, Anthony. "The Jewish Leaders." In *Jesus among Friends and Enemies: A Historical and Literary Introduction to Jesus in the Gospels,* edited by Chris Keith and Larry W. Hurtado, 199–217. Grand Rapids: Baker, 2011.

Lee, David. *Luke's Stories of Jesus: Theological Reading of Gospel Narrative and the Legacy of Hans Frei.* JSNTS Supplement 185. Sheffield: Sheffield Academic, 1999.

Legaspi, Michael C. *The Death of Scripture and the Rise of Biblical Studies.* Oxford Studies in Historical Theology. Oxford: Oxford University Press, 2010.

Leithart, Peter J. *Deep Exegesis: The Mystery of Reading Scripture.* Waco, TX: Baylor, 2009.

Levine, I. S. and J. D. Zimmerman. "Using Qualitative Data to Inform Public Policy: Evaluating 'Choose to Defuse.'" *American Journal of Orthopsychiatry* 66 (1996) 363–77.

Lewis, C. S. "Bluspels and Flalansferes: A Semantic Nightmare." 1939. In *Selected Literary Essays,* edited by Walter Hooper, 251–65. Cambridge: Cambridge University Press, 1969.

———. *An Experiment in Criticism.* Cambridge: Cambridge University Press, 1961.

———. "Hamlet: The Prince or the Poem?" 1942. In *Selected Literary Essays,* edited by Walter Hooper, 88–105. Cambridge: Cambridge University Press, 1969.

———. "Meditation in a Toolshed." 1945. In *First and Second Things: Essays on Theology and Ethics,* edited by Walter Hooper, 50–54. London: Fount, 1985.

———. "Sometimes Fairy Stories May Say Best What's to be Said," 1956. In *On Stories: And Other Essays on Literature,* edited by Walter Hooper, 45–48. London: Harcourt, 1966.

Loman, Susan E., and Leslie J. Francis. "The Loman Index of Biblical Interpretation: Distinguishing between Literal, Symbolic and Rejecting Modes among 11 to 14 Year Olds." *British Journal of Religious Education* 28 (2006) 131–40.

MacDonald, George D. "The Imagination: Its Function and Culture." 1867. In *A Dish of Orts,* 9–35. Reprint, London: Prime Classics, 2004.

MacIntyre, Alasdair. "Epistemological Crises, Dramatic Narrative, and the Philosophy of Science." In *Why Narrative? Readings in Narrative Theology*, edited by Stanley Hauerwas and L. Gregory Jones, 138–57. Eerdmans: Grand Rapids, 1989.

Marguerat, Daniel, and Yvan Bourquin. *How to Read Bible Stories: An Introduction to Narrative Criticism*. 1998. Translated by John Bowden. London: SCM, 1999.

Marshall, I. Howard. *The Gospel of Luke: A Commentary on the Greek Text*. New International Greek Testament Commentary. Grand Rapids: Eerdmans, 1978.

———. *Luke: Historian and Theologian*. Carlisle, UK: Paternoster, 1970.

Martin, Dale B. *Pedagogy of the Bible: An Analysis and Proposal*. Louisville: Westminster John Knox, 2008.

Maxwell, Kathy Reiko. *Hearing Between the Lines: The Audience as Fellow-Worker in Luke-Acts and Its Literary Milieu*. London: T. & T. Clark, 2010.

May, Tim. *Social Research: Issues, Methods and Process*. 2nd ed. Buckingham: Open University Press, 1997.

McComiskey, Douglas S. *Lukan Theology in the Light of the Gospel's Literary Structure*. Milton Keynes, UK: Paternoster, 2004.

McGrady, Andrew G. "Metaphorical and Operational Aspects of Religious Thinking: Research with Irish Catholic Pupils, Part 1." *British Journal of Religious Education* 16, no. 3 (1994) 148–63.

McIntyre, John. *Faith Theology and Imagination*. Edinburgh: Handsel, 1987.

Meek, Margaret. *How Texts Teach What Readers Learn*. Stroud: Thimble, 1988.

Merenlahti, Petri. "Reading as a Little Child: On the Model Reader of the Gospels." *Literature and Theology* 18, no. 2 (2004) 139–52.

Mikkelsen, Nina. *Powerful Magic: Learning from Children's Responses to Fantasy Literature*. New York: Teachers College Press, 2005.

Moberly, R. W. L. *The Bible, Theology, and Faith: A Study of Abraham and Jesus*. Cambridge: Cambridge University Press, 2000.

Morgan, David L. "Focus Group Interviewing." In *Handbook of Interview Research: Context and Method*, edited by J. F. Gubrium and James A. Holstein, 141–59. London: Sage, 2002.

Morris, Leon. *Luke: An Introduction and Commentary*. Tyndale New Testament Commentaries. Rev. ed. Leicester: IVP, 1988.

Morse, Janice M. "Principles of Mixed Methods and Multimethod Research Design." In *Handbook of Mixed Methods in Social and Behavioural Research*, edited by Abbas Tashakkori and Charles Teddle, 189–208. Thousand Oaks, CA: Sage, 2003.

Nesbitt, Eleanor. "Researching 8 to 13-year-olds' Perspectives on Their Experience of Religion." In *Researching Children's Perspectives*, edited by Ann Lewis and Geoff Lindsay, 135–49. Buckingham: Open University Press, 2000.

Nipkow, Karl Ernst. "Elementary Encounters with the Bible." *British Journal of Religious Education* 5, no. 3 (1983) 162–68.

Nolland, John. *Luke 1—9:20*. WBC 35A. Dallas: Word, 1989.

———. *Luke 9:21—18:34*. WBC 35B. Dallas: Word, 1993.

Oatley, Keith. *Such Stuff as Dreams: The Psychology of Fiction*. Oxford: Wiley-Blackwell, 2011.

Ovwigho, Pamela Caudill, and Arnold Cole. "Scriptural Engagement, Communication with God, and Moral Behaviour among Children." *International Journal of Children's Spirituality* 15, no. 2 (2010) 101–13.

Parker, Walter Chalmerse. "Interviewing Children: Problems and Promise." *Journal of Negro Education* 53 (1984) 18–28.
Parsons, Mikeal C. *The Departure of Jesus in Luke-Acts.* JSNTSup 21. Sheffield, UK: Sheffield Academic, 1987.
———. *Luke: Storyteller, Interpreter, Evangelist.* Peabody, MA: Hendrickson, 2007.
Peatling, John H. *Religious Education in a Psychological Key.* Birmingham: Religious Education, 1981.
Pennington, Jonathan T. *Reading the Gospels Wisely: A Narrative and Theological Introduction.* Grand Rapids: Baker, 2012.
Peskin, Joan, and Janet Astington. "The Effects of Adding Metacognitive Language to Story Texts." *Cognitive Development* 19 (2004) 253–73
Phillips, Anne. *The Faith of Girls: Children's Spirituality and Transition to Adulthood.* Farnham, UK: Ashgate, 2011.
Piaget, Jean. *The Child's Conception of the World.* Translated by Joan and Andrew Tomlinson. London: Routledge, 1929.
Pike, Mark A. "Belief as an Obstacle to Reading the Bible." *Journal of Beliefs and Values* 24, no. 2 (2003) 155–64.
———. "The Most Wanted Text in the West: Rewards Offered for Reading the Bible as Literature." *Use of English* 54, no. 1 (2002) 29–42.
———. "Transactional Reading as Spiritual Investment." In *Teaching Spiritually Engaged Reading,* edited by David I. Smith et al., 83–94. Journal of Education & Christian Belief 11/2. Nottingham: Stapleford, 2007.
Polanyi, Michael. *Personal Knowledge: Towards a Post-Critical Philosophy.* London: Routledge, 1958.
Powell, Mark Allan. *Chasing the Eastern Star: Adventures in Biblical Reader-Response Criticism.* Louisville: Westminster John Knox, 2001.
———. *What Are They Saying about Luke?* New York: Paulist, 1989.
———. *What Is Narrative Criticism?* Minneapolis: Fortress, 1990.
Prince, Gerald. *A Dictionary of Narratology.* Rev. ed. Lincoln: University of Nebraska Press, 2003.
Pyper, Hugh. "What the Bible Can Do to a Child: The Metrical Psalms and *The Gammage Cup.*" In *An Unsuitable Book: the Bible as Scandalous Text,* 135–53. Sheffield, UK: Sheffield Phoenix, 2005.
Rhoads David, and Donald Michie. *Mark as Story: An Introduction to the Narrative of a Gospel.* Philadelphia: Fortress, 1982.
Rich, John. *Interviewing Children and Adolescents.* London: Macmillan, 1968.
Riches, John, ed. *What Is Contextual Bible Study? A Practical Guide with Group Studies for Advent and Lent.* London: SPCK, 2010.
Ricoeur, Paul. *From Text to Action: Essays in Hermeneutics.* London: Athlone, 1991.
———. *Time and Narrative.* Vol. 1. Chicago: University of Chicago Press, 1990.
Ritchie, Jane. "The Application of Qualitative Methods to Social Research." In *Qualitative Research Practice: A Guide for Social Science Students and Researchers,* edited by Jane Ritchie and Jane Lewis, 24–46. London: Sage, 2003.
Ritchie, Jane, et al. "Designing and Selecting Samples." In *Qualitative Research Practice: A Guide for Social Science Students and Researchers,* edited by Jane Ritchie and Jane Lewis, 77–108. London: Sage, 2003.

Roberts, Helen. "Listening to Children: And Hearing Them." In *Research with Children: Perspectives and Practices,* edited by Pia Christensen and Allison James, 260–75. 2nd ed. London: Routledge, 2000.

Robinson, Chris, and Mary Kellett. "Power." In *Doing Research with Children and Young People,* edited by Sandy Fraser et al., 81–96. London: Sage, 2004.

Rogers, Andrew P. *Congregational Hermeneutics: How Do We Read?* Farnham, UK: Ashgate, 2015.

Rosenblatt, Louise M. *Literature as Exploration.* 1938. 4th ed. New York: Modern Language Association, 1983.

———. *The Reader, The Text, The Poem: The Transactional Theory of the Literary Work.* Carbondale: Southern Illinois University Press, 1978.

Rowe, Arthur J. "Children's Thinking and the Bible." *Journal of Christian Education* 70 (1981) 18–32.

Rowe, C. Kavin. *Early Narrative Christology: The Lord in the Gospel of Luke.* Grand Rapids: Baker, 2006.

Rowland, Christopher, and Jonathan Roberts. *The Bible for Sinners: Interpretation in the Present Time.* London: SPCK, 2008.

Rowling, J. K. *Harry Potter and the Goblet of Fire.* London: Bloomsbury, 2000.

Rugg, Gordon, and Marian Petre. *A Gentle Guide to Research Methods.* Maidenhead, UK: Open University Press, 2007.

Schaffer, H. Rudolph. *Introducing Child Psychology.* Oxford: Blackwell, 2004.

Schneiders, Sandra M. "The Gospels and the Reader." In *The Cambridge Companion to the Gospels,* edited by Stephen C. Barton, 97–118. Cambridge: Cambridge University Press, 2006.

Scott, Drusilla. *Michael Polanyi.* Rev. ed. London: SPCK, 1996.

Searle, Alison. *The Eyes of Your Heart: Literary and Theological Trajectories of Imagining Biblically.* Eugene, OR: Wipf and Stock, 2008.

Seim, Turid Karlsen. "Feminist Criticism." In *Methods for Luke,* edited by Joel B. Green, 42–73. Cambridge: Cambridge University Press, 2010.

Sharpe, Eric J. *Understanding Religion.* London: Duckworth, 1983.

Shillington, V. George. *An Introduction to the Study of Luke-Acts.* London: T. & T. Clark, 2007.

Slee, Nicola. "Goldman Yet Again." *British Journal of Religious Education* 8, no. 2 (1986) 84–93.

Smith, David. "The Bible and Education: Ways of Construing the Relationship." *Journal of Education and Christian Belief* 5, no. 2 (2001) 119–33.

Smith, Peter K., et al. *Understanding Children's Development.* 5th ed. Chichester, UK: Wiley & Sons, 2011.

Snape, Dawn, and Liz Spencer. "The Foundations of Qualitative Research." In *Qualitative Research Practice: A Guide for Social Science Students and Researchers,* edited by Jane Ritchie and Jane Lewis, 1–23. London: Sage, 2003.

Spencer, F. Scott. *Salty Wives, Spirited Mothers, and Savvy Widows: Capable Women of Purpose and Persistence in Luke's Gospel.* Grand Rapids: Eerdmans, 2012.

Spinks, Christopher D. *The Bible and the Crisis of Meaning: Debates on the Theological Interpretation of Scripture.* London: T. & T. Clark, 2007.

Squires, John T. "The Gospel according to Luke." In *The Cambridge Companion to the Gospels,* edited by Stephen C. Barton, 158–81. Cambridge: Cambridge University Press, 2006.

St. Ignatius of Loyola. *The Spiritual Exercises of St Ignatius*. 1533. Translated by Anthony Mottola. Garden City: Image, 1964.

Steiner, George. "Critic/Reader." *New Literary History* 10 (1979) 423–52.

Stout, Jeffrey. "What Is the Meaning of a Text?" *New Literary History* 14 (1982) 1–12.

Strauss, Anselm, and Juliet Corbin. *Basics of Qualitative Research: Grounded Theory Procedures and Techniques*. London: Sage, 1990.

Talbert, Charles H. *Literary Patterns, Theological Themes, and the Genre of Luke-Acts*. Missoula, MT: Scholars, 1974.

Tannehill, Robert C. "Freedom and Responsibility in Scripture Interpretation, with Application to Luke." In *Literary Studies in Luke-Acts: Essays in Honor of Joseph B. Tyson*, edited by Richard P. Thompson and Thomas E. Phillips, 265–78. Macon, GA: Mercer University Press, 1998.

———. *Luke*. Abingdon New Testament Commentaries. Nashville: Abingdon, 1996.

———. *The Narrative Unity of Luke-Acts: A Literary Interpretation*. 2 vols. Philadelphia: Fortress, 1986, 1990.

Tatar, Maria. *Enchanted Hunters: The Power of Stories in Childhood*. London: Norton, 2009.

Thompson, John Lee, and Marianne Meye Thompson. "Teaching the Bible to Your Children: The Risks and the Rewards." *Word and World* 17, no. 3 (1997) 295–300.

Thompson, Neil. *Understanding Social Work: Preparing for Practice*. Basingstoke, UK: Palgrave, 2005.

Tolkien, J. R. R. "On Fairy-Stories." 1947. In *The Tolkien Reader*, 33–99. London: Allen & Unwin, 1966.

Tsai, J. L., et al. "Learning What Feelings to Desire: Socialization of Ideal Affect through Children's Storybooks." *Personality and Social Psychology Bulletin* 33 (2007) 17–30.

Van Ness, Patricia W. *Transforming Bible Study with Children: A Guide for Learning Together*. Nashville: Abingdon, 1993.

Vanhoozer, Kevin J. *First Theology*. Leicester, UK: Apollos, 2002.

———. *Is There a Meaning in this Text? The Bible, the Reader, and the Morality of Literary Knowledge*. Grand Rapids: Eerdmans, 1998.

Village, Andrew. *The Bible and Lay People: An Empirical Approach to Ordinary Hermeneutics*. Aldershot, UK: Ashgate, 2007.

Vincent, John. "How We Got Here." In *Mark Gospel of Action: Personal and Community Responses*, edited by John Vincent, 9–14. London: SPCK, 2006.

Warnock, Mary. *Imagination*. London: Faber & Faber, 1976.

Wellington, Jerry, and Marcin Szczerbinski. *Research Methods for the Social Sciences*. London: Continuum, 2007.

Wengraf, Tom. *Qualitative Research Interviewing: Biographic, Narrative and Semi-Structured Methods*. Thousand Oaks, CA: Sage, 2001.

West, Gerald O. *The Academy of the Poor: Towards a Dialogical Reading of the Bible*. Sheffield, UK: Sheffield Academic, 1999.

Westcott, Helen L., and Karen S. Littleton. "Exploring Meaning in Interviews with Children." In *Researching Children's Experience: Methods and Approaches*, edited by Sheila Greene and Diane Hogan, 141–57. London: Sage, 2005.

Wiarda, Timothy. *Interpreting Gospel Narratives: Scenes, People, and Theology*. Nashville: B & H Academic, 2010.

Wolterstorff, Nicholas. "A Response to Trevor Hart." In *Renewing Biblical Interpretation*, edited by Craig Bartholomew et al., 335–41. Carlisle, UK: Paternoster, 2000.

Worsley, Howard. "The Bible in Family Context." *International Journal of Children's Spirituality* 15, no. 2 (2010) 115–27.

———. *A Child Sees God: Children Talk about Bible Stories*. London: Kingsley, 2009.

———. "How Children Aged 9–10 Understand Bible Stories: A Study of Children at a Church-Aided and a State Primary School in the Midlands." *International Journal of Children's Spirituality* 9, no. 2 (2004) 203–17.

———. "Insights from Children's Perspectives in Interpreting the Wisdom of the Biblical Creation Narrative." *British Journal of Education* 28, no. 3 (2006) 249–59.

Wright, N. T. *Evil and the Justice of God*. London: SPCK, 2006.

Wright, Stephen I. "An Experiment in Biblical Criticism: Aesthetic Encounter in Reading and Preaching Scripture." In *Renewing Biblical Interpretation*, edited by Craig Bartholomew et al., 240–67. Carlisle, UK: Paternoster, 2000.

Yamasaki, Gary. "Point of View in a Gospel Story: What Difference Does It Make? Luke 19:1–10 as a Test Case." *Journal of Biblical Literature* 125, no. 1 (2006) 89–105.

Author Index

Abrams, M. H., 19–21, 19n38, 22, 24, 26
Adam, Jean-Michel, 13n17
Alasuutari, Pertti, 87, 87nn25–26, 114, 114n39
Alderson, Priscilla, 82, 82nn12–13, 83, 83n15, 90, 90n41, 101, 101n6
Alexander, Loveday, 10n3, 10n4, 12, 12nn12–13, 13, 13n18
Alter, Robert, 73–74, 74n117, 176, 176n17, 185, 185n33
Applebee, Arthur N., 5n2, 40–42, 40n35, 41nn36–40, 42n41, 43, 51, 56, 56n22, 59–60, 200, 200n30, 237, 237n7, 237n11
Appleyard, J. A., 5n2, 35, 35n5, 42–44, 42nn42–44, 43nn45–51, 44nn52–55, 51, 59–60, 68, 74, 74n119, 215–16, 215n9, 215n11, 216n12, 223, 223n29, 237–39, 237n7, 237n12, 238n14, 238n17, 239n19
Ashton, Elizabeth, 58n30
Astington, Janet, 47n66
Auerbach, Erich, 11n7
Aulén, Gustaf, 231n43
Austin, J. L., 193n6

Bailey, Kenneth E., 204–5, 205n41
Barbour, Rosaline, 114n38
Barth, Karl, 67n78, 218n20
Bartlett, Frederic C., 47n66
Barton, John, 19–21, 19n39, 22, 24, 26
Bauckham, Richard, 20, 20n41, 30–31, 30n85, 31nn86–87

Bauer, David, 23n53
Bazeley, Pat, 112n32
Bennett, Zoë, 27, 27n69
Benny, Mark, 86nn23–24
Birnie, Ian, 57n23
Bottigheimer, Ruth B., 67n79, 68n86
Bourg, Tammy, 186n36
Bourquin, Yvan, 13, 13nn15–17, 19n40, 24, 24nn59–61, 62, 62n49, 134, 134n15, 139, 139n21, 171, 171n1, 197n21, 208, 208n48
Boyd, Gregory A., 231n43
Brierley, Peter, 89n35
Briggs, Melody, 184n31
Briggs, Richard S., 192–93, 193nn6–7
Brock, Tim C., 47n69
Brooks, Peter, 11, 11n8, 212–13, 213n3, 213n5
Bryman, Alan, 80n2, 81, 81n10, 113n35, 114n37, 120n50
Burman, Erica, 34n1, 39, 39n28
Burrell, David, 202–3, 202n37
Burridge, Richard A., 10nn2–3

Cadbury, Henry J., 10n1
Campbell, Joseph, 214–15, 214nn7–8, 216, 216n14
Carpenter, Humphrey, 154n19
Carroll, Lewis, 195, 195n14
Casey, Mary Anne, 119n48
Chambers, Aidan, 102–4, 102n9, 103nn10–11, 103nn13–14, 103n16

AUTHOR INDEX

Chapman, Stephen B., 167–68, 168nn41–42
Charmaz, Kathy, 105n17, 110n25, 111nn26–29
Chatman, Seymour, 11, 11n11, 23n54, 131, 131n3, 146, 146nn37–38, 154, 154n21
Clark, Andrew, 48, 48n72
Clines, David J. A., 63n54
Cole, Arnold, 57, 57nn25–26
Coleridge, Samuel Taylor, 166n36
Conzelmann, Hans, 228n35
Copley, Claire, 63n55, 64nn58–59
Copley, Terence, 63–65, 63nn53–54, 64nn56–57, 64nn60–61, 241n30
Corbin, Juliet, 112n33
Cosgrove, Charles H., 200, 200n31
Cox, Rosemary, 70–71, 70nn100–1, 71n102, 72–73, 73n115, 240n22, 241n30
Craddock, Fred B., 134n14, 142n26, 169, 169n45, 188, 188n41, 198, 198n25, 220, 220n24
Creswell, John W., 80n4, 81, 81n7
Csanyi, Daniel A., 69–70, 70nn93–94, 71
Culler, Jonathan, 22, 22nn48–49, 24n59, 131, 131n2, 212, 212n1

Darr, John A., 18, 18n33, 22, 22n47, 147, 147n39, 182–83, 182nn28–29, 187, 187n39, 236, 236n5
Dawsey, James M., 144, 144n31
De Hulster, Izaak J., 151n6
Dinkler, Michal Beth, 229–30, 229nn37–38, 229n39
Donaldson, Margaret, 35, 35nn6–7, 73
Dornisch, Loretta, 30, 30n83

Eco, Umberto, 13, 13n19, 18, 18n30, 18n34, 20n41, 23n55, 24, 24n61, 69, 197, 197n21
Eder, Donna, 86n20, 88, 88n31, 111n30, 115, 115n42, 115n44
Erikson, Erik H., 34, 37, 37n16, 37nn18–19, 39, 42, 227–28, 227n33
Evans, C. F., 169n44

Fee, Gordon D., 97, 97nn54–55
Fewell, Danna Nolan, 68, 68nn82–85, 69
Fingerson, Laura, 86n20, 88, 88n31, 111n30, 115, 115n42, 115n44
Fish, Stanley, 21n42, 192n2
Fokkelman, J. P., 17, 17n25, 193, 193n8, 213, 213n4, 228, 228n36
Forster, E. M., 171, 171n2
Fowl, Stephen, 192, 192nn2–3
Fowler, James W., 37–38, 38nn20–23
Fowler, Robert M., 21, 21n46, 23n58, 27–28, 28nn72–73, 160, 160n31, 207, 207n46
France, Alan, 89, 89n34, 89n38
Francis, Leslie J., 57, 57n24, 58n29, 61–63, 61nn43–45, 62nn46–47, 62n51, 74, 240, 240n25, 240n27
Frei, Hans W., 10n4, 11, 11nn9–10, 28, 28n76
Fry, Donald, 48, 48n74–75, 50, 163, 163n34

Genette, Gérard, 22n50, 97n56, 144n30
Gerrig, Richard J., 21n45, 45–46, 45nn56–61, 47, 166n36, 179, 179n23, 196, 196n20, 237, 237n8, 238, 238n15
Glaser, Barney G., 112n34
Gobbel, Gertrude, 71–73, 71nn103–7, 72nn108–11, 76, 233, 233n1, 240, 240nn23–24
Gobbel, Roger, 71–73, 71nn103–7, 72nn108–11, 76, 233, 233n1, 240, 240nn23–24
Goldman, Ronald J., 58–60, 58nn27–28, 58n30, 59nn31–37, 60n39, 60nn41–42, 61, 71, 240n25
Gooder, Paula, 62, 62n48
Gowler, David B., 176n16, 187n38, 189, 189n44, 216n13, 217, 217nn17–18, 226, 226n32
Green, Garrett, 151, 151n9, 151n11, 156, 156n25, 161, 161n32
Green, Joel B., 10n4, 11, 17, 17n24, 17n27, 18n30, 19n36, 28, 28n75, 31–32, 31nn91–92,

AUTHOR INDEX

32n93, 133, 133n9, 134n12, 137, 137n18, 144–45, 145n33, 145n36, 147, 147n40, 158n28, 159–60, 160n30, 178, 178n21, 187, 187n40, 199, 199n26, 200–1, 201n32, 212, 212n2, 220, 220n22, 222, 222n27, 231, 231n44
Green, Melanie C., 47, 47nn69–70
Greene, Sheila, 82n12, 83, 83n14, 90n44, 114n40
Greer, J. E., 58n30
Greig, Anne, 82n12, 84n17, 89, 89n36, 90nn39–40, 91n45

Harris, Paul, 46, 46nn62–64, 51, 66, 151n10, 237, 237n9
Hart, Trevor, 151n6, 175, 175n14, 179, 179n22, 196, 196n18
Hartin, Patrick J., 57n23
Hauerwas, Stanley, 202–3, 202n37
Hays, Richard B., 209, 209n49
Heary, Caroline, 114n41, 115n44
Hennessy, Eilis, 114n41, 115n44
Hill, Malcolm, 82n12, 83, 83n14, 86n20, 88, 88n32, 90n44, 95n51, 114n40
Holland, Norman N., 21n42, 21n45, 192n2
Holm, Jean L., 58n29
Holmes, Robyn M., 86n20
Hume, David, 150n5

Iser, Wolfgang, 21, 21nn43–44, 23n54, 26, 27n68, 28, 28n74, 47, 133, 133n8, 149–50, 150n3, 155, 155n22

James, Allison, 34n1
James, Henry, 213, 213n6
Johnson, Luke Timothy, 142, 142nn26–27, 145n36, 153, 153n18, 158, 158nn28–29, 169, 169n43, 177, 177n18, 205–6, 206n43, 222, 222n27
Johnson, Mark, 25, 25nn64–65, 70, 70n95
Jowett, Benjamin, 96n53

Kant, Immanuel, 150n5
Karris, Robert J., 19n36, 230–31, 230n42
Kay, W., 58n30
Keen, Suzanne, 172–73, 173nn4–5, 173n7, 174n9, 175, 175n13, 186, 186n36
Kellett, Mary, 87, 87n28
Kermode, Frank, 196, 196n17
Kingsbury, Jack Dean, 15n23, 216–17, 217n16, 217n18, 219, 219n21, 221, 221n26, 230, 230n40
Knight, Peter T., 119n47, 120, 120n49
Kohlberg, Lawrence, 34, 36–37, 36nn11–14, 37n15, 39, 39n29, 39n31, 203
Krueger, Richard A., 119n48
Kvale, Steiner, 86n21, 101n4, 102, 102n7, 106n20, 107, 107n23

Lakoff, George, 25, 25nn64–65, 70, 70n95
Landy, Francis, 67–68, 67nn80–81, 68, 69, 72n114
Lawrence, Louise J., 5n1, 31, 31nn89–90, 56, 56nn18–21, 201, 201n34
Le Donne, Anthony, 216, 216n15, 217, 217n19, 221n26, 224, 224n30, 225, 225n31
Lee, David, 141, 141n24, 143, 143n28
Legaspi, Michael C., 28, 28n77
Leithart, Peter J., 74, 74n120
Levine, I. S., 114n41
Lewis, C. S., 25–26, 25nn62–63, 27–28, 32, 44, 46, 49, 72, 74, 74n121, 130, 132, 132nn6–7, 152, 166, 166nn37–38, 173, 188, 188n43, 208n47, 235, 235n4, 236
Littleton, Karen S., 87–88, 88n29
Loman, Susan E., 61–63, 61nn43–45, 62nn46–47, 62n51, 74, 240, 240n25, 240n27

MacDonald, George D., 152–53, 153n16
MacIntyre, Alasdair, 198, 198nn23–24
Marguerat, Daniel, 13, 13nn15–17, 19n40, 24, 24nn59–61, 62,

62n49, 134, 134n15, 139, 139n21, 171, 171n1, 197n21, 208, 208n48
Marshall, I. Howard, 28-29, 29nn78-80, 133, 133n10, 134n13, 169, 169n46, 228, 228n35
Martin, Dale B., 60, 60n40, 157, 157n27
Maxwell, Kathy Reiko, 18, 18n31, 19, 19nn36-37, 31, 31n88, 196, 196n19, 234, 234nn2-3
May, Tim, 93n49, 94n50
McComiskey, Douglas S., 15, 15n21, 29, 29n81
McGrady, Andrew G., 58n30
McIntyre, John, 151n7, 151n10, 153, 153n17, 175, 175n14
Meek, Margaret, 49, 49nn76-78, 50, 69, 69n91, 136, 136n16, 162, 162n33, 242, 242n34
Merenlahti, Petri, 69, 69nn89-90, 69n92
Michie, Donald, 23n51
Mikkelsen, Nina, 5n2, 49-50, 49n79, 50nn80-85, 52, 152, 152n15, 174, 174n11, 180, 180n24, 239, 239n21
Moberly, R. W. L., 192, 192n5
Morgan, David L., 115, 115n43
Morris, Leon, 169n44
Morrow, Virginia, 82, 82nn12-13, 83, 83n15, 90, 90n41
Morse, Janice M., 113n36, 118, 118n46

Nesbitt, Eleanor, 84n16, 101, 101n5, 106, 106n21
Nipkow, Karl Ernst, 72, 72nn112-13, 240n23
Nolland, John, 133, 133n9, 134n11, 145n36, 147-48, 148n41, 169, 169nn43-44, 220, 220n23, 220n25

Oatley, Keith, 46-48, 46n65, 47nn66-71, 48nn72-73, 51, 56, 56n22, 66, 152, 152nn13-14, 173, 173n6, 194, 194n9, 237-38, 237n10, 238n13
Ovwigho, Pamela Caudill, 57, 57nn25-26

Parker, Walter Chalmerse, 90, 90n42
Parsons, Mikeal C., 19n36, 156, 156n24, 232n46
Peatling, John H., 58n29
Pennington, Jonathan T., 6n3, 10n2, 10n4, 17, 17n26, 75-76, 76n122, 130n1
Peskin, Joan, 47n66
Petre, Marian, 62n50
Phillips, Anne, 38, 38n24, 40n34
Piaget, Jean, 34-36, 35n3, 35n6, 37, 39, 39n32, 41, 51, 58, 59, 71, 73, 167
Pike, Mark A., 38-39, 38n25, 39nn26-27, 70, 70nn97-99, 71, 205, 205n42, 240n22
Polanyi, Michael, 26, 26n67, 199, 199n27
Powell, Mark Allan, 11n7, 12, 12n14, 19n36, 20n41, 23, 23nn51-53, 23nn56-57, 174, 174n12, 194n10, 230, 230n41, 232, 232n46
Prichard, Mari, 154n19
Prince, Gerald, 228n34
Prout, Alan, 34n1
Pyper, Hugh, 69, 69nn87-88, 240, 240n28

Rhoads David, 23n51
Rich, John, 87, 87n27
Riches, John, 5n1, 55, 55nn11-13, 204n39
Ricoeur, Paul, 12, 13n15, 19n40
Ritchie, Jane, 91n46, 100, 100nn1-2
Roberts, Helen, 89, 89n37
Roberts, Jonathan, 5n1, 55-56, 56n17
Robinson, Chris, 87, 87n28
Rogers, Andrew P., 54, 54nn8-10
Rosenblatt, Louise M., 17, 17n28, 50, 50n81, 50n83, 131, 131nn4-5, 173n8, 184-85, 184n32
Rowe, Arthur J., 70, 70n96, 71
Rowe, C. Kavin, 14, 14n20, 209, 209n50
Rowland, Christopher, 5n1, 55-56, 56n17
Rowling, J. K., 140, 140n22
Rugg, Gordon, 62n50

Schaffer, H. Rudolph, 34n2, 35n4, 36, 36nn9–10, 37n17, 40n33, 103n12
Schneiders, Sandra M., 25, 25n66, 197n22
Scott, Drusilla, 199n28
Searle, Alison, 150n4, 151n7, 166n36, 167, 167n40, 199, 199n29
Seim, Turid Karlsen, 29–30, 30n82
Sharpe, Eric J., 92, 92n47
Shillington, V. George, 19, 19nn36–37
Slee, Nicola, 58n30
Smith, David, 57n23
Smith, Peter K., 35n8, 39n30, 39n32
Snape, Dawn, 80nn5–6, 81n9, 82, 82n11
Spencer, F. Scott, 30n84, 206, 206n44
Spencer, Liz, 80nn5–6, 81n9, 82, 82n11
Spinks, Christopher D., 192n1
Squires, John T., 15n22
St. Ignatius of Loyola, 140n23
Steiner, George, 28n72
Stout, Jeffrey, 192n2
Strauss, Anselm L., 112nn33–34
Strauss, Mark L., 97, 97nn54–55
Szczerbinski, Marcin, 63, 63n52, 101n3, 107n22

Talbert, Charles H., 10n2, 74, 74n118
Tannehill, Robert C., 18, 18n32, 29n81, 134n11, 136, 136n17, 139n19, 141, 141n25, 142n26, 143, 143n29, 144, 144n32, 145n34, 145n36, 157, 157n26, 158, 158n29, 169, 169n47, 176n16, 178, 178nn19–20, 181, 181n26, 183, 183n30, 185–86, 185n34, 186n35, 188, 188nn41–42, 195, 195n16, 207n45, 215, 215n10, 231, 231n45, 236, 236n6
Tatar, Maria, 5n2, 51, 51nn86–87, 181, 181n25, 238, 238n16
Thompson, John Lee, 67, 67n78, 69
Thompson, Marianne Meye, 67, 67n78, 69
Thompson, Neil, 92n48
Tolkien, J. R. R., 151, 151n8, 194–95, 195nn11–13
Tsai, J. L., 47n69

Van Ness, Patricia W., 72, 72n114, 240n23
Vanhoozer, Kevin J., 27, 27n71, 152, 152n12, 192n4
Village, Andrew, 53–54, 53n1, 54nn2–7, 59, 59n38
Vincent, John, 27, 27n70

Warnock, Mary, 150n5, 151n7
Wellington, Jerry, 63, 63n52, 101n3, 107n22
Wengraf, Tom, 106, 106n19
West, Gerald O., 55, 55nn14–16
Westcott, Helen L., 87–88, 88n29
Wiarda, Timothy, 17, 18, 18n29, 19n35
Wilkins, R., 58n30
Wright, N. T., 231n43
Wright, Stephen I., 74n121
Wolterstorff, Nicholas, 186, 186n37
Worsley, Howard, 65–67, 65nn63–68, 66nn69–70, 66nn72–75, 67nn76–77, 75, 242n35, 244, 244n37

Yamasaki, Gary, 139, 139n20

Zimmerman, J. D., 114n41

Scripture Index

Genesis
1–2	65

Exodus
14:1–31	59

Esther
	244

Psalms
	244

Matthew
4:1–11	59, 60

Mark
	196
9:14–29	54

Luke
1:1–4	144–45
1:1–2	96–97
1:1	11
1:4	19, 145
1:5	11, 15, 144
1:11–17	15
1:26–37	15
1:32–33	14, 15
1:35	15
1:46–56	16
1:57–66	15
1:67–79	16
1:69–79	15
2:1–15	15
2:6–7	158
2:13–14	16
2:14	208
2:28–32	16
2:40–52	163, 183–84
3:7–18	16
3:19–20	15
3:22	15
4:1–13	15
4:14	15
4:16–21	14
4:41	15
4:43	14
5:1–11	16, 157
5:12–15	14
5:17–26	14, 97, 138–39, 156, 168–69, 188–89, 221–22, 240
5:18	168
5:19	169
5:20	168–69
5:21–26	15
5:23	222
5:27–32	16
6:1–5	14
6:6–11	14, 16, 226
6:12	16

Luke (continued)

6:19	15
6:20–49	16
6:20–25	17
6:27–49	14
6:27–36	197
6:27	203
6:37–38	202
6:41–42	141, 156, 236
6:43–45	118–19, 122–23, 137, 156, 165, 166–67, 177–78, 196, 202, 208
7:1–10	16
7:11–16	14
7:18–23	14
7:36–50	16, 17, 195–96
8:4–15	14
8:4–8	145, 207
8:11–15	145
8:16–17	132–34
8:16	236
8:22–25	14, 16
8:26–39	14, 15
8:40–56	14, 158
8:42–48	142, 175, 200–1
8:49–56	158
9:1–6	15
9:7–9	15
9:10–17	14, 141, 142–43
9:21–22	16
9:23–26	205
9:30–31	16
9:35	15
9:37–43	14, 15, 159–60
9:46–50	15
9:46–48	17
9:57–62	16
10:6	208
10:17–24	15
10:25–37	14, 64, 64n62, 177, 206–7
10:38–42	118–19, 121, 143, 171–72, 182–83, 205–6, 251
11:1–13	16
11:5–8	187–88
11:14–26	15
11:14–22	15
11:37–54	16
12:8–12	16
12:13–34	17
12:22–34	16
12:41–48	17
12:41–47	16
12:49–53	164
12:49	86n22
13:10–17	14
13:18–21	16
13:31–35	15
14:1–6	222
14:7–35	16
14:7–14	17
14:15–24	172–74, 198
14:25–35	16
15:1–32	14, 16, 29
15:1–7	31, 118–19, 121–23, 202, 204–5, 252
15:1–3	204
15:4–7	29, 147–48
15:8–10	28–29, 30, 31–32, 137–38, 143, 178–79
15:11–32	202–3
16:19–31	17, 178, 241
17:5–6	16
17:7–10	17, 207
17:11–19	15
18:1–14	16

18:1–8	4	22:33–34	182
18:9–17	17	22:47–62	15
18:9–14	14, 16, 186–87	22:47–48	218, 229
18:15–17	16, 183	22:61–62	182
18:18–30	17	22:66–71	229
18:31–34	175		
18:31–33	16	23:1–26	15
18:35–43	14, 15, 157–58	23:1–3	229
		23:6–12	229
19:1–10	16, 143, 198–99	23:26	164–65
19:11–27	14, 210	23:27–38	189–90
19:45–46	207–8	23:33–46	213–14, 241
		23:39–43	185–86, 236–37
20:1–47	219–20		
20:9–19	64, 64n62	24:1–49	231
20:9–18	14, 144, 209, 241	24:25–27	16
20:19–26	118–20, 223, 226–27	24:50–53	231–32

John

6:16–21	69

21:1–4	17

Acts

232, 232n47

22:1–6	15, 218, 229
22:7–13	160–61
22:13	161

www.ingramcontent.com/pod-product-compliance
Lightning Source LLC
Chambersburg PA
CBHW071241230426
43668CB00011B/1540